splendor in the short grass

splendor in the

short grass

THE GROVER LEWIS READER

edited by Jan Reid and W. K. Stratton

foreword by Dave Hickey

remembrance by Robert Draper

UNIVERSITY OF TEXAS PRESS   AUSTIN

The editors are grateful to Dave Hickey and
Robert Draper and the following publishers
for permission to include these essays:

© 1992 *Texas Monthly.* Grover Lewis, "Farewell to
    Cracker Eden" (September 1992). Reprinted by
    permission.
© 1995 *Texas Monthly.* Robert Draper, "Cracker's
    Farewell" (June 1995). Reprinted by permission.
© 1997 The Foundation for Advanced Critical
    Studies, Inc. Originally published as "Grover
    Lewis: An Appreciation" by Dave Hickey in
    the *Los Angeles Times* (June 1995) and revised
    and reprinted in *Air Guitar: Essays on Art &
    Democracy* (Art Issues Press, Los Angeles, 1997).
    Reprinted by permission.

Requests for permission to reproduce
material from this work should be sent to
    Permissions, University of Texas Press,
    P.O. Box 7819, Austin, TX 78713-7819.

♾ The paper used in this book meets the minimum
    requirements of ANSI/NISO Z39.48-1992 (R1997)
    (Permanence of Paper).

Library of Congress Cataloging-in-Publication Data

Lewis, Grover.
    Splendor in the short grass : the Grover Lewis reader /
edited by Jan Reid and W. K. Stratton ; foreword by
Dave Hickey, remembrance by Robert Draper.— 1st ed.
        p.   cm.

ISBN 0-292-70559-X (hardcover : alk. paper)
I. Reid, Jan.   II. Stratton, W. K.   III. Title.
PS3562.E943A6   2005
818'.54—dc22   2004020328

*Every effort has been made to trace photographers.
The University of Texas Press will be happy to hear
from any who proved impossible to contact.*

Photo credit page iii: Fred Hamill

to **Rae Lewis**

contents

Magazine Writer
Dave Hickey

Air Guitar, 1997

SINCE MY OLD pal Grover Lewis no longer walks among us, let me begin by saying that, as a physical creature, by the standards of the culture, Grover was nobody's dream date. But he had an air about him, something likable and complicated. He had this lanky Texas stance, a big mouth with a big smile, and attired as he usually was, in boots, jeans, and some goofy forties shirt, faintly squiffed and glaring at you through those thick Coke-bottle glasses, he was a caricaturist's delight: all eyes, mouth, angles, sweetness, and ferocious intelligence. Moreover, he was a Southern boy to the end. He believed in truth and justice, and through all the years of dope and whiskey, Deadheads and deadlines, movie stars and rented cars, he remained an alumnus of that old school.

Women always called my attention to Grover's "courtly manner"—alluding to his charm even. But to me, he was always Prewitt in *From Here to Eternity*, a clenched fist in a frail package—prince and pauper in equal parts—always passing some outrageous, absolute judgment on your life and work, while appealing to your sympathy by bumping into a chair. Which is pretty much my definition of "exasperating"—that uncanny ability to break your heart while making you smile—so you never knew whether to thank Grover or forgive him for his impertinence. In my own case, since we were old and permanent friends (and Texas boys, too, cagey with mutual respect), I usually settled for neither.

Grover was, after all, the most stone wonderful writer that nobody ever heard of and blind as a cave bat in the bargain. He had been since birth, so he had to wear those wonky glasses. So, when he really ticked me off, I comforted myself with imagining Grover and his old running mate, Larry McMurtry, back at North Texas State in the fifties, as campus pariahs: two skinny, four-eyed geeks in goofy forties shirts scuttling along the sidewalk head to head, toting copies of *The Evergreen Review* and plotting their mutual apotheosis—in the aftermath of which they would both be famous authors, claiming any female who fell within their view.

The pleasure I took in this imagined tableau of pathetic geekdom was considerably enhanced by the improbable fact that both Larry and Grover, each in his own way, actually *achieved* their apotheosis (and its consequent surfeit of feminine companionship)—so rapidly, in fact, that by the time I met them in the early 1960s they were no longer geeks. They were "promising Texas writers." McMurtry had published his first novel, *Horseman, Pass By.* It was soon to be made into a movie called *Hud,* and, in the interim, he was teaching creative writing at TCU, while resisting attempts to ban *Horseman* from the university library. Grover had been booted out of grad school for publishing "communist pornography" in a state-funded journal and had begun publishing essays in national magazines. He had also written a bleak, feral book of poems called *I'll Be There in the Morning, If I Live* and could be found reading from it in coffeehouses and other fugitive venues. So, far from being geeks, when I met them, Grover and Larry were on their way, marking the path I fully intended to follow out of town.

By the early 1970s, McMurtry was producing novels at a steady clip and living like a fugitive out on the highway. Grover and I had seen the blessed vision—Texas in the rearview mirror. We were ensconced on opposite ends of the country practicing something called "New Journalism," which, in fact, was nothing more than Victorian reportage with neon punctuation—Dickens and Stevenson and DeQuincey in meaner streets with stronger drugs. Grover was in San Francisco working for *Rolling Stone,* writing landmark stories about movies and rock-and-roll—inventing pop genres like "the location story" and "the tour story." I was in New York, writing about art for *Art in America* and about rock-and-roll for *The Village Voice.* As a consequence, our paths began crossing in airports and bars, in press trailers and at country music festivals. We forged a friendship based on our mutual distaste for bar-ditch Texas and on our fatal love for the life we found ourselves leading. Both of us had read enough books and seen enough highway to know what a lovely moment it was.

We had grown up with the myth of the open range, with that unreflective, visceral cowboy hatred for fences, and, just for that moment, the fences were down. The institutions that strung them were in disgrace, and the borders were open: the president was a crook; the generals were losers; corporate culture was in disarray; and the universities were irrelevant. So there was a sense of making it up as you went along, with new rules in a new place, where, if you wished, you could bring your Deleuze and your Stratocaster, too. And there was plenty of sleazy fame to go around—except that, back then, it was still the colossal joke that Warhol intended it to be, still marketing and not yet a religion.

You could still write a tight, astringent literary piece about a rock-and-roll band or a pop mogul or a movie set, or even an evangelist, and it would pass for hype—the assumption being that people were cool, and everybody was in on the joke. So we wrote as well and as wittily as we could; then, with what we thought of as profligate generosity, we sailed our pieces out, like paper air-planes, into the woozy, ephemeral ozone of Pop America—feeling ourselves part of this vast conspiracy of coolness that extended all the way from Keith Richards, in extremis somewhere in France, to the vast republic of scruffy kids flipping albums in minimalls across the heartland. The sustained ironies of this new world distressed utopians and conservatives alike, but it was very Victorian, really. As Grover put it, we wrote about cottage industries that bubbled up out of the rookeries. We did pieces about people doing pieces, out there in the savanna between the corporate jungle and the ivory tower.

Ultimately, however, the fences would go back up, and as the eighties progressed, that space would evaporate. Suddenly, it was all Demi Moore and no more demimonde. Somehow, in a twinkling, "celebrity" had become a *class* in America, not an aberration, and celebrities themselves were no longer cool people, no longer edge-walkers like Ray Davies and Dennis Hopper, amazed and bemused by their new ludic status. Suddenly, they were hopeless, helpless dweebs, nervous and afraid of losing what they knew they didn't deserve; and the people who worked for them in the celebrity game (who used to lay out lines for us and let us borrow the limo) ceased to be cool, as well. More and more, Grover and I found ourselves dealing with hysterical, defensive bureaucrats—guardians of the inner temple—who wanted to write our stories for us. The days of midnight rides with the Allman Brothers were over. Opportunities to write hip stories about pop subjects disappeared. Pop stories about hip subjects were the vogue, and it was no fun anymore.

As I told Grover at the time, "Either we got old, or the president did." Probably it was both, but it hit Grover hard. He *loved* what he did and the status associated with it. And he *hated* where he came from. By the time he was ten, Grover explained, he had known enough hard times and chaos to last the entire population of Newport Beach into the next century. He hadn't liked it then and he didn't like it now. But he remained a Southern boy, stubborn as red dirt, bound and determined to stick to his last, lost cause or not, and to believe forever in that brand of truth and justice that had first set him free. And he was a *magazine writer*. His job was to hammer the detritus of fugitive cultural encounters into elegant sentences, lapidary paragraphs, and knowable truth; and, in truth, the loveliness and lucidity of Grover's writing always rose to the triviality of the occasion.

His burden was to suffer that chronic, Promethean anguish known only to slow writers with short deadlines and absolute standards, and he had lived with that. Whatever it cost Flaubert to conjure up *le mot juste* for Madame Bovary's trousseau, Grover paid comparable prices to evoke the butch camaraderie on the location of some lamentable movie, to capture the joy and desperation of some unremembered rock concert in a gym in southeastern New Mexico, to dramatize the antic absurdity of lunch with Paul Newman at the Pump Room. He accepted that discipline and bowed to it, soothing the anguish with whiskey, amphetamines, and carloads of cigarettes.

But the work dried up anyway. In Grover's view, this was because editors, at present, were either corporate swine or academic twits and he, Grover Lewis, had his fucking standards. I suggested that Marie Antoinette had her fucking standards, too, but to no avail. So there were several years in the eighties when, to put it mildly, Grover was a very grumpy dude, prowling like a blind lynx around the apartment in Santa Monica where he and his wife Rae had finally come to rest. I would drop by and find him reading ten books, one page at a time, making encyclopedic tapes of all his favorite songs, fulminating against things in general and writing at a pace that was stately even by Grover's standards.

It was not a good time, but finally, with nothing much to look forward to, Grover began looking back, tentatively at first, but then with a longer, stronger gaze at his final, terrible treasure, that brutal world of Texas white-trash geekdom from whence he sprang — at the redneck tribes of sharecroppers, well-diggers, religious maniacs, and petty thugs from whose blunt ignorance he had struggled so mightily to liberate himself. Opening up those raw memories gave him nightmares for a while, but even so, in 1992, he accepted the assignment to return to Texas and write a piece for *Texas Monthly* about Oak Cliff, the working-class suburb of Dallas where he spent the best part of a childhood that, in truth, had no best part at all.

"Farewell to Cracker Eden" turned out to be a hard and beautiful piece of writing, and Grover was heartened by its reception. So, finally, in his most Faulknerian manner, he "resolved to track the black beast to its lair." He wrote a proposal for an autobiographical book about those years. It was to be called *Goodbye If You Call That Gone*, and it began like this:

> *History and legend bind us to the past, along with an unquenchable memory.*
>
> *In the spring of 1943, my parents — Grover Lewis, a truck driver, and Opal Bailey Lewis, a hotel waitress — shot each other to death with a pawnshop pistol. For almost a year, Big Grover had stalked my mother, my four-year-old sister, and me across backwater Texas, resisting Opal's decision to divorce him. When she finally did, and when he finally cornered her and pulled the trigger as he'd promised to do, she seized the gun and killed him, too.*

To no one's surprise but his own, Grover got a contract to write this book, his first, for real money. About a month after that, Grover and I had a long conversation about the book. By this time he was fully aware of the ironies that swirled around the project. It was not a story he was born to write, he said: he had already written that in a thousand magazines with the shelf life of milk. It was, however, the book he *had* to write because he was born where and when he was, and to whom. And he planned to write it with a vengeance because, at one level, he had been "Lonesome Doved," as he called it, referring to the experience of his friend McMurtry, who after twenty years of writing first-rate novels about living Americans in the contemporary moment, had been rewarded finally for a mythic novel based on an old screenplay about archetypal cowboys.

So Grover had a little litany that he had clearly worked up with me in mind: "They will admire you for writing about the present, oh yeah. But they will *love* you for writing about the past. They will praise you for writing about housewives and showgirls, bookworms and businessmen. But they will *pay* you for cowboys and rednecks. They will admire you for writing about the world before your eyes. But they will *adore* you for spilling your guts. And somehow," he said, "I'll subvert that crap and still write this book." *Bam!* He hit the table with his hand. It was the only violent gesture I ever saw him make. I was heartened by it.

But there was more to it than that, because in essence, by writing this book, Grover was dismantling the engine that drove the words that wrote it. He knew, and I knew too, that by writing the story of his parents, he was handing every armchair psychologist we knew a false key to his heart, because, clearly, the crazy, loving, violent figure of Big Grover flickered behind half the people he had written about, behind all the bad guys, roughnecks, and broken poets, behind Robert Mitchum, Duane Allman, Lee Marvin, Lash LaRue, Art Pepper, John Huston, and Sam Peckinpah, and Grover knew it.

"I can see it now, of course," he said, "how I would want to talk to somebody who was like Big Grover, who was bad and good, sweet and violent. How I would want to speculate on how he might have survived, done well, and been redeemed. That's a reasonable interest, I think, but it doesn't *explain* anything. That was just the *assignment*, you know, and I'm too good a reporter to let the assignment distort the story. I always got the story that was there. From all these people. The only difference Big Grover made, I think, was that I was really interested in those guys and predisposed to forgive them for their rough edges. That made better stories, I think."

It would have made Grover's book a better book, too, I think, but about two months after we spoke, Grover hurt his back moving something on his desk. He went to the doctor with it and was diagnosed with terminal lung cancer. He was immediately thrust into chemotherapy, which scalded his throat, so we never spoke again. He died six weeks later and was buried in Kanarraville, Utah, Rae Lewis's hometown, in a little Mormon cemetery in a high mountain meadow on a day full of wind and scudding clouds, hard rain, and banners of angled sunshine.

A small group of us stood in the mud around the grave, hunched against the rain and blinking in the shafts of dazzled sunlight. A girl in a country dress played an Irish melody on the fiddle. It was so damn cinematic I could barely stand it. All it needed was Beau Bridges and a commissary truck, so, to distract myself from the proliferation of easy ironies, I thought about the fragment I had read of *Goodbye If You Call That Gone*. About these lines: "The fatal events took place in my hometown of San Antonio when I was eight. By then I had experienced first hand such a numbing amount and so many varieties of violence that I was left with a choice between an invitation to death and the will to live." Grover, of course, being Grover, chose both.

Star-Crossed

A BIOGRAPHICAL SKETCH OF GROVER LEWIS

Jan Reid and W. K. Stratton

THE GUNMAN WORE cowboy boots with bulldogging heels. He chased the woman into the bathroom of the boarding house at the intersection of Presa and Arciniega Streets in San Antonio at around six o'clock in the morning of Monday, May 10, 1943. An old man who lived there was scrubbing the bathroom floor when she ran in. "Stay by me, Dad!" she cried out to the man. "He's going to kill me!" Before the old man could do anything to help her, the gunman fired two shots from his revolver, dropping the woman. Then he stood over her, shot her three more times, and let the gun fall to the floor. He was stepping back from the fallen woman when another shot rang out — the last bullet in the pistol. It hit the gunman in the eye and lodged in his brain. When the police arrived just minutes later, Grover Virgil Lewis was barely alive. Opal Bailey Lewis, a waitress at the Menger Hotel who had been granted a divorce from Big Grover just six weeks earlier, was already dead. The police had Big Grover, as he was known in his family, rushed to Robert B. Green Hospital, where he died a short time later.

At least that was how the astounding story played in the police report and in Grover Jr.'s head down through the years. Many years later, Big Grover and Opal's son, the writer Grover Lewis, tried to make sense of this horrendous episode as he was entering the last months of his own life. Drawn to the brute pathos of that explanation, he had in his writing reconstructed the scene in ways that rang true. But the premise relied on a coroner's ruling that Opal — despite having been shot five times, with mortal injuries convening in not the steadiest rush, and with no known experience handling a gun — managed to pick up the revolver and fire the perfect fatal shot into Big Grover's eye. It was as if God himself hurled down a thunderbolt of outrage and retribution. For a long time, Grover believed the coroner's account, but from studying the scant evidence he decided that the old man in the bathroom retrieved the pistol; and he was the one who put Big Grover down. The San Antonio police assessed the situation, decided Big Grover deserved shooting, and let the old man walk.

Whatever happened, the killings culminated one catastrophic phase of Grover's life and opened the door to another phase that was as terrible in its own way. That he was able to survive what he did in childhood and go on to become a highly regarded magazine journalist and popular-culture critic is testament to a courage and stamina beyond what most people could ever hope for.

Grover Virgil Lewis Jr. was born November 8, 1934, in San Antonio. A daughter was born to Big Grover and Opal two years later. Big Grover worked as a truck driver, but he drank away much of his earnings, and by the early 1940s, the family lived in San Antonio's Victoria Courts, a low-income housing project. Big Grover and Opal's marriage seemed doomed from the start. He was a rough-cut, scarcely educated man who'd grown up in the small Texas towns of Lampasas and Bowie. Opal came from Dallas and possessed a level of sophistication far beyond Big Grover. She loved books and movies, passions that she passed on to her son. Young Grover Lewis himself seemed to be a source of conflict within the marriage. He was born with a congenital eye condition that manifested itself in a severe astigmatism that left him with only 17 percent of normal vision. The condition was common among the Baileys, and Big Grover came to blame Opal for giving him a four-eyed, geeky son instead of a "normal" child. When disputes with Big Grover became too violent for Opal to bear, she hit the road with her children. Big Grover stalked her until the shooting in San Antonio.

After the deaths of his parents, the boy and his sister were sent to live with Opal's sister and her husband on the outskirts of Fort Worth. The aunt and uncle were cut from a lot of the same cloth as Big Grover. Caught up in fundamentalist religion and not trusting education or culture, they were cruel to the boy with the intellectual airs. He frequently was beaten. At times, they withheld food from him as a penalty for some perceived wrongdoing. At other times, they required him to eat food he didn't like as punishment. As a result, Grover developed eating disorders that dogged him for the rest of his life. At one point, Grover saved up precious nickels earned from a newspaper route and bought a relative a copy of *The Grapes of Wrath* as a present. Spotting the book in Grover's room, his uncle became furious, convinced that it was some form of pornography. He forced Grover to burn the book in the backyard. Not long after that, Grover ran away from home and made his way to San Antonio. He was all of thirteen years old.

Shortly after he arrived, the police in San Antonio picked him up at a bus station. His uncle in Fort Worth wasn't much interested in having him back. And Grover was dead set against returning. The family decided that he should stay with an uncle from the Bailey side of the family who lived alone in a shabby apartment in the Dallas suburb of Oak Cliff. This turned out to be one of the few good decisions made about Grover in his younger years. This uncle nurtured him rather than stymied him, encouraging his jaunts to nearby movie theaters and the local library. His terrible eyesight forced him to read like a robot, literally moving his head slightly to the right as he read each word, then jerking it to the left to start a new line. Yet he began compulsively consuming two or three books a week, a habit that continued for the rest of his life. And in the dark recesses of Oak Cliff theaters, Grover developed an encyclopedic knowledge of the works of actors, directors, and screenwriters, plus a deep understanding of how movies are made.

A lackluster student while in Fort Worth, Grover now earned top grades. He graduated from W. H. Adamson High School in 1953, then headed north to Denton to attend North Texas State College (now the University of North Texas), where he took a B.A. in English in 1958. At North Texas, Grover flourished. He won student writing awards for poems, short stories, and essays. He helped found a student-faculty society for "the study of cinematic arts" and acted in theater productions. His stories and poems began to appear in prestigious literary magazines like *Carolina Quarterly* and *New Mexico Quarterly*. *The Nation* bought one of his satirical works while Grover was still an undergraduate. Samuel French Inc. published his play *Wait for Morning, Child* after it won the company's national collegiate writing contest. And Grover developed an important friendship with another North Texas student with writing ambitions, Larry McMurtry. The two discussed books they'd read, bouncing theories off each other. Grover later fondly remembered times when he and McMurtry would drive for hours just to get a milkshake at some out of the way drive-in restaurant they'd heard about, talking about books the whole time they were on the road. Students of other enthusiasms might react to them as a couple of odd-looking ducks wearing the unflattering spectacles of the time, but they were the undisputed star literati on campus. Their poetry and prose carried and dominated issues of *Avesta*, the student literary magazine (copies of it became a rare treasure in the world of collectors that would beckon McMurtry). Though McMurtry subsequently changed the dedication in later editions after their friendship had grown distant, the first edition of McMurtry's *Horseman, Pass By* carries a dedication, in part, to Grover Lewis.

Grover's time at North Texas had its rough moments, too. As soon as he discovered that there was such a thing as a counterculture, he championed it. In the 1950s, that meant embracing the Beat movement while snubbing his nose at the extremely conservative political views in vogue in Texas. His writings expressed these interests and brought about howls from some faculty and administrators at North Texas. And, in a place dominated by Southern Baptists and Campbellites, Grover proudly proclaimed himself to be a Unitarian. He had turmoil in his personal life as well. At nineteen he had married, and while still a college student, he fathered a son and a daughter. Money was tight. Grover was learning he had little in common with his wife, so the marriage grew tense. Compounding the situation was that, like his father, Grover had begun drinking — hard. Eventually the young couple divorced. Grover signed away his parental rights when his ex-wife remarried, creating an estrangement between him and his children that he came to regret later in life.

After graduating from North Texas, Grover spent a year teaching high school English in Wylie, Texas, before returning to Denton to enter grad school. Between classes, he held down a full-time job as a philosophy instructor at North Texas (in one class he formed a lasting bond with a lanky small-town student named Don Graham, who became a prominent writer and scholar of the cultural life of the Southwest). Grover also found the time to hold a job as a staff book reviewer for the *Dallas Times Herald*. In 1960, he was named a National Defense Act fellow and moved to Lubbock to pursue a Ph.D. in English at Texas Tech. At Tech, he encountered an environment that was even more hostile to his freewheeling ideas, and he was not happy, though he distinguished himself as a graduate assistant, a speaker, and a proponent of roots music, particularly Southwestern folk music. Frustrated by the cultural environment in Lubbock, he left Tech in 1963 without his doctorate and traveled to California to sample a less restrictive lifestyle.

Later that year, he was back in Texas, working as a copy editor and music and book critic for the *Fort Worth Star-Telegram*. He was one of a number of talented writers performing groundbreaking work on Dallas and Fort Worth newspapers in that period — Dan Jenkins, Edwin "Bud" Shrake, A. C. Greene, and Gary Cartwright among them. He was not as close to Shrake and Cartwright — nor their legendary bacchanals — as he would have liked; he came to know them and gained their respect in later years. He was drawn to writers who shared his Texas origins and his ribald aspiration to transcend those roots. Of all the writers he knew over the years, he admired none more than Billy Lee Brammer, another Oak Cliff native who wrote the novel *The Gay Place*, and the all-purpose critic and stylist Dave Hickey, who came up on the brick streets of Fort Worth. During Grover's Fort Worth days, he made a name for himself by serving as featured speaker at various arts programs around town, and he collected a Sigma Delta Chi award for a series of features he wrote about blues singer Lightnin' Hopkins—he later drew on this material for a celebrated *Village Voice* series about Hopkins. His expertise on blues music prompted Chess Records to invite him to write liner notes for albums by Little Milton and Mitty Collier.

After leaving the *Star-Telegram* in 1965, he worked in advertising and public relations before taking another metropolitan newspaper position in 1966, this one as a state desk reporter at the *Houston Chronicle*. When Ken Kesey, Neal Cassady, and the rest of the Merry Pranksters showed up in Houston aboard their fabled bus to visit Kesey's old friend Larry McMurtry—the novelists had met while on Wallace Stegner writing fellowships at Stanford— Grover wrote about psychedelia's big-time coming to town for the *Chronicle*, pre-dating Tom Wolfe's *The Electric Kool-Aid Acid Test* by more than three years. During these years, he also served as fiction editor for a local arts magazine and helped the David Gallery in Houston with its advertising. He left the *Chronicle* in May 1968 for a job writing copy for a Houston advertising and PR firm, but within a year, he'd taken a big step forward in moving his career to the national stage.

In January 1969, *The Village Voice* published his Lightnin' Hopkins series. With it, Grover was able to leave Texas newspapers and PR agencies and move to California. He went there to cover the booming counterculture for the *Voice*. The calm and frightful vividness of his piece on the Altamont rock festival–disaster caught the eye of many discerning readers. While still on the *Voice* staff, he coedited a publication called *Focus: Media*. One issue contained the bylines of Nelson Algren, Tim Cahill, Tom Buckley, Jack Thibeau, the great San Francisco sportswriter Wells Twombley, and two young writers who would make their marks in Texas, C. W. Smith and Gregory Curtis. But Grover scored the coup with an article about an upstart counterculture magazine, *Rolling Stone*. On the basis of that piece publisher Jann Wenner hired him as a *Rolling Stone* associate editor—and put him at the white-hot center of American journalism.

During the early '70s, he enjoyed the widest reading audience of his career as a major *Rolling Stone* writer at a time when the magazine was being lauded as the best publication in America. His most important pieces were written from the sets of films like *The Getaway* and *The Friends of Eddie Coyle*.

Early in his *Rolling Stone* career, he was cast in a small role in the film version of McMurtry's *The Last Picture Show*. As Sonny's dad, he appears on screen for only a few moments with a couple of brief lines of dialogue during the Christmas dance scene. It was not enough to open the doors of an acting career for him. But he kept careful notes about his experiences on the set, and the article he wrote from them turned out to be pure gold in terms of his writing career. "Splendor in the Short Grass" became one of the longest, best-written articles ever to run in the magazine, and it was a breakthrough achievement for him.

His snapshot of the set of *Picture Show* and other articles won plaudits from many people in Hollywood. But Grover never was one to respect inflated egos, and his experiments in style left some subjects of his articles thinking they'd been exploited. Pieces like "Splendor in the Short Grass" tested the waters of "gonzo journalism," an over-the-top form of the New Journalism first crafted by Grover's fellow Texan Terry Southern in the pages of *Esquire* and perfected by Hunter S. Thompson. One of the principals profiled in "Splendor" later claimed everything that Lewis wrote about him was a lie and expressed surprise that no one sued the magazine over the article.

Style was his long suit but it wasn't perfect. The New Journalism encouraged lengthy articles (in proclamation of its newness Tom Wolfe, future author of lengthy novels, boasted that inventive magazine nonfiction had supplanted the novel). Grover ran off across the prairie with those free reins flapping, jerked from the hands of editors who must have given up and just tried to hang on. He wrote *long:* his pace for a narrative gallop seemed to be about 8,000 words, and some of his strongest articles exceeded 12,000 words. Though gonzos of the day routinely made themselves prominent characters in their stories, Grover was strangely out of sorts with himself in recounting interviews he conducted. He had a tremendous ear for the spoken word, and unlike some of the practitioners of the new form, he recognized the utility of a tape recorder. But he had his subjects answer his questions as if they had thought of them rhetorically. The resulting soliloquies had an archaic stiffness that contrasted with the swirl of exceptional prose around them.

As a reporter he also had a reputation for being ruthless, if not brutal. He was fundamentally a beatnik, an aficionado of jazz and blues; at *Rolling Stone*, of all places, he put a grumpy sign on his desk that read "I Do Not Write No Rock 'n' Roll." But like all journalists moving a publication to press he did not get to choose every one of his assignments; in more than one article, his contempt for the glorification and self-indulgence of the rock world showed. Grover's fireworks piece was his profile of the Allman Brothers Band on tour, which painted the band as rough-cut boys with cracker roots and a taste for loose women and mounds of cocaine. These guys, he intimated strongly, were not the brightest bulbs in the Old South's war-torn chandelier. Between the time Grover finished the article and its publication date, the superbly talented guitarist and bandleader Duane Allman died in a motorcycle crash. Given the circumstances, Grover was unenthusiastic about printing the article, but Wenner insisted it should run. And so it appeared, just days after the accident. The roar out of Macon, Georgia, was ferocious. The band in general and Duane in particular had found Grover to be an irritating presence while he traveled with them, so the pro-Allman camp laid blame for the article squarely on the writer, not the publication. Word has it that the name Grover Lewis can still raise Greg Allman's ire, all these years later.

Behind the scenes at *Rolling Stone*, Grover assigned and edited stories, took part in the meetings that budgeted money and space, and in general helped chart the magazine's direction. He fought the good fight for the copy of Tim Cahill and Texan Chet Flippo, who became star contributors. He bought a strangely appealing piece about the armadillo as countercultural motif from another fellow Texan, Stephen Harrigan, later a *Texas Monthly* mainstay and much-praised novelist. For a while, subscribers to *Rolling Stone* received a pamphlet printed on expensive paper containing Grover's spoof, "The Last Poem: All My Friends Are Going to Be Published." In 1973, *Rolling Stone's* book publishing arm, Straight Arrow Press, brought Grover's first book into print, a collection of poems entitled *I'll Be There in the Morning, If I Live*, most of them dating from the 1960s. And it was at *Rolling Stone* that he met the love of his life.

After his divorce, Grover had relationships with several women, including the writer Gina Berriault. But they were not cut from the same cloth as Rae Ence, a self-proclaimed "jack Mormon" originally from the small town of Kanarraville, adjacent to Zion National Park in southwestern Utah. Rae was free-spirited, well-read, and tough-minded, and she possessed an artistic bent. The descendant of Utah sheep ranchers, she, too, reacted aversely to inflated egos and other forms of phoniness — exactly the kind of woman who appealed to Grover. Rae was emerging from a crumbling marriage and working for *Rolling Stone's* lawyers when they were introduced. The attraction was immediate and grew into a love that lasted for the rest of Grover's life.

That love was tested, though. Like many writers and editors who have worked at *Rolling Stone*, Grover eventually found himself on the outs with Wenner. By the mid-1970s, the rancor between them forced Grover to leave the magazine. Grover and Rae left San Francisco for San Antonio to collaborate with Texas writer Sherry Kafka on a Straight Arrow Press book about John Connally, the former Texas governor and presidential aspirant. The book never got off the ground, and Straight Arrow published instead a collection of Grover's *Rolling Stone* articles as *Academy All the Way*. While the trade paperback developed a cult following, Grover disavowed *Academy*, believing it to be a poorly planned and edited throwaway put out by Straight Arrow to satisfy a contractual obligation.

After the collapse of the Connally book, Grover felt adrift in San Antonio. He and Rae would stroll along the River Walk, stopping at an outdoor tavern for a drink and to listen to Johnny Rodriguez moan his early hit, "Pass Me By If You're Only Passing Through." As Grover's career bottomed out, his drinking spun out of control. But Rae stuck by him. She knew if she was going to rescue him she had to get him out of San Antonio, away from the ghosts of Big Grover and Opal. Whenever Rae needed refuge herself, she went back to her Utah hometown. She convinced Grover to spend some time with her at Kanarraville. It worked. Grover came to love the people of Kanarraville and the surrounding countryside. While he didn't quit drinking, he did cut back and was able to get focused on his career again. And in future years, whenever he needed to recharge, Kanarraville was where he went.

He and Rae returned to California, settling in Santa Monica. Grover continued to contribute to a variety of national magazines (including *Playboy*, for which he wrote a memorable dispatch from Oregon during the filming of *One Flew over the Cuckoo's Nest*). He also signed on as a contributor for *New West* magazine, a sort of California equivalent of *New York* or *Texas Monthly* magazines founded by New Journalism pioneer Clay Felker and edited by Texan Joe Armstrong. Unfortunately short-lived, *New West* was a comeback venue for Grover. During their association he published several excellent pieces, including "Buried Alive in Hype," which won a National Magazine Award nomination.

Grover finished out his career working as a freelancer. His stories appeared in everything from the *Los Angeles Times Magazine* and *LA Weekly* to fairly obscure film publications, frequently focusing on all-but-forgotten movie presences like Lash LaRue. He also started a novel of Hollywood, *The Code of the West*, that he could never finish. In the 1980s, the years of bad diet, smoking, and drinking began to take their toll; his health began to fail. On three occasions in the 1980s, he suffered eye infections that threatened to destroy what little vision he had. Sensing that his time was growing short, Grover set out to make peace with his past. He reconnected with his sister and his children, with mixed results. After his son, who was now grown, spent a holiday with Grover and Rae, he expressed concern about how much his father drank. Grover responded by quitting drinking cold turkey. And he never backslid.

Grover and Rae traveled to Texas to allow him to visit his childhood haunts while researching his family history. Out of this came his last major magazine piece, "Cracker Eden," an account of a return trip to Oak Cliff, which appeared in *Texas Monthly* in 1992. Robert Draper had written a book about *Rolling Stone* that Wenner hated but Grover loved, for it gave him his due. (He had been removed from the magazine's authorized history, like those Bolsheviks erased from the revolution's photos during the Stalin purges.) Grover had published short fiction by *Texas Monthly* editor Greg Curtis two decades earlier, in *Focus: Media*. But Grover wasn't going to scrape and bow in gratitude; he may have aged, but he was still feisty. He delivered the story past the deadline and fought *Texas Monthly* over edits and cuts as well as his expenses. But "Cracker Eden" turned out to be a beautiful piece of writing. Book editors in New York took notice, and soon he had a contract with HarperCollins for a memoir, *Goodbye If You Call That Gone*.

Grover had begun work on his memoir when one day he felt some pain after moving some furniture. This felt like more than just a pulled muscle. He confided to Rae that he feared something was seriously wrong—he went to see a doctor, whose diagnosis was grim, terminal lung cancer. Grover went downhill quickly, never returning to work on his memoir. He died on April 16, 1995, almost seven months shy of his sixty-first birthday. Rae chose to bury him in Kanarraville, the place that had revived him when he was at his lowest ebb.

Splendor in the Short Grass

THE MAKING OF THE LAST PICTURE SHOW

Rolling Stone, 1971

Flying west, through Texas, you leave Dallas–Fort Worth behind and look out suddenly onto a rolling, bare-boned, November country that stretches away to the horizon on every side—a vast, landlocked Sargasso Sea of mesquite-dotted emptiness. There are more cattle down there ranging those hazy, distance-colored expanses than people, and in turn, more people than timber topping out at five feet, for this is cowdom's fabled domain, the short-grass country—*yipi-ti-yi-yo, little pardners*—the Land of the Chicken-Fried Steak, where if your gravity fails you among the shit-kickers, chili-dippers, and pistoleros, negativity emphatically won't pull you through.

Below, there are few houses, fewer roads, and scarcely any towns. As the dun landscape slides past under the plane's port wing, the overwhelming sense of the vista is solitude, and if you happen to hail from that iron killing floor down there, as I do, you begin to feel edgy and defenseless, moving across so much blank space and drenching memory.

The shuttle plane, an eighteen-seater De Haviland–Perrin, seems infernally slow after the rush of the Delta jet from San Francisco; its engines are loud, too, and it bucks around in the brown overcast between Dallas and Wichita Falls like a sunfishing busthead-bronc. Fitfully, I'm riffling through the pages of an underground sheet called *Dallas Notes*—"Narc Thugs Trash Local White Panthers"—but the lonesome countryside below keeps drawing my mind and eye away from the real-enough agonies of Big D's would-be dope brotherhood. Somewhere down there slightly to the south, a pioneer Texian named William Medford Lewis—my paternal grandfather—lies buried in the Brushy Cemetery, hard by the fragrant dogwood trails of Montague County where he and I once tramped together in less fitful times. Beside him, that fierce, pussel-bellied old man I remember above all other men, lies his next-to-youngest son, Cecil—a ghostly wraith-memory of childhood, a convicted bank robber and onetime cohort of Bonnie and Clyde who was paroled from the Huntsville pen in 1944 just in time to die fifty-six days later in the invasion of Sicily—and beside Cecil, in turn, lies my grandmother, who once lifted an uncommonly sweet contralto in whatever Pentecostal church lay closest to hand.

Somewhere down there, too, slightly more to the west, in a decaying little ranching hamlet called Archer City, a protean-talented young Hollywood writer-director named Peter Bogdanovich is filming Larry McMurtry's novel *The Last Picture Show* in its true-to-life setting. McMurtry—Archer City's only illustrious son—previously wrote *Horseman, Pass By*, from which the film *Hud* was made. *Picture Show*—there may be a title change before the film's release, to avoid confusion with Dennis Hopper's *The Last Movie*—is to star Ben Johnson, Clu Gulager, Cloris Leachman, Jeff Bridges, and a couple of promising young unknowns, Timothy Bottoms and Cybill Shepherd. And, save us all, I'm to be in it, too, playing a small supporting part.

The Ramada Inn on the Red River Expressway, where the sixty-odd members of the *Picture Show* troupe are quartered, is big, seedy, and expensive, a quadrant of fake-fronted Colonial barracks overlooking a dead swimming pool and a windswept compound full of saw grass and cockleburs. "Hah yew today?" the desk clerk, a platinum-streaked grandmother in a miniskirt, trills cheerily as I check in at midafternoon.

My room—at least a city block from the lobby as the crow flies—is de rigueur institutional ugly, distinguished only by a tiny graffito penciled beneath the bathroom mirror: *People who rely on the crutch of vulgarity are inarticulate motherfuckers.* In sluggish slow motion, I stretch out across the bed to doze and await instructions from somebody in Archer City, forty miles to the southwest, where the day's shooting has been under way since early morning. When the phone jangles a few minutes later, I snap alert, sweating, disoriented. Waking up in Whiskey-taw Falls storms my mind; less than twenty-four hours ago, I was bombed-and-strafed in the no name bar in Sausalito.

Through a crackling connection and a babble of background din, the film's production manager is shouting to ask what my clothing sizes are. "Peter wants you out here on the set as soon as possible," he commands, barking out staccato directions of how I'm to connect with a driver who'll fetch me to the location site.

Feeling wary and depressed, I wander downstairs and wait in the lobby. Christ, I haven't done any acting I'd admit to since college, when I was typecast as the psycho killer in *Detective Story*. Now, I'm supposed to play

"Mr. Crawford"—the village junkie-geek of Archer City circa the Korean War era, a character maybe twenty years my senior. More typecasting, I figure sourly.

The driver, a large, loose-limbed black man named James, lifts my spirits on sight. "Fuck them long cuts, ain't I right, Grovah? I'ma take a short cut and git you to the church *on time*," he announces, pumping my hand like a handle and grinning through dazzling silver teeth. On the way out of town in a Hertz station wagon, we pass the M-B Corral, a notorious hillbilly dive where, fourteen or fifteen years ago, Larry McMurtry and I stood among a circle of spectators in the parking lot one drizzly winter night and watched a nameless oilfield roughneck batter and kick Elvis Presley half to death in what was delicately alluded to afterwards as a difference of opinion about the availability of the roughneck's girlfriend. McMurtry and I were wild-headed young runners-and-seekers back then, looking, I think, for a country of men; what we found, though, together and apart, were wraithlike city women in blowing taffeta dresses. And the shards and traceries of our forebears, of course, trapped in the stop-time aspic of old hillbilly records.

Out on the open highway, James stomps down hard on the accelerator and free-associates about his Army days to pass the time and the miles: "Twenty-two years in all I served in the arm service. . . . I ony been back in Wichita, lessee, oh, about goin' on three years now. . . . Yeah, I seen action in World War II, in Korea, and in Veet-nam. Never kilt nobody, though, far's I know, and never got kilt my own self, neither. Hah! . . . If it's anything I despise to be in, it's a conflick. . . . I swear, this ol' State 79 here, it's the lonesomest stretch of miles I've ever drove, you know it? Sheeit."

With a practiced snick, James spits out the window and falls silent. Beyond the weed-choked bar ditches paralleling the road, the stringy mottes of mesquite trees and stagnant stock tanks and the Christmas-tree oil rigs flash past at eighty mph under an unutterable immensity of hard blue sky. It is bluer even than I remember it, the sky, and I remember it as being blue to the point of arrogance, a galling reminder that it is harder to live in this hard-scrabble country than tap-dancing on a sofa in a driving rain. Up ahead, a rusty water tank towers over what looks like an untended automobile graveyard, and the .22-pocked city limits sign appears to identify the harsh tableau: *ARCHER CITY—Population 1924.*

The Spur Hotel, a rattletrap cattlemen's hostel commandeered by the film troupe as production headquarters, hasn't seen as much elbow-to-ass commotion since the great trail drives to Kansas in the Eighties. Throngs of stand-ins, crew technicians, bit players, and certified Grade A stupor-stars course in and out of the makeshift office like flocks of unhinged cockatoos. Phones ring incessantly; nobody moves to answer them. The location manager mutters into a walkie-talkie, and the agile-fingered men's wardrobe master deals out seedy-looking Western outfits to a queue of leathery-faced extras like soiled cards from the bottom of the deck.

Making faces into the mouthpiece, the location manager does a fast fade on the field phone, pours a couple of cups of coffee, and broken-fields across the crowded room to say hello: "You play 'Mr. Crawford,' right? Far out, good to meet you. . . . Don't let this spooky dump spook you, hear? Looks like a rummage sale in a toilet, don't it? Well, that's show biz. . . . As of this minute, Anno Domini, the production is—well, we're behind schedule. Which means that Bert Schneider, the producer—you won't meet him, he only feels safe back in Lotus Land—Bert's begun to act very producer-like and chop out scenes. Peter just had to red-pencil the episode where the gang of town boys screws the heifer, and I hated like hell to see it go. That sort of material is disgusting to a lot of people, but, shitfire, man, it's true-to-life. These hot-peckered kids around here still do that kind of thing as a daily routine. You've read McMurtry's book, haven't you? Why, Christ, to me, that's what it's all about—fertility rites among the unwashed." Grinning amiably, he lifts his cup in a sardonic toasting gesture: "Well, here's to darkness and utter chaos, ol' buddy."

Polly Platt materializes out of the crush, her hands in her jean pockets, Bette Davis–style. A poised, fine-boned blonde with sometimes complicated hazel eyes, she is the production designer, as well as Bogdanovich's wife. After an intense discussion with the wardrobe master about what constitutes a village geek, she coordinates my spiffy "Crawford" ensemble — baggy, faded dungarees, a shirt of a gray mucus color, and a tattered old purple sweater that hangs halfway to my knees.

Humming off-key, Polly waits while I change into my new splendor between the costume racks, and then the two of us stroll across the deserted courthouse square toward the American Legion Hall. She laughs with girlish delight as we pass the long-shuttered Royal Theater—the Last Picture Show in both fact and fantasy—and chats fondly about Ben Johnson, who's already completed his part in the film and departed:

"He's the real thing, Ben is—an old-fashioned country gentleman from his hat to his boots. Why, he didn't even want to say 'clap' when it came up in dialogue. Peter and I were both flabbergasted. Later, I asked Ben about the nude bathing scene in *The Wild Bunch*. It turns out Sam Peckinpah had to get him and Warren Oates both knee-walking drunk to get the shot, which wasn't in the original script. . . . But Ben and Peter ended up working beautifully together. Wait'll you see his rushes"—she gives a low whistle of admiration— "Academy stuff all the way, as they oom-pah in the trades."

Inside the ramshackle Legion Hall—a confusion of packed bodies, snarled cables, huge Panavision cameras, and tangled mike booms and lighting baffles—Polly leads the way to a quiet corner and begins tinting my hair gray with a makeup solvent recommended to Bogdanovich by Orson Welles. In the crowd milling around the center of the hall, I single out Cloris Leachman, whom I've just seen in *WUSA*; Bogdanovich, head bent in intent conversation with cinematographer Bob Surtees, whom I recognize from a press book promoting *The Graduate*; Clu Gulager, foppish-perfect-pretty in Nudie's finest ranch drag and manly footwear; and several teasingly familiar faces I can't quite fit names to. Glancing our way, Bogdanovich smiles and waves to indicate that he'll drop over to chat when he's free.

"Orson may turn up down here, you know," Polly muses as she dabs at my temples with a cotton swab. "The old rogue's making a picture about a Hollywood director—*Jake Hanniford*—and as usual he wants to steal scenes from somebody else's setup, if he can. Orson thinks Peter's some kind of nutty intellectual, so he's written him into the script in that sort of burlesque part. Peter says *Hanniford's* going to be the dirtiest movie ever made. . . . Whew, you sure get to know people fast, having to fool with their hair. Let's see what you look like. Oh, fantastic, great! I like your face—it's so *ravaged*. With the hair jobbie and those grungy old clothes, you look lunchier than Dennis Weaver in *Touch of Evil*." Typecasting, I mumble under my breath.

Bogdanovich, a slight, grave-faced young man wearing horn-rims and rust-colored leather bell-bottoms, shakes hands in greeting, eyes my scruffy getup narrowly, and nods agreement; yes, he likes my ravaged face, too. "Just don't wander out on the streets without a keeper," he murmurs, deadpan. "I don't want you getting arrested." Motioning for me to follow, he strides briskly across the dense-packed room toward the camera setup, stopping along the way to introduce me to Cloris, Gulager, Surtees, Cybill Shepherd, and because she's standing nearby, a pale, pretty young bit player from Dallas named

Pam Keller. Finally, I make my shy hellos with Tim Bottoms, the tousle-haired, James Dean–ish actor who's to play my estranged teenaged son in the upcoming scene: "Hi, son." "Lo, dad."

Oblivious to the racketing noise and movement around him, Bogdanovich blocks out our paces and patiently coaches Tim and me on our lines. It's a muted confrontation scene the two of us are involved in, a long, Wellesian dolly shot set against the backdrop of a country-and-western dance. Tim and I rehearse our moves until Surtees signals Bogdanovich that he's ready to roll; Peter, in turn, motions for Leon Miller's string band, arrayed on a platform at the head of the dance floor, to strike up "Over the Waves." The cameras whir; we go through the motions of the complicated shot twice. The second time around, it feels good. "*Cut,*" Bogdanovich calls. "Print both takes. Good work, everyone. *Stel-lar!*"

"*Academy,*" a disembodied voice bawls from behind a bank of glaring klieg lights.

Feeling washed-out and blank, I settle in a folding chair on the sidelines next to Pam Keller, who is "almost twenty" and who plays the part of "Jackie Lee French"—"Clu's dancing partner," she explains with a wry laugh, "which makes her a kind of semipro floozy, I guess." As if on cue, Gulager wanders by with chat-up on his mind; playfully, he makes a feint at Pam's ribs and bottom. "Oh, don't be such a wimp," she protests, frowning. Gulager, who speaks in a deep glottal rattle like Jimmy Stewart, gives her a pained look: "What was that you said, little lady?" "I don't stutter, buster," Pam snaps icily.

Dismissing him with a stare, Pam turns to ask what I do besides playing village junkie-geeks. Polly, who's stood by watching the exchange, grins and flashes Pam the V-sign as Gulager stalks disgustedly away: "Way to go, sweetheart. He's a real Hollywood showboat, that yo-yo."

The interminable delays between takes stretch into hours that elide past like greased dreams. Late in the evening, Pam is saying, between polite yawns, that she absolutely adores books, particularly Kahlil Gibran's *The Prophet,* and have I, by any chance, met Eric Hoffer, who she's heard somewhere also lives in San Francisco?

Around midnight, the tedium shades off into stuporous exhaustion, and abruptly seven or eight of us are headed back to the Ramada Inn in an over-stuffed Buick sedan. Pam falls asleep instantly, looking frail and vulnerable enough to resemble somebody's sister, maybe my own. To pass the time and the miles, Cloris and Gulager harmonize on old Baptist hymns, then trail off to silence. In the darkness beyond the swath of the headlights, the stringy mottes of mesquite trees and stagnant stock tanks and the Christmas-tree oil rigs flash past at eighty mph. Startled by the sight, I glimpse my bone-white hair and ravaged face in a window as I light a cigarette.

The conversation rises and falls desultorily. "Do we work tomorrow?" Gulager asks Cloris edgily. "Maybe we don't work, huh? That'd be nice. I'd like to spend the day limbering up at the Y." Cloris doesn't know, shrugs fatalistically. "God, I've just been thinking about that gross asshole who plays my husband. . . . This is the saddest picture," she reflects with a wilting sigh.

The next day begins and ends with the ritual viewing of the dailies in the hotel's cavernous banquet room. Sitting with Bogdanovich, who seems tense and distracted, and Bob Surtees, who is always medium cool, I watch enough footage to confirm Polly's estimate of Ben Johnson's performance as "Sam the Lion," the dying proprietor of the Last Picture Show—he's magnificent. Academy all the way. Then I hurry off to board the charter bus headed for Archer City.

On the hour-long ride to the set, I share a seat with Bill Thurman, who plays "Coach Popper," Cloris Leachman's husband in the film. Thurman, whose meaty, middle-aged face is a perfect relief map of burnt-out lust and last night's booze, is kibbitzing across the aisle with Mike Hosford, Buddy Wood, and Loyd Catlett—*Picture Show*'s resident *vitelloni*. The term springs automatically to mind to describe the three randy young studs because, in essence, they're playing themselves; on screen and off, they're the high-strutting young calves of this short-grass country, always on the prod for excitement, and maybe a little strange to boot. Loyd, who is seventeen and something of a self-winding motormouth, is plunking dolefully on a guitar and munching a jawful of Brown Mule. "Terbacker puts fuel in mah airplane," he explains expansively. "Say, look-a-here, Thurman, you seen our scene the other night—you thank we was any good?"

Thurman puts on a mock scowl and snarls: "Shit naw, kid, I thought yall sucked—buncha little piss-aint punks." "Hmph," Loyd snorts, "that's what that dollar whiskey'll do to your brains, Ah guess." Under his breath, he hisses: "Kiss mah root, you boogerin' ol' fart." Without preamble, he breaks into the Beatles' song about doing it in the road, and the other boys join in the singing with gusto, if no clear command of harmony.

"Me and Cloris are gettin' along real good together in our scenes," Thurman remarks, looking as if he'd give a princely sum to believe it. "I guess the production's been a little bit disorganized up to now, but all things considered, I b'lieve we got a real grabber on our hands here, don't you agree?" The *vitelloni* strike up "A Boy Named Sue," and Thurman starts reminiscing about the various "stars and gentlemen" he's had the privilege of working with. "Les Tremayne," he says. The boys segue into "Don't Bogart That Joint." "Bob Middleton . . . Paul Ford . . ." Thurman intones reverentially. *"They're — gonna — put — me — in — the — movies,"* Loyd is yowling as the bus pulls up at the Spur Hotel.

After changing into our costumes, Loyd and I walk over to the Legion Hall together. He says he wants to be an actor or maybe a stunt man — "for the money and the thrills . . . There's flat nothin' to do around these parts but fistfight and fuck, and Ah ain't even got a girlfriend," he laments. "Sometimes Ah feel lower than whaleshit, good buddeh, and that's on the bottom of the ocean. . . . Drama in high school — that's the only thang Ah was ever any good at. That and rodeoin', but mah folks made me give up ridin' bulls 'cause it's dangerous and they didn't like the company Ah was keepin'. Now, though, Ah've got mah foot in the door to the movies — shit, son, Ah'm gonna make $1,600 on this picture just by itself — and all Ah gotta do is take the ball and run, don't you thank?"

On the set, which is being busily readied for another take in the dance sequence, the wardrobe master sits slumped on a camp stool, firmly clutching the prop purse that Cloris Leachman will need in the upcoming scene. Striding past him, the first assistant director fakes an ogling double take: "Somehow, Mick, I don't think it's the real you — but would you be my *bubeleh* tonight?" The wardrobe master grins and lazily flashes him the bird.

"We need a huge container of water, Lou," Bogdanovich calls out to the second propman. "Waterloo!" the first assistant director crows. "That's what this whole deal is about, right?" "We hired Rube for his wit, not his talent," Bogdanovich murmurs as he peers through a viewfinder.

The hall is chill and drafty; the first raw gusts of a blue norther are rattling the windowpanes and doors. I find a chair near a gas heater and sit down to scribble some notes. Nearby, Bill Thurman, Clu Gulager, and several extras are seated around a card table, playing Forty-two. "Pass, fade, or die, you mis'able sonsabitches!" Thurman keeps bawling. Pointedly ignoring him, Gulager asks his partner, a barrel-gutted oil rigger from Olney: "Are you fellows deep-bleed drilling? Are you draining off all the oil over there?" "Sheeit," the rigger drawls, "I ain't been dreenin' off nothin' lately, what with this recession got me by the short hairs."

The second assistant director stops to survey the domino game for a minute. "Sweet baby Jesus," he mutters, "if I ran into this bunch in Tarzana, I'd turn out the lights and call the law."

Speaking of which, there's Joe Heathcock, the lanky apparition who plays the county sheriff in the film, proudly displaying his prop .38 police special to John Hellerman, who portrays "Mr. Cecil," a high school English teacher unjustly stigmatized as a homosexual. "My, oh, my," Hellerman, a dainty-featured little man, keeps murmuring as Heathcock waves the pistol around airily, explaining that Texas lawmen don't carry .45s much anymore — "That's just what you might call a lingerin' myth. They mostly tote these leetle ol' boogers like this here now. . . . Did I tell you? I just missed gettin' hijacked to Cuba with ol' Tex Ritter oncet. He tole me later they treated him like royalty down there — fed him a steak thick as a horse blanket." "My, oh, my," Hellerman repeats uneasily, his eyes keeping track of the gun.

Heathcock, I'm not surprised to find out, was famous long ago as "Jody" in Bob Wills' Texas Playboys (*"A-Ha! Come on in, Jody!"*), and nowadays gigs around Hollywood, Vegas, and Nashville for an enterprising $2,500 a week. As he talks, his movements and gestures aren't so much direct thrusts as sidelong indirections — furtive, elliptical — as if he's swimming through syrup toward some improbable lover. I mark him down on sight as an all-around *rara avis*, this homely, likable old bird, and move in closer to listen as he launches into a scarifying yarn about getting tossed in jail in Bowie, a shirttail burg not far to the south of Archer City.

"Wellser, I was a drankin' man back in them days," he recalls, sucking fire into his pipe and cackling now and then with the force of an exploding boiler. "As I recollect it, I was drivin' up from San Antone to Tulsa to meet Bob and the boys in the band, and I was about half-drunk — the last half, that is — hah! — so I pulled off the road and was gonna catch a leetle nap of shut-eye. Now, understand, I wasn't nothin' but a hahrd hand back then, but I had six-seven hunnerd dollars stuffed in my boot, so when somebody started shakin' my laig in the middle of the night, why, I just natcherly kicked whoever it was flush in the face. Wellser, be damned if whoever it was didn't turn out to be a Bowie constable, and he done the same thing right back to me — I left the better half of my teeth strung out along that highway when he brang me in to the lockup. Still and all, it was kiley a Mexican standoff — I shinered both of his eyes and bust his nose, too, before I realized he was a po-lice. Wellser, as it happens, that leetle set-to turned out to be a turnin' point for me—I ain't had a drank since, and that was right at twenty years ago. I figgered I'd been down so long it looked like it was all up to me at that point, so I—"

"But what happened?" Hellerman asks, jaw ajar.

"Happened?" Jody blinks. "Why, I awready told you. I quit drankin'."

"I mean at the *jail*," Hellerman persists.

"Oh, *that*." Jody relights his pipe with the timing of a paid assassin. "Well, I got out with a leetle hep from some friends."

Taking a few minutes' breather, I sit down on the sidelines, idly thumbing through the pages of a paperback copy of the novel version of *Picture Show* (Dell, 75¢, out of print). Set in a grim, mythical backwater called Thalia in 1951 (and "lovingly dedicated" to Larry McMurtry's hometown), the story focuses on a loose-knit clique of teenagers who have ultimately nowhere to go except to bed with each other, and to war in Korea.

The adults who alternately guide and misguide their young—even Sam the Lion, the salty old patriarch who rules over the town's lone movie theater—are no less disaffected by the numbing mise-en-scène of Thalia; in Dorothy Parker's phrase, they are all trapped like a trap in a trap.

The tenor of life in Thalia is described this way by a wayward mother to her soon-to-be-wayward daughter:

"The only really important thing I [wanted] to tell you was that life here is very monotonous. Things happen the same way over and over again. I think it's more monotonous in this part of the country than it is in other places, but I don't really know that—it may be monotonous everywhere. I'm sick of it, myself."

As far removed from grace or salvation as the Deity is reputed to be distant from sin, the town boys haunt the picture show, where they're permitted a few hours of "above the waist" passion with their girls on Saturday nights. Inexorably, boys and girls together careen into out-of-control adulthood in the Age of the Cold Warrior. But as they do, the symbols and landmarks of their childhood become lost to them, and in the end, even the picture show is gone.

Weighing the book in my hand, I try to weigh it in my mind as well— objectively, if possible. The narrative is sometimes crude, more often tasteless, and always bitter as distilled gall. But it is true—true to the bone-and-gristle life in this stricken, sepia-colored tag-end of nowhere. So it goes in the short-grass country. It's hardly a thought to warm your hands over, but it occurs to me that I've been in Archer City only a scant few hours, and like that daughter's mother in Thalia, I'm already a little sick of it, my own self.

"What previous movie work have you done, little lady?" Gulager asks Pam as they idle at their toe marks for the still-stalled dance sequence. Pam darts him a quizzical glance, decides his tone is neutral if not exactly friendly, and says that she was Charlotte Rampling's nude stand-in in an unreleased picture shot in Dallas called *Going All Out*. "Charlotte who? Never heard of her," Gulager shoots back, not neutral after all as he bends over to dust off his hand-tooled boots with a handkerchief. "Oh, you know — that girl in *The Damned*," Pam stammers, looking flushed. "You saw *The Damned*, didn't you? . . . I remember seeing you in *The Killers* with Lee Marvin. I thought you were — really quite good in it."

Gulager smiles crookedly and tucks the handkerchief back in his pocket: "Everybody thought I was good in that one, including me, honey. It was made for TV, and I expected to win an Emmy nomination for it. Turned out, the picture was too violent for family viewing and none of the networks would touch it . . ." Gulager pauses, then spits out coldly: "I hate acting, anyway — despise it. *San Francisco International* on NBC this season — you seen it yet? Don't bother. It's a piece of fuckin' trash. I'm only working on that series and this picture for the money. My main drive from now on is to become a filmmaker. Control — that's the only thing worth having in this business."

Unsure what to reply, Pam clears her throat and delicately observes that Gulager sounds a lot like Jimmy Stewart at certain odd moments. Gulager laughs shortly: "I wish I had Stewart's money." "Oh, money's not everything —" she starts to scold. Gulager cuts her off: "I can't think of anything I want to do that money can't buy. Money buys talent. Talent makes movies. I want to make movies. It's that simple."

Up on the rostrum, Leon Miller's string band — two guitars, a bass, and a fiddle — saws away wearily on "Put Your Little Foot" as the two assistant directors supervise endless dance rehearsals. A grip threads his way across the dance floor, bawling, "*Hot stuff — comin' through.*" The box he's carrying is marked: DON'T TOUCH — PROOFS TO TUESDAY'S SHOOTING. As they advance *one-two* and return *three-four*, Gulager and Pam continue their muted bickering until finally he flares up and calls her a "know-it-all little shit." Eyes snapping, Pam tartly informs him that you have to be a little shit before you can be a big one—"Ness pah, Big Shit?" Out on the floor, one of the extras faints, and there's another long delay. Pam wanders over to the sidelines, looking flustered. Jody, strumming Jeff Bridges' gleaming D-28 Martin, serenades her, Jimmie Rodgers–style:

> *If I can't be yo' shotgun, mama*
> *I sho ain't gonna be yo' shell*

Pam blushes pleased pink and mercurially changes moods. Maneuvering around to catch a glimpse of my notes, she puts on an impish smile and cajoles in an orphan-of-the-storm falsetto: "Oh, make me famous, will you, please? Are you famous by any chance? Clu Gulager is famous, you bet. He's famous-er than anybody, in fact. Just ask the rat bastard."

Near one of the too-few heaters scattered around the hall, Bob Glenn, who plays a nouveau-dumb oil baron in the film, is remarking that he appreciates the unstructured makeup of the location company—"No snotty star types, all the lead actors mingling with everybody else." Fred Jackson bobs his head in agreement: one of the stand-ins, he's a tall drink of water from over Throckmorton way who looks uncannily like Buck Owens. "Hail yes, Bawb," he says. "So far, ever'body high and low's just acted like we'us all in this thang together, you know what I mean? Dju meet ol' Ben Johnson while he'us down here? Shit, he's just *folks*, that ol' boy. He's sposed to come back one a these times and go huntin' with me. You ever do any huntin'?"

Looking sulky and bored, Loyd Catlett saunters past and overhears Jackson's question. "You damn betchy Ah go huntin'," he grumps, "but that don't mean Ah never ketch nothin'. Same thang with this picture—Ah missed out on all the good parts. Ah never git no pussy, and Ah don't git in no fights. Ah'm just a kind of sidekick for Jeff and Tim, Ah guess." "Well, I reckon you just got to keep on keepin' on, boy," Jackson says affably. Loyd can't maintain his pout for long. Soon, he's grinning toothily despite himself: "Aw, slap hands with me, you sorry hillbilly dip-shit. *Rat-on!*"

Over an electric bullhorn, the first assistant director booms out: "All right, everybody be of good cheer. All together now, let's have some *SMILES!*" "Let's have some liquor," somebody groans in reply. Scowling distractedly, Bogdanovich kicks at a thick hummock of recording cable. "Let's have some lunch," he sighs quietly.

With manic zest, Gulager titillates the townspeople dining at the Golden Rooster, Archer City's lone indoor eatery, by pasting pats of butter on his cheeks and forehead. "It wouldn't melt in your mouth, honey," Cloris observes acidly. Cybill Shepherd, who plays "Lacy," the film's teenaged sexpot, looks pained at the buzzing commotion Gulager is causing among the diners; wordlessly, she picks up her book—Thomas Mann's *The Magic Mountain*—and leaves before the meal is served. It's an interesting choice of reading and an interesting reaction; I determine to try to talk to her if a chance arises.

A local filling station owner approaches the table and shyly asks Gulager for his autograph; the big, sunburned man pretends not to notice the trickle of butter oozing down the actor's jaw. Not to be overlooked in the crowd, Cloris launches into a rambling singsong recitative about George Hamilton taking a sleeping-pill suppository during a cab ride in Paris. She projects the maybe-apocryphal story just like an actress, but she breaks just like a little girl when nobody but Jeff Bridges laughs at the punch line. Gratefully, she tousles his hair: "Give my love to your daddy, Jeff-boy. Is he still all water-puckered from *Sea Hunt?*" Jeff grins bashfully and mumbles something into his plate.

Gulager, milking the butter schtick to the last drip, scrapes the runny yellow goo off his face and spreads it on a slice of bread, then wolfs it down with extravagant gusto. To a man, the diners across the crowded room crane around to watch his every move, but nobody quite applauds.

Pam, who's sat rigid with distaste throughout the meal, looks pensive during the two-block walk back to the Legion Hall. "Clu Gulager," she announces at last in a tiny, constricted voice, "is just another pretty face. All smeary with butter, at that. *Blechh!*" She reminds me of someone, Pam does. Like Loyd, in his way, and Jody, too, she reminds me of everybody decent I ever knew in this empty, perishing, hard-scrabble country.

Back on the set, the crew members are beginning to trundle the monstro Panavision equipment out into the parking lot where the night's shooting is to take place. By this time, it's 6:30, dark as the grave, and biting cold. Jody is warming his hands over a feebly flickering heater. "You awder this bad weather, darlin'?" he teases Pam. The prop master wanders among the clusters of actors and extras huddled around the stoves, asking, "Has anybody seen a can of snow?" General laughter trails him around the room. The chief camera operator is telling a spectacular-breasted teen queen from the neighboring town of Electra about working on *Drive, He Said.* "Well, it was a weird experience, I tell you that, sugar. Jack Nicholson's what they call far out, you know? Dope and rebellion, all that shit. Me, I'm more or less a law-and-order person myself, so I told him after we saw the rough cut: 'Jack, it's a cute picture, but it's not anything I'd want to take my wife and kids to see.' Listen, uh . . . Dottie . . . I'll probably have to work here until pretty late, but, uh . . . what're you going to be up to around midnight?"

Loyd Catlett rushes in with the news that the generator truck has caught on fire. "The *lost* picture show," Mae Woods, Bogdanovich's secretary, groans, dashing outside to take a look. Fred Jackson grasps Loyd's elbow and probes for his funnybone: "You hear about that ol' hippie kid, he got the first asshole transplant?" Loyd shakes his head: "Naw—*ouch*, you sombitch!" "It re-jected him," Fred guffaws. On a rump-sprung sofa near a fireplace that doesn't work, Jody strums patient accompaniment while Cybill Shepherd and Jeff Bridges try to remember the words to "Back in the Saddle." A rash of new domino games breaks out around the fires.

Outside, towering floodlights illumine the '52-vintage cars ringing the entrance to the hall. The minor generator blaze has already been dispatched by the Archer City Volunteer Fire Department, some of whose members remain behind, striking stalwart poses. As usual, the shot Bogdanovich plans is diabolically complicated:

(1) Cybill, as "Jacy," is to park her '48 Ford convertible near the hall's entrance, get out of the car, and be greeted by Randy Quaid, who plays "Lester," a goofy-looking idle-rich suitor. They're to exchange a page or so of dialogue before (2) Jeff and Tim Bottoms, as "Duane" and "Sonny," respectively, barrel into the parking lot in a battered Dodge pickup against a moving frieze of extras shown in deep focus getting out of cars, walking across the lot toward the hall's side entrance, etc. Tim exits from the truck toward the rear door while Jeff advances to embrace Cybill. During the clinch and subsequent dialogue, the camera pans around to show (3) Clu Gulager, as "Abilene," escorting Pam Keller—"Jackie Lee French"—through the front door.

"All of that in one so-called fluid take," the dolly operator groans piteously. "Hell, Peter, it's not only difficult, it's impossible." "With patience and saliva," an electrician pronounces sagely, "the elephant balleth the ant."

"Peter, can we shoot this shit?" the boomman screams out from overhead. "Or not?" "Strictly speaking, Dean," Bogdanovich mumbles, squinting at the setup, "possibly." He motions toward the first assistant director: "Meester Ru-

Timothy Bottoms (left) and Grover Lewis in a scene from **The Last Picture Show**. Lewis played the father of Sonny, Bottoms's character, in the classic movie based on Larry McMurtry's novel.

bin I theenk it iss time ve vill take a live vun." "Damn, Peter," the second assistant director snorts, "you're getting to sound just like Otto. That prick." "Ready when you are, C. B.," shouts the first assistant director.

In a sudden hush, the cameras begin to roll, but Cybill blows the take by missing her mark parking the convertible. When she stammers out an apology, the sound mixer stage-whispers gruffly: "Sympathy can be found in the dictionary between shit and syphilis, sister."

After the eighth consecutive take has gone down the tube—this time because Jeff has rammed the pickup into the side of the building—Bogdanovich murmurs though blue lips, "Well, back to the old drawing board." "We're as shit out of luck tonight as a barber in Berkeley," the key grip grumbles. Polly Platt wanders around looking worried-in-general; Fred Jackson pats her on the shoulder in paternal commiseration. "Ain't a horse that can't be rode," he philosophizes solemnly, "and ain't a cowboy that can't be thrown." "Our l-left foot doesn't seem to know what our other left f-foot is d-doing tonight," Polly complains through chattering teeth.

Down on the shoulder of the highway, where despite the cold a sizeable crowd has gathered to watch the filming, a bandy-legged cowboy and his woman—both drunk—are quarreling bitterly about money. "Aw, hush up about it, honey," she snaps, reaching for his arm. "C'mon—less you and me *vámanos a casa*. Piss on a buncha movie stars, anyhow." "*Naw, goddamnit!*" he cries in a strangled fury, bristling away from her and fishing feverishly through his pockets. "I ain't about to haul-ass home till we get this thang settled, oncet and for all! Here, goddamn your bitchin' eyes—here's 99 cents in change. Put a fuckin' penny with that and you can buy a dollar anywheres!" Starting to sob, the woman slaps the change out of his hand and stumbles off into the darkness. After a minute, the cowboy spits toward the coins scattered in the gravel and sways off after her, howling: "Hey Trudy! Wait up a goddamn minute! I'm comin', darlin'!"

It's a wrap at last on what must be the eleventh or twelfth take. The actors and crew look numb and gray-faced with exhaustion; Pam looks distressed, as well. Her face is wind-chapped, she has a big red bump swelling on her forehead, and she's worried sick that she may lose her receptionist's day-job at the Royal Coach Inn in Dallas because Bogdanovich says he needs her for an additional day's shooting. "I didn't count on this movie changing my *whole darn life!*"

The troupe works till the midnight hour, then falls apart like some hydra-headed beast sawed off at the knees. In a station wagon speeding back to Wichita Falls, Gulager asks Jody how he happened to get involved with *Picture Show*.

"Wellser, ol' Reba Hancock, Johnny Cash's baby sister, she recommended me for the part," Jody answers, tamping his pipe. "She's a darlin' woman, Reba is. You know her by any chance?"

Gulager leans forward, interested: "No, but I've met John. Worked on a benefit with him once: Has he cleaned up his act, like they say? Is he walkin' the line these days?"

Jody grins broadly: "Aw, you bet yore sweet ass he is. Ol' John's livin' real good now, real straight. I recollect he tole me oncet that he used to take up to a hunnerd pills a day—you know, what they call them, uppers? But that's all spilt milk under the bridge now. . . . Yep, John's just bought hisself a nice home over at Nashville from Roy Osborne—and, a course, he's got June, too, which that leetle ol' girl has just done wonders for his health and his life." "Is that where you make your home—Nashville?" Gulager asks.

"Yesser," Jody nods, "and mah own self, I couldn't be happier noplace else in the world. Shoot, I got more work comin' in anymore than I can get around to, seems like. I'm a reg'lar member of the *Grand Ole Opry*, I work on *Gunsmoke* three-four times a year. The Mills Brothers just recorded a leetle ol' song that I wrote—'It Ain't No Big Thang'—and I seen just the other day in *Cashbox*, I b'lieve it was, where that sucker's awready in the Top One-Hunnerd.

"Hell's bells, I had to flat up and quit *Hee-Haw*—it'us too corny for my sights, you know what I mean? Buncha sorry, white-trash mow-rons settin' around on the floor cuttin' up like fools. Then, too, Junior Samples, he's got a terrible drankin' problem, and not much sense to start with, and I got sick and tahrd of readin' his idiot cards for him. . . . But, y'know, that eggsuckin' show shot up to 15 in the Nielsens last week, and John Cash's fell off to 65. Somebody's givin' John some bum goudge on per-duction, seems like to me . . .

"Yesser, I lead an awful full and happy life these days. Play goff every chancet I get. I shot a few rounds with Dean Martin not long back. You know Dino, by any chancet? Well, lemme tell you, he's a fine ol' boy—he wants to record in Nashville sometime soon. And Frank, y'know, he's awready got studio time booked over there."

Gulager coughs delicately: "That's . . . uh, Sinatra you mean?"

"Yesser," Jody nods, sucking serenely on his pipe, "that's the one."

During the postmidnight screening of some late-arriving rushes in the hotel's banquet room, Bogdanovich, Polly, Bob Surtees, and six or seven other production aides drowse through some routine interior establishing shots, then snap alert at a brace of electrifying takes showing Gulager, as "Abilene," seducing "Jacy"—Cybill Shepherd—in a deserted pool hall. Even in its unedited form, the scene has a raw and awesome power; at one point, Gulager's right eye, slightly cocked, gleams out of the eerily lit frame like a malevolent laser beam. "Academy," the first assistant director murmurs reverently in Surtees' direction. "Wow—Clu looks positively *ogreish*," the second assistant director crows in delight. A brittle female voice pipes out of the dark at the back of the room: "Nothing that mental and spiritual plastic surgery couldn't cure, honey."

I spend the better part of an hour the next morning reviewing the reactions of some of the local gentry to the filming of *Picture Show* on their home turf, as expressed in letters to the editor of the weekly *Archer County News*. These are heartfelt communications, I'm given to understand by a hard-drinking production secretary, from "Baptists and worse."

From the paper's October 22, 1970, edition:

> . . . I understand that (Larry McMurtry's) book, if it can be called that, is to be translated into a movie and that portions are to be filmed in Archer City with the support and approval of the Citizenry. No doubt, a certain glamor and glitter is to be anticipated from having a few Hollywood types in the city during the filming, and perhaps some economic benefit may ensue, but if the City Dads and the School Board Members have taken the precaution to read the book, then no question can prevail as to the type of movie that will result. I, for one, feel that Archer City will come out of this with a sickness in its stomach and a certain misgiving about the support the City is lending to the further degradation and decay of the morals and attitudes we foist upon our youth in this Country . . .
>
> Where are the voices that should be raised in opposition to this travesty?
>
> Wake up, Small Town America. You are all that is left of decency and dignity in this country . . .
>
> Yours truly, Noel W. Petre

In the November 5 edition, the publisher, Joe Stults, mills about smartly over the issue in a signed column called "Joe's Jots":

> Let me be fast to point out that I do not endorse or purchase dirty or obscene books, nor do I attend or endorse dirty movies. Neither do I consider myself a literary or movie critic. I must admit I have read only a few excerpts from the book and from what I read the book "stinks." However, on the other hand, a Wichita Falls school teacher (woman) told me that she has read all of McMurtry's books and thought they were tops . . .
>
> I definitely cannot see where Archer City will suffer a "black eye" for permitting the movie to be filmed here. It has already proved to be an educational experience for many and if our morals are affected by this book or movie then maybe we need to cultivate a little deeper.

Later in the morning on the set in Archer City, the cast assembles and waits fretfully for the final hours of shooting on the dance sequence to begin. Polly Platt, renewing the tint job on my hair, is saying from behind her enormous blue oval shades: "I was a Boston deb—can you believe it?—so I had a different notion about dances when I first got here. . . . Now, I'm miserable and deliriously happy at the same time. I miss my baby girls to the point of pain—they're with Peter's family out in Phoenix—but I'm elated about the way the movie's coming along. . . . Of course, part of the agony is that Peter is no longer my friend or lover or companion; Peter is making a movie. . . . He has a terrific nostalgia for his teenage years in the Fifties—Holden Caulfield ice-skating at Rockefeller Plaza with wholesome young girls in knee socks, like that. . . . Somehow, he's managed to transfer those feelings about his own adolescence to the totally different experience of the kids in the film. . . . Have you noticed? He's very tender with the young actors. . . . So, I ended up 'doing' Cybill—her overall appearance as 'Jacy'—to lock into those longing fantasies of Peter's. In reality, I created a rival for myself, I guess. . . . Well, anything for art, huh? There, now—you look properly geekish again. Get out there and wow 'em, kid: Win this one for the Gipper."

"Who's the Gipper, coach?" Cloris inquires brightly, making room for me in the shivering circle massed around a heater. Nearby, one of the never-ending Forty-two games is in progress, generating more heat than the stove. John Hellerman is dourly predicting that Mae Woods, Bogdanovich's secretary, will turn pro and start hustling in the L.A. domino parlors when she gets back home. "Forty-two again!" Mae squeals, flashing Hellerman a deep-dish grin. Chording Jeff's guitar from his perch on a prop crate, Jody serenades Ellen Burstyn, who plays "Lois," a cynical, bed-hopping socialite in the film:

> Sick, sober and sorry,
> Broke, disgusted, and blue.
> When I jumped on that ol' Greyhound,
> How come I set down by you?

By the fake fireplace, Bob Glenn is recalling the years he spent working in a repertory group in a remote area of Canada: "Only the National Geographic reviewed us," he concludes ruefully. When I laugh, he sidles nearer and asks out of the lower half of his mouth if I'm holding anything "interesting to smoke from Frisco." I give him a puzzled look; he looks at me as if I'm peculiar, too, then turns away to listen to Bill Thurman, who's describing his lady agent in Dallas: "Gawddamn, boy, her fuckin' laigs look like a sackful of door-knobs, and they run clear up to right under her tits. Shit, I can't figger out a-tall how her ol' man ever gets any." Later in the day, I do a double take when Bogdanovich, who's been standing within earshot, incorporates the remarks almost verbatim in a colloquy between the character "Coach Popper" and his beer-guzzling cronies.

"Domino contingent," the first assistant director rasps over a bullhorn, "please hold it down to a roar. We're having a rehearsal." Warmed up by now, I stroll around for a while among the extras. Most of the men are unsmiling, stiff-starched, gleaming with brilliantine. The women, as a hard rule, are pinch-faced, mean-spirited cunts who make me wonder how I managed to couple with their spitting images so long without turning raving queer. Near the coffee urn, Gulager, his concho-studded hat tilted forward rakishly, is chousing a couple of the younger, prettier ones: "You got a boyfriend, do you, sugar? And you, too, hon? Back in Alvarado? Wahl, what do those two lucky ol' boys think about you pretty little things bein' way up here all by your lonesome makin' a moom pitcher? Wahl, wahl, wahl . . ."

Over by the bandstand, where Leon Miller and his boys sit slumped like zombies after having played "Put Your Little Foot" for approximately the 527th time, Loyd is dogging the heels of the casting director. "Ah heard they gonna aw-dition three nekkid girls from Dallas today," he whispers to me with a wink, "so Ah'm ona see if ol' Chason'll let me sneak a little peek."

It's a moment of truth for Pam, too, who's just had a long, nerve-rattling talk on the phone with her boss in Dallas. While Bogdanovich blocks out the paces of her final scene with Gulager, Thurman moseys by, notices her woebegone expression, and asks, not unkindly: "Whatsa matter, sugar? You look like somebody cut yore piggen strang." Pam makes a fetchingly grotesque face at him, but doesn't answer. "Yeah, Pam, what's up?" Bogdanovich prods with fond amusement. "You gonna get fired or what?" "I don't *know!*" she bursts out, an oyster's tear away from real tears. "A fat lot you care, anyway, Mr. Bigtime Director—you're making a *movie*, right? The show must go on, right?" "Right," Bogdanovich says evenly, turning away. Polly, who's been following the conversation, bites her lip but says nothing.

"Hell, Pam, you think *you* got problems," Thurman interjects gloomily. "Today's mah birthday—I'm fifty years old. Syrup just went up to a goddamn dollar a goddamn sop." "That so?" Gulager asks, flicking imaginary specks of dust off his glove-tight trousers. "I'll be forty-two this month myself. But that's all right, I guess—Antonioni was thirty-eight before he directed his first feature." Polly makes a deep, gagging sound in her throat that Gulager pretends not to notice.

Out on the dance floor, Bogdanovich has a setup at last. When the actors are all in position, he sings out: "This is a take, folks. Movies are better than ever! Roll 'em!"

"Mark it," the sound mixer growls.

"Five-nine-charlie-apple — take one," a grip intones, clapping a slapstick.

"And . . . *dancing!*" the first assistant director booms out.

It's a wrap in one so-called fluid take, and the crew lustily yodels its approval: "Way to go, Pam baby!" "*Academy!*" "Nice work, Clu."

Over on the sidelines, where Pam goes to fretfully await transportation to the airport in Wichita Falls, a spry old lady from Vernon in a bird-nest hat is reminiscing about her honeymoon on the Goodnight Ranch in 1923; wearing a new fur coat, she tells Pam with a wan smile, she lost her footing crossing a fence stile and sank neck-deep in a snowdrift. "My swan," she marvels in remembrance, "it took four big drovers to pull me a-loose. Of course, it got much colder in those days than it does now —"

Straight-arming her way up close, a blue-haired matron of fifty-odd in a psychedelic-splotched pantsuit interrupts to ask Pam: "Hay yew today?" "Just fine, thank you." "Listen, can I git your autograph, dumplin'? You do play 'Jacy,' don't you?" "No, ma'am, I play 'Jackie Lee French' —" "Aw, well," the woman sniffs, "that's about as good, I gay-ess." Looking stricken, Pam signs a paper napkin, then quickly scratches off her home phone number on a sliver of envelope and hands it to me. "If you happen to see the rushes I'm in," she blurts, "call and let me know what you think, would you? I'm not sure I ever want to be in any more movies, but I'd like to know if I did good or not in this one." Hugging Polly good-bye, she hurries off after a driver who'll take her the first leg of the way back to Dallas.

Loyd watches Pam leave, then turns to Polly: "She say she don't wanna be in no more movies? Is that what she said? Sheeit, boy, Ah do! Ah'd lahk to be in about a million of 'em."

"Hush, Loyd," Polly says in an absent tone.

Feeling twitchy and fogged-out, I cash in my costume early and hitch a ride back to the Ramada Inn in Bill Thurman's blue Lincoln. Bob Glenn takes the wheel next to Gulager, while Thurman stretches out over most of the backseat, drinking what he calls "toddy for the body" — Old Taylor out of the bottle.

Between jolts, Thurman is gossiping about a Dallas-based sci-fi film impresario for whom he's worked in a total of thirteen Grade Z pictures: "Ol' Larry's a good ol' boy, you understand, but he cain't keep his pecker out of his pocketbook." Pause for a deep swallow. "'Course now, Mr. Bogdanovich . . . you know, Peter . . . he's somethin' else altogether, cain't you agree, Clu?" Every time Thurman addresses Gulager, he calls him "Clu"; sometimes at both ends of the sentence.

Gulager, slumped in the front passenger's seat, doesn't deign to answer at once. Thurman goes on: "I mean, to me, I thank he's got the makin's of, uh, well . . . a great artist, maybe." "Meb-be," Gulager concedes, sounding unconvinced: "Personally, I don't like the script cuts he's making, but I guess he doesn't have much choice about it. I'm gonna fight for that scene of yours in the gym, Bill—you know, where you tell the boys they're too ugly to be girls and too short-peckered to be men."

"Clu, would you do that, Clu?" Thurman entreats softly. "Gowddamnit, ol' buddy, I shore would appreciate it, Clu."

"Well, I don't have any real power to do anything," Gulager snaps irritably. "I'm just another Okie from Muskogee, myself—just another hired hand working for day wages—"

Bob Glenn cuts his eyes off the road an instant: "You really from Muskogee?"

"Tahlequah," Gulager says, "twenty-nine miles outside. . . . But shit, look, Thurman, that's the only reason I took my role—which is a fat zero of a nothing part—because there was a lot of other good stuff in the script. It read good to me, it read *honest*. As to whether Mr. Bogdanovich makes it or not, that pretty much depends on how this picture comes out. Both of you guys work mainly out of Dallas, right? Well, I make my living in Hollywood, and they write you off quick if you fail in my city." The cutting edge of finality in his voice is chilling. Glenn suddenly brakes the car up short; a herd of high-stepping whiteface cattle stream across the highway. Thurman tips up his bottle for a long instant. Abruptly, it is spectral dark, and the night's chill is on us all.

San Francisco International is on TV that night. I watch part of it in my room, then drift off to the hotel bar to belt back a few healing brandies. Gulager was square on the money in his estimate of the show; with lines like "A killer in an airport full of emotional people is a bad situation," it's a disaster area looking for a landing site. Half-tight, I vow soberly never to broach the topic to him.

Later, on my way to bed, there's a phone message for me at the desk from the Yankee Lady out in California: *Sleep warm.* After a bit, I do just that, dreaming at some surreal point that I'm Dennis Weaver in *Touch of Evil*, only *Touch of Evil* has somehow become a Saturday-afternoon Western playing at the Last Picture Show in Archer City—the old shuttered Royal Theater—and my grandfather and I are sitting in the hushed dark alongside—who're those two ol' boys in the seats next to us?—Larry McMurtry and Elvis?—yes—and suddenly my own ravaged face swims into focus on the silvery screen, bigger than life, and the camera pulls back to show me tap-dancing on a sofa in a driving rain while Bill Thurman, Bob Glenn, and Clu Gulager ping away at my feet with six-shooters. My grandfather leans forward as the scene unreels, lifts one liver-speckled old man's hand as if to greet his own surprise, and says with an expiring sigh: "*Academy, boy. Academy all the way!*"

The next day's call sheet lists the setting to be used as EXT GRAVEYARD, and summons all the principals of the cast and crew, plus "20 atmos. mourners," a location van, the generator truck, a bus, two station wagons, the director's car, and one (1) Ritter wind machine to the Spur Hotel at 9:30 sharp. From there, the assembled caravan will converge on the Archer City Community Cemetery, where the funeral of "Sam the Lion" is to be shot.

The Archer City cemetery, a barren but neatly tended tract with a few knobby trees jutting up here and there, forms a strong, stark tableau, so devoid of ornament that each stone and plant and ruptured fissure of the land plays an intense part in the composition, subtly forcing the eye out to the horizon and up to the sky. The weather, fortunately for Bogdanovich and us all, has turned mild, almost balmy, and the wind from the sea of mesquites to the west soughs along the yellow, grassy swells that ascend in all due homage to the burial ground's only imposing structure—the Widow Taylor's marble-columned crypt, with twin potted cactus plants flanking the door like spikey tribunes. As the actors file off the bus and mill curiously about a freshly dug grave to be used in the scene, the first assistant director unslings his ever-present bullhorn and intones solemnly: "Let us now praise famous men, ladies and gents. Welcome to Lenny Bruce's cafeteria."

Bogdanovich sets up the master shot of the funeral scene with uncommon speed, but close-ups and dialogue fakes last well into the morning. In off minutes, the *vitelloni* caper among the gravestones. "*It's Boot Hill, son,*" Kenny Wood squalls in the distance, "*the last roundup, motherfuckers.*"

Jeff, who's by now as hooked on dominoes as Bogdanovich's secretary, starts up a game a few paces away from Larry McMurtry's family burial plot. The markers for McMurtry's paternal grandparents read:

Louisa F.		*William J.*
	and	
1859–1946		*1858–1940*

The sight of the stones sets up an aching urge in me to be away from the place; I've been to too many of these country boneyards for real, listening to shiny-suited shamans with faces like sprung mousetraps gibber piously over old men and women who were, somehow, in their lifetimes, a little better than they ought to have been anyway, given the time and place.

Over by the wind machine, Bill Thurman is sounding off to Bob Glenn about how loaded he'd gotten the night before: "I was so pissed outa mah mind, boy, I couldn't have drove mah dick in a can of lard. You orta been there." Glenn surveys the empty horizon and spits: "Everybody from here to the damn Atlantic Ocean is three drinks and two fucks behind, you ask me." Nearby, Clu Gulager is chatting up a pretty young hot dog from Anson: "You got a boyfriend up there, do you? What's he think about you comin' down here to make a moom pitcher? Wahl, wahl, wahl . . ."

A grizzled old extra in a string tie and Mexican-tooled boots squints disapprovingly at Tim Bottoms, who's lying face down on a grassy slope beyond the last row of gravestones. "Wouldn't know a gol-danged rattler if one taken a gol-danged bite out of him," he sneers, pouring together the makings out of a Prince Albert can.

Downwind from the action, Jody strums quietly on a guitar. "Oh, I had a friend named Ramblin' Bob," he sings, then looks up and notices Barc Doyle, who plays a Baptist preacher's son in the film. "Yore daddy shore dresses you tacky, boy," he cackles. Unlucky at dominoes, Jeff sprawls out in the grass to drowse in the sun, his head cushioned on a pile of jackets. John Hellerman stumbles through the maze of film equipment strewn about on the ground, looking viscerally shaken by the barrenness of the land. "Texas is almost all depleted now," Gulager tells him with a brooding scowl. "It's 20 million square acres of fucked-up land, that's it."

After a while, when the cameras move elsewhere, I go look into the open grave wherein Ben Johnson — "Sam the Lion" — is supposed to be laid. The brand name on the casket-lowering device says *FRIGID*, and you'd better believe it, little pardners.

Everything about him is gigantic, this sixty-odd-year-old cowboy spook who braces me later that day outside the Spur—his immense hands dangling out of the kind of gangrene-colored Western tent-suit you can buy at Leddy Bros. in Fort Worth for around $400, his watermelon-sized skull bulging out of a spotless XXXXX Stetson beaver, even his blinding-white dentures glistening like a wholesaler's display of cue balls out of a massive, rutted face that looks to have been marinated a winter or two in creosote and brine. He's M. B. Garrett, as it turns out, from over in Prairie Grove—lived over there all his life, he says, has a little spread over there, in fact, just a few thousand acres, the place mostly takes care of itself these days, even though his boys have up and moved off to Dallas on him, so he's chancing a one-day flyer in this crackerjack movie-extra game . . .—and say, look-a-here, do I mind some company over to the commissary for a leetle snack to eat? He's heard the food over there is right tolerable today—steak, fresh greens, and biscuits—and, anyway, he's curious about that little spiral notebook he's noticed me scratching in all day.

Sure, be glad to have you, I say, shaking hands and moving off in the direction of the dining hall. But he detains me with a polite thumb and forefinger encircling my upper arm: "You don't wanna *walk* over there, do you?" he asks anxiously. Why not? I shrug, it's only a block or two—"Because *my whiskey* is under the seat in the *truck*," he explains patiently, pointing to a dusty Ford pickup at the curb with a bumper sticker that reads: *When guns are outlawed, only outlaws will have guns.* Oh, I hear myself saying in a faraway voice.

This M. B. Garrett from over there in Prairie Grove turns out to be a self-cooled, rapid-firing, semi-automatic sagebrush yenta as he fishes a fifth-sized bottle in a brown paper bag from the accumulated detritus on the floorboard and guides the Ford at a creep across the square and into a mire of unpaved streets. Between bowel-stinging jolts from the bottle, which we pass gingerly back and forth like the hot stuff it is, he geysers out jocular gossip about the McMurtry clan, past and present, and says as we pass a local doctor's pretty daughter: "Married twicet, divorced twicet. She's been warmed-over for the next feller in line twicet-over, you might say." He brakes to peer up a side road: "Might as well take the long way around. Give us another excuse to take a leetle snort."

When we pull up at the dining hall several excuses later, Garrett puts on a

long, sorrowing face and announces that he has a "confession" to make—
"That toddy you been drankin'? Well, I'm obliged to tell ye it was half vodka
and half Old Crow. I didn't have no full dram of neither when I set out this
mornin', so I just taken and mixed 'em both up in the same bottle. Hah! Bet
you never knowed it, am I right? That's a good one on ye, ain't it?" Garrett is
still guffawing when we unload our lunch trays at a table where the location
manager is poking apprehensively at his greens and reading a paperback copy
of *One Flew over the Cuckoo's Nest.*

At the sight of the book's title, Garrett imitates a little boy reciting a nursery rhyme for the PTA:

> *Wire, briar, limber-lock,*
> *Three geese in a flock.*
> *One flew east, one flew west,*
> *One flew over the cuckoo's nest . . .*

"*And shit a big gob,*" he concludes in the little-boy falsetto, clicking his den-
tures to underscore his wickedness. Wolfing his food so he can get home and
hay his stock before nightfall, Garrett slyly intimates that he himself has been
interested in books for quite a spell now—for years, in fact. Yesser, why, he
himself even buys a book now and again from what they call—what is it
now?—aunty-quarian book dealers? Up there in New Yowrk and so on? Yesser,
he himself, in matter of active fact, concentrates mainly on collecting rare editions of Texans. In matter of goddamn active fact, he owns one of the only
complete collections of J. Frank Dobie in existence, and he reckons it's worth
a right smart of money—at least, that's what those aunty-quarian whoosits up
there in New Yowrk claim, if you can take such people at their word, sight unseen and all. Sight unseen, because he doesn't get up to New Yowrk much anymore—his wife's health ain't all that it might be now, and she never did cotton much to missing Sunday services over there in Prairie Grove, anyhow. But
if my friend there and me are interested in such truck—J. Frank Dobie and all
such as that—and we ever happen to get over there to Prairie Grove, why, you
know, just look him up, everybody knows where his place is at . . .

After the old man takes his leave, the location manager shakes his head in
wonderment. "What in the name of God's body," he whispers, "was *that?*"
Somebody who's been trying to kill me all my life, I tell him as a joke. Only,

judging from the way he cranes around to peer at me, it doesn't quite come out that way.

Getting dressed to go back to Wichita Falls that night, Loyd Catlett calls out to Jeff Bridges with studied nonchalance: "Whyn't you'n me run over by the high school tonight, Jeff — you know, fool around some?" Jeff explains that he isn't feeling well; when he gets back to the hotel, he says, he's going to bed and stay there for the evening. "Aw, sheeit," Loyd grumbles, crestfallen.

My part in the picture is finished by now — *Academy all the way, William Medford Lewis* — so I'm essentially hanging out the next day when the shooting commences with a brief picnic sequence in Hamilton Park — the Beverly Hills of Wichita Falls, kind of — then shifts to the Cactus Motel on Old Iowa Park Road for the exteriors of a tryst scene involving Cybill and Tim.

Every hole-in-the-road town in the short-grass country has its version of the Cactus, a sagging row of plaster-and-lath cabins beneath an eternally winking "Vacancy" sign. Next door is a franchise tamale joint, and beyond that lies a solid mile of truck stop cafes, liquor stores, used car lots, filling stations that solicit all known varieties of credit cards, and about a hundred or so of the baddest beer bars in the Western world.

As the troupe disgorges from the bus, the sun beats down, fleets of semi trucks roar by on the highway, and a gaggle of townspeople gather to gawk and shyly shake hands with the actors they recognize. "*It's so inneresting,*" a rabbit-toothed woman in pedal pushers exclaims. "Look," somebody hisses softly, pointing at Jeff, who's hunkering down alongside Loyd on a plot of dead grass beside the generator truck, "there's Beau Bridges." "Who?" "Lloyd Bridges' kid." "Oh."

While the propmen are dressing the scene, Bogdanovich lounges against the hood of a car, doing a fair-to-middling imitation of Peter Lorre. As all good secretaries do on such occasions, Mae Woods registers 100 on the laugh-meter. Cybill sits off to one side, intently squinting into the pica-choked pages of *Crime and Punishment.* Nearby, one of the grips is trying to shmarm over a tushy piece of the local Freez-Kreem talent: "What we're doing, see, is making a lap-style horror flick — *It Came to Eat the Freeways,* you dig. Stars eight thousand Datsuns and a beat-up old VW bus. There're still a few bit parts open, though. Sa-ay, do you think you could play a topless sheriff at a Missis-sippi kill-in? *I'll* speak to the director about it myself. Like, gimme your phone number and I'll get on the horn to you first thing tonight . . ."

Slack-jawed but firm-butted, the girl dutifully pokes through her bag for something to write on. There isn't even the faintest quiver of comprehension in her face.

Meanwhile, on their tiny plot of dead grass, Jeff and Loyd are embarked on an extraordinary exchange of their own. Jeff is saying in a casual, offhand way that he knows Loyd doesn't do much reading, but anyway, he's got this spare copy of a book called *Steppenwolf* in his room at the hotel, and he wants to lay it on him . . . you know, whatever . . . just in case Loyd ever gets the urge to read something in an off minute.

"Steppenwolf. Is that that rock group?" Loyd asks. "Shit, boy, Ah lahk rock — it puts fuel in mah airplane."

No, Jeff explains — still ever so offhandedly, casually — the rock group in all likelihood took its name from the book, which is about — well, about this dude named Steppenwolf, Loyd'll just have to read about it for himself to under-stand. . . . But if there's an overall *message* to the book . . . you know . . . well, maybe it's something like — *Keep movin'*. . . . Or, whatever. . . . It's only a book after all, but still and all, Loyd might get something out of it that might, you know . . . change his way of thinking, his values, stuff like that —

"Ah ain't good at books — Ah don't have to tell you that — but Ah lahk that message, whatever you call it," Loyd says, worrying at his teeth with a stem of grass. "*Keep movin'* — shit, that's mah meat, awright. Listen, Jeff — you reckon Ah'd make a fair Western star? Ah'm savin' mah money so's Ah can go out to California when this outfit's done shootin' here, but what happens then? How do Ah go about gettin' in the union, do you know? The Screen Actors Guild? Mr. Surtees said he wants to do some stills of me if Ah ever make it out to Hollywood. And John Hellerman — you know, he's an awful fahn little man — he gimme a mixed drank last night up in his room at the ho-tel and tole me Ah could bunk at his place when Ah git out there. Well, shit fahr and save matches, maybe ever'thang's gonna turn out awright, you thank so?"

Jeff, no longer offhand or casual, hunches his shoulders forward intensely and gestures in an agitated circle: "I don't *know*, Loyd. Nobody knows anything for sure, so nobody can tell you anything for sure. If some dude says he can, then he's bullshitting you. That's why it's important to *keep moving* —

keep tryin' to understand yourself better in the world, the *real* world of true recognitions.

"OK, so Surtees and Hellerman say they'll try to help you. Well, I'll try, too—I'll give you my L.A. address, to start with. But I don't want you to get your hopes pumped up too high, because you might not make it. Probably won't, in fact. Hell, you might even find out you don't *want* to be a movie star, blah-blah-blah. Follow me? You might find you want to be something altogether different, you know? The thing everybody has got to learn is—*channel that energy*. I mean, like in your case, don't fight with your fists anymore, all that jiveass shit you've told me about. Fuck, or eat, or climb a mountain, or do something useful instead."

Unused to such talk, Loyd passes a troubled hand across his face, then blurts impassionedly: "Gawddamn it to hell, Jeff, it's hard for me to keep thoughts lahk that in mah head, but Ah'll try, and you got mah word on it, buddeh! Hell, Ah wanna know about all that stuff you mean—values and thankin' and all that shit. You just way out ahead a me, is all, and it's hard as hell to catch up. Ah guess just bein' in this movie, gettin' to know a guy like you and all—that's changin' mah lahf, ain't it? . . .

"Ah was thankin' the other night at the house—you know, just settin' around thankin', lahk a guy'll do—and all of a sudden, Ah was on the subject of God. *Jesus Christ*, Ah says to mahself, what's goin' on here? Ah never did figger it all out to suit me, but anyways, what Ah was thankin' was you limit yourself to God, but He don't limit Hisself to you, does He? Ah mean God can be whatever he takes a notion to be—a tree or a rock or whatever the fuck. . . . But a guy cain't be nothin' but a human man, see what Ah'm gittin' at? And you know what? Alla that made me feel—lonesome, somehow. Ah don't know how to explain it, but Ah guess you cain't hep but feel lonesome sometimes, can ye?"

Later, leaving to go back to the hotel, I draw Loyd to one side and thank him for being in my movie. He looks surprised for a minute, then gives me a gentle poke on the arm. "You're kiddin' me, ain't ye, doctor," he says pleasantly.

The next afternoon, under a lowering sky, Cybill puts aside her books and sets out with a male companion for a meandering stroll to the Wichita Cattle Company auction barn, located about a mile from the hotel across the kind of middle-class black ghetto that would have been unthinkable anywhere in

Texas a decade ago. Along the way, she languidly waves at children playing in the scrupulously clipped yards and ticks off the key events of her *vita brevis* with the heatless detachment of a NASA lifer selecting trinkets for inclusion in a time capsule:

A wealthy "philistine" upbringing in Memphis . . . growing up absurd, all that . . . winning a "Model of the Year" contest . . . moving to Barrow Street in the Village . . . meeting an "older man," a Manhattan restaurateur, who introduced her to the Truly Important Things — music, the theater, abstract expressionism, the European literary heavies. . . . "I never learned how to make friends," she reflects moodily, peering down into the dung-pungent shadows of the deserted auction arena. "But . . . I learned early how to fill needs."

Prowling around the barn's maze of tunnels and chutes, she wanders out on a raised plank walkway overlooking pens of cattle being fattened for sale. "What do cows do mostly?" she asks abruptly. The usual things animals do, she is told. "Eat, you mean? Sleep? Make love? I think I might like to be a cow."

On the way back to the Ramada, she chews on a piece of straw and confides that the illusionary business of making a movie is troubling her. "It's like living in a hall of mirrors," she says, smiling a fragile, very private smile. "It's like being dumb but reading Kafka, anyway."

The *Picture Show* cast begins to scatter in all directions like M. B. Garrett's limber-lock geese; by now, Bob Glenn has returned to the sci-fi mother ship in Dallas, Cloris Leachman and Clu Gulager have departed on separate flights back to L.A., and I'm scheduled on a San Francisco flight out early the next morning. While I'm packing, it occurs to me that I've missed seeing Pam Keller's rushes. Debating whether or not to call her, anyway, and try to bluff it through — *Terrific, Pam baby. Academy all the way* — I head down to the hotel restaurant and join Jody Heathcock and Eileen Brennan for coffee.

Eileen, who plays a salty-tongued barmaid in the film, has just boosted a pair of 89¢ sewing scissors from a five-and-dime store, and she crows about her petty thievery elatedly as she knits and purls on something gruesome and fuzzy spilling out of her lap. Jody is slyly jiving the waitresses, Carole and Winnie, as he's done with their sisters-in-aprons a thousand times before, playing one-night stands from Yazoo City to Weed. The two girls are loving it; they can't, in fact, get enough of that cool, adenoidal *a-ha*, because this guy is *Jody Heathcock*, after all, who used to be a famous big shot with Bob Wills, that famous old-timey bandleader their folks used to rave about after drunken Saturday night stomps at the M-B Corral. Besides, Jody *knows—is friends with plays golf with*—all the famous big shots in the world—Faron Young, Roy Acuff, Dean Martin, Marvin Rainwater, Sonny James, Frank Sinatra, Stringbean, Lefty Frizzell, Ray Price, Merle Haggard, Waylon Jennings, Glen Campbell, Jim Nabors, Engelbert Humperdink, Cowboy Copas, Johnny Cash—the list is endless. . . . *Hot damn!*

Winnie, arms akimbo on the counter, initiates the flirty ritual as Carole serves Jody an open-faced sandwich: "Well, hah yew today, Mr. Heachacallit?"

"Aw, I'm sick in the bed, honey. Say, look-a-here, when're you'n me goin' down the road for a leetle piece, you sweet thang?"

"Don't you take me for granite, Jody," she sniffs. "Besides, you'll have to ast my ol' man about *that.*"

Jody winks at her and turns to Carole: "What kinda sangwich is this you brang me, anyways, dear heart?"

"Freench dip. What you awdered, ain't it?"

"Well, bless mah heart, Ah must have. Listen, set down here beside me and Freench mah dip agin, darlin'."

Carole cracks her gum and pretends not to know what he means: "Naw. I've awready eat."

"Anybody Ah know?"

"Oh, *you.* You're the filthiest-mouthed thang I've ever saw!"

"*Me?* Why, you're shore one to talk. Least Ah don't let mah meat loaf, lahk you do. What's a sorry, mattress-assed ol' gal lahk you doin' in a nice place lahk this, anyways?"

"Hmnph—*you're* gonna be the sorry one, you ol' letch. You'll never know what sweet lovin' you missed, neither."

Jody looks her up and down for a minute, from bouffant topknot to rubber soles: "Bah damn, Ah bet if you ever got to sunfishin', you'd break a man's back. What time you git off tonight? I'll be Don Ameche in a taxi, honey—all you got to do is bend over and I'll drive you home."

"Well . . . I don't know about *that.* I'm not even sure I lahk you anymore."

Jody drowns a final hunk of bread in his gravy boat, then rises and hitches up his trousers: "Well, that's purely up to you, dumplin'. 'Cause Ah'm *likable.*"

Late that night, there's a small birthday gathering for me in Jeff's room; from Mae Woods or somebody, word has gotten around that my ravaged face is a year older. Cybill Shepherd shows up, and so do Eileen Brennan and Jody, Loyd, Tim Bottoms, and the location manager. Soon, some imported Mexican hors d'oeuvres are making the rounds, and Jagger is bleating "Sympathy for the Devil" on a tinny cassette machine. Jody, sucking contentedly on a pipeful of something pungently contraband-smelling, buttonholes me to ask, "Say, look-a-here Grober, you got anythang sharp and shiny to carry in yore pocket?" As a present, he gives me his bone-handle whittling knife. As my last sober act of the evening, I hand him back a penny, because when a man gives you a knife in the short-grass country, you can't accept it without giving a gift in return for fear of severing your friendship.

Loyd, his hat shoved back at an angle on his dark hair, is sitting in the middle of the floor, taking the first toke of his life in the real world of true recognitions. He sputters and coughs and grins lopsidedly: "Sheeit, that stuff makes ye feel boneless, don't it?" Before the Stones have given way to Elton John, he's sprawled out full-length, asleep. The music and the Mexican imports burn on. Sure, you can go home again, I hear myself telling someone much later, if you're making a movie.

Sam Peckinpah in Mexico

OVERLEARNING WITH *EL JEFE*

Rolling Stone, 1972

Limping delicately as if his boots are a couple of sizes too tight, so rockinghorse loaded on Juárez tequila he'd flunk a knee-walking test, Roy Jenson, one of the neo–Wild Bunch of characters and character actors that Sam Peckinpah has flushed out of the Hollywood woodwork to play the cutthroat band of thieves in his ultraviolent new thriller *The Getaway,* lurches against a red light into the rushing cabal of noonday traffic at Oregon Street and Missouri Avenue, a stone's throw away from the Holiday Inn–Downtown (El Paso), where most of the film's location troupe is quartered. Impervious to the abruptly bleating horns, the squall of brakes, and drivers' outraged yelps, Jenson, a barrel-gutted factory-second Forrest Tucker–type, stops dead in the center of the swirling traffic, squints up at the broiling late-April sun, blinks rapidly, and with agonizing deliberation puts on a pair of those mirrored wraparound shades that Vietnam chopper pilots wear on the Six O'Clock News every night. Then, hitching up his baggy-seated twill ranch pants and flashing an up-yours salute to the world at large, Jenson resumes his peristaltic cha-cha-cha to the opposite side of the street, where a startled onlooker, out on a stroll from the hotel, has stood riveted to the sidewalk watching the actor's near-calamitous weave through volleys of cars slipstreaming close enough to Jenson's body to lift his longish, graying topknot to a whipping boil.

"*Hah,*" Jenson snorts, dabbing at his damp temples with a crumpled red bandanna as he hobbles up on the curb, jerking a thumb for the onlookers' benefit at the tire-screeching melee in the street behind him. "Ony fuckin' safe place in a fuckin' war is to be dead, anyways." Pursing his lips narrowly, Jenson looks the second man — a writer from San Francisco, as it happens — up and down, from English-cut black velvet jacket to faded bell-bottoms to well-traveled Tony Lama boots. Expelling a long, warm rush of alcohol fumes, Jenson politely encircles the writer's upper arm between thumb and forefinger and begins guiding him, firmly but gently, up the block toward a basement place called Miguel's: "C'mon, doctor, you look *real* . . . innersting. I gotta

45

headache and a hard-on both. Less you and me go get us a drank before I lose my fuckin' high."

The downstairs bar-restaurant is dim and quiet and pleasantly cool. A blonde waitress in a miniskirt fetches the two men's drinks, and as she leans over the table to put the coasters in place, Jenson, without preamble, attempts to stick his tongue in her ear. Startled, horrified, the young girl recoils. "Aw, it's awright darlin'," he assures her soothingly. "Listen here, lady—you gotta boyfriend?" Keeping her distance, the girl stiffly nods yes. Jenson grins wolfishly: "Tell you what, then, hon—you tell that ugly sombitch to be down here at closin' time tonight and I'll blow his fuckin' head off with a fuckin' Thompson machine gun. Can you remember that?" Wordlessly, the girl scurries off white-faced, heel-and-toe, heel-and-toe. Jenson looks after her fondly: "Hot damn, she's a real motor scooter, you know it? I purely love to give these little ol' country girls somethin' to remember me by. It's a real thrill for 'em."

Belching, Jenson drains off half his martini and helps himself to one of the writer's cigarettes. Then he slaps his palm down on the tabletop with a crack like a rifle shot. Heads crane around all across the restaurant. "So you came down here to the fuckin' El Paso del Norte to write a story about ol' Sam Peckinpah, did you?" he sneers, striking a match with his thumbnail. "*Sheeit*. Big deal, haw-haw, boy." Jenson pronounces the word "Baw-uh." "Sheeit, Sam probly won't even talk to you—who the fuck are *you*, anyways? Anyways, he just got shut of some lame-brained cunt from *Esquire* who spent ten days hangin' around tellin' him how great she was. Listen, baw-uh, would you care to arm rassle or knife-fight or somethin'?"

When the writer grinningly declines, Jenson grumbles unintelligibly to himself for a minute, stubs out his freshly lit cigarette, then immediately lights another. "Listen, baw-uh—you wanna know the real honest-to-God goudge about ol' Sam Peckinpah? I'll just bet you do. Well, let me tell you—he's a lowlife sorry sonofabitch, a mean, shifty-eyed backstabbin' motherfucker— he's shitty, he's beautiful, he's great, he's a fuckin' wizard and he's also a saint. *He's a goddamn man, baw-uh. A goddamn natural man.*"

Shaking his head as if there's something rolling around loose inside it, Jenson takes off his mirrored shades and rubs his mucus-crusted eyes delicately with the tips of his fingers before going on: "You been to college, right, stud? Yeah, well, you must of—you look about smart enough to make change for a dollar. What outfit'd you say you worked for? Naw, I never heard of it. But looky here—you recollect how some of your college professors leaned toward underlearnin' you and others toward overlearnin' you? Well, ol' Sam Pee will overlearn you every time — every single friggin' time . . ."

Poking at the dregs of his drink with a swizzle stick, his meaning obscure and his expression undecipherable, Jenson trails off to stony silence. Warily, the blonde waitress returns, but this time she's careful to keep at arm's length from him. "Y'all want anything else to drink?" she inquires in a small voice. "Damn right, you sexy motor scooter," Jenson drawls, straightening up from his slump and putting on a boozy, lopsided grin. "How about you and me eelopin'? Right now, today — go get a clean toothbrush and your fastest walkin' stick. Hell, I'm a married man with three kids, but I don't give a rat's ass about any of that if you don't. Why, I'll sell my $750,000 ranch in the San Fernando Valley and give you the whole bundle, and we can run off to Mexico and be cowboys or somethin'. And I promise not to gun down your boyfriend, neither — I'll just maim him a little, maybe. Besides, my part's done in the pitcher, and I've already turned in my machine gun to Property, anyways. How about it, hoss? You hot to trot?" "Aw, you don't have no $750,000 ranch *anywheres*," the girl scoffs scornfully. Jenson lumbers heavily to his feet, groping blindly for the check, fumbling in his wallet for a bill. "Naw, I don't, darlin'," he concedes in a thick, weary voice. "Naw, lady, 'deed I don't."

Left a little sandbagged by his happenstance encounter with Jenson, the writer returns to the Holiday Inn to spend a couple of uneasy hours spot-reading through Walter Hill's screen treatment of Jim Thompson's novel *The Getaway*. From time to time, reflecting on the fact that he's, in effect, been barred from observing the day's shooting by Sam Peckinpah's fiat — relayed discreetly, of course, down the production chain-of-command via the film's unit publicist, Mack Hamilton — and recalling Jenson's sardonic jibe — *Sam probly won't even talk to you — who the fuck are YOU, anyways?* — the writer paces restlessly around the room, stopping on each heel-turn at the sliding balcony doors to gaze out over a squalling freeway toward the haze-shrouded mountains of New Mexico, the somber Organ ranges, where a bellicose magenta nimbus formation is gathering force. A couple of floors below, the hotel's pool gleams blinding-bright in the sun, surrounded by ersatz-green Astroturf, and huddled at the far end of the deck, a red-haired matron in white go-go boots sits alone in a webbed beach chair, sobbing into her hands over something or other.

Hill's screenplay, dedicated "to Raoul Walsh," is taut, fast-paced, and chilling. The story concerns a bank robbery in a small Texas town and its blood-spattered aftermath as the thieves begin to double-, triple-, and quadruple-cross each other in a scramble for the loot. The holdup is financed by a corrupt LBJ-type politician and his accountant brother, played respectively by Ben Johnson and John Bryson, and executed by a professional thief, "Doc McCoy"—Steve McQueen—his wife "Carol"—Ali McGraw—and a shrink's surfeit of sadistic gunsels portrayed by Roy Jenson, Al Lettieri, Bo Hopkins, Bill Hart, and Tom Runyon.

After a couple of grisly shootouts early-on in the action, "Doc" and "Carol" flee across the Texas plains with the money, hotly pursued by the politician's henchmen and separately by "Rudy"—Al Lettieri—who, because he's wounded and unable to drive, abducts a terror-stricken veterinarian and his hot-to-get-it-on wife, who obligingly balls the gangster in a succession of motel rooms while her bound-and-gagged husband looks helplessly on. Eventually, all the surviving thieves converge on the seedy Laughlin Hotel in downtown El Paso for an apocalyptic, gut-spattering showdown. When the smoke clears, "Doc" and "Carol" hightail it for Mexico with the loot, in the clear for the present, but their future clearly tense.

On the whole, the characters in *The Getaway*, including the principals, are depicted as sordid, grubby, essentially conscienceless psychopaths, pretty much lacking in either basic human scruples or redeeming social value. But far and away the most repellent—and fascinating—character in the script is "Fran," the veterinarian's distinctly polymorphous-perverse wife. The production credit sheet lists "Fran" as being played by Sally Struthers.

Sally Struthers . . . can youse believe it? She plays Gloria, Archie Bunker's nineteen-year-old clean-machine daughter, the plump WASP dish married to that Styrofoam hippie on the TV show *All in the Family*.

Late that afternoon, a big Sony stereo cassette machine is brassily booming out behind her when Sally Struthers greets the writer in the foyer of her comfortably cluttered ninth-floor suite. Suppressing a girlish titter and executing a saucy little two-step, she rolls her eyes mock-coquettishly and sings falsetto accompaniment to her own home-recorded rendition of "Me and Bobby McGee" as she leads her visitor toward a sling chair near the sundeck.

"Isn't that *great*? Don't you just love it?" Sally squeals, clapping her hands in childlike glee. "That's what I do to entertain myself when I have to sit here for four or five hours on a 'Will Notify' call. Would you like anything to drink or anything?" Snapping off the tape machine, she orders beer and orange juice from room service and plops down in the center of the bed, her legs drawn up under her lotus-fashion, gesticulating extravagantly as she talks and chain-smokes Winstons. A big-busted woman with electric-blue eyes, she's wearing light blue sailor pants that bell completely over her feet, an orange waist, and a Buster Brown wristwatch that ticks as loud as a dollar alarm clock.

"Everybody thinks I'm stoned all the time, ducks dear," she whispers confidentially, "but I'm not really—I'm just crazy. I'm a Leo." Pealing with laughter, she twines and untwines a lock of honey-colored hair around a finger. "Well, everybody and everything's crazy, you know? Like this part I play in the picture—a really far-out, loose Texas lady. That's quite a switch, you know, from being Archie Bunker's cute, sweet daughter—Little Miss Do-Goody Two-Shoes—to playing a . . . *lewd* woman. I think it'll shock my family and it'll shock America. But sometimes you've got to do that to be remembered. In *Five Easy Pieces*, for instance, I was on screen for—Listen, would you be horribly offended if I took off my shoes?"

With a smile that accentuates her sensual overbite, Sally slips off her peach-colored wedgie espadrilles and drops them to the floor, massaging the soles of her feet with ecstatic "oo's" and "ah's."

"They're not dirty or anything—my feet, I mean," she giggles. "Uh . . . where was I? Oh, yeah. In *Five Easy Pieces*, I was on screen for less than five minutes. But because I played such a different sort of person from myself, I was noticed more on the street, even though I'd been on TV for a year already—*The Smothers Brothers Summer Show, The Tim Conway Show*, various talk shows, and so forth. Well, not that I was exactly dying to be noticed, but as soon as *Five Easy Pieces* came out, everybody recognized me."

At a knock, Sally bounces up to admit a bellman with the refreshments from room service. After he's deposited the tray and gone, she takes a long, thirsty swallow of orange juice and tumbles backward onto the bed, bicycling her legs with furious energy. When she sits up, erect again, she grasps her ankles and leans forward intently:

"*The Getaway* is, let me think . . . my fourth film, I guess. Three years ago, I did a hot-cha $2 million Warner Brothers' extravaganza which you may recall from all the hot-air advance hype in the trades. It was called *The Phynx*, and it had a bunch of over-forty stars in it like Desi Arnaz, Butterfly McQueen, and Johnny Weissmuller in cameo roles. The guy who directed it—I didn't get along with him too well, so I've got a cast-iron block against remembering his name—he'd never done a big musical before, only television. When the film finally opened, it played for one day only in Milwaukee, and it grossed like $17 and they hid it away in a can someplace and there it sits. That's show biz, huh?"

Draining off what's left of her orange juice, she pouts prettily for a minute, then snaps her fingers, *pop:* "Katzin! That's the guy who directed *The Phynx*—Lee H. Katzin. I never knew what the 'H' stood for. Hopeless? Help? Ho-ho-ho?

"Nah, I'm only kidding. Katzin was probably a fabulous director in his own right, but we didn't see eye-to-eye, and he was about 180 degrees turned around from someone like Sam Peckinpah. Sam is . . . well, I don't even like to call him Sam. Somehow, it doesn't seem respectful to a man as great as he is, you know? So I always call him Mr. Peckinpah. And if I go up to him with an idea, which I've done often in the last few weeks, he listens, he usually likes the idea, and he always at least lets me try it out. He lets the actors invent, and he spurs you on to think of bits of business to add, and he never puts a damper on that which is great. It really helps you build a part when you can feel free to add a word here or a prop there that wasn't specified in the original script. Like, Mr. Peckinpah's let me do some really weird things—wearing earphones so I don't have to listen to my wimpy husband whining. Lots of funny stuff like that.

"Of course, he teases me a lot, too—me and Ali McGraw both. When we were shooting in San Marcos, I had to do a scene with Al Lettieri. He plays a gangster, you know, and he's sitting there with a gruesome bullet hole in his shoulder, and I'm making eyes at him because I find him more attractive than my husband"—Sally springs to her feet to pantomime the scene—"so the situation turns into a kind of strange, *blech* triangle. Since the scene takes place in a veterinary hospital, this adorable little black kitten is playing around on Al's lap. Well, the kitten starts to screech a little and scratches Al a couple of times. So Mr. Peckinpah, acting real mad, yells: 'Goddamnit, somebody get a pair of pliers and pull that cat's goddamn claws out.' So one of the grips dashes off to get some pliers, and I panic and run off the set crying before I snap that it's all just a rib to spook me.

"Well, that's pretty typical of the kind of fun-and-games that goes on. Yesterday and the day before that, I had to do a scene sitting in a hallway at the Laughlin Hotel screaming my lungs out and leaping up and running like crazy when I heard gunshots. Oh, my God, I can't tell you!" Sally rocks back and forth on the balls of her feet, holding her head piteously. "They shot those blankety-blank guns off so close to my ears that I shook for hours afterward. Mr. Peckinpah has the guys in the cast pull little stuff like that on Ali and me just to get our reactions on film, I guess, but it's sort of hard to take, 'cause neither of us is violence-oriented at all.

"Steve McQueen did a scene with me a few days ago where he hit me right smack in the middle of the face and knocked me cold in that same hallway at the hotel. I didn't want a stunt girl — you can always tell when there's a stand-in. Right now, if I lowered my pants or pulled up my blouse, you could see how many bruises I've got all over my body from that scene, because Steve went straight for my face. He didn't do the other actor snaps his head to the side and just pretends to be hit. Steve did a shot that hasn't been seen in the movies in a long time — straight to my jaw so my head had to snap straight back. And every time my head snapped back, it hit the wall, and I had to drop like a sack of potatoes to the floor. My whole right hip is still bruised black and blue, and I've got little knots all over the back of my skull from slammin' against that darned wall so many times."

Perching on the edge of the bed, Sally rests her deep-dimpled chin against her drawn-up knees. "Violence," she sniffs with a cross toss of her hair. "There was some off-camera violence in the production office at the Laughlin today — well, almost. This crazy young guy crashed the set last week and said some outrageous things to Ali — I mean, horrible things, not even repeatable. So, when he wouldn't leave her alone, the police came and carted him off to jail. But he showed up again today right after lunch and started talking to Roy Jenson about me — about all the creepy-crawly things he wanted to do to me if he got me alone. Have you met Roy Jenson? He's a very groovy guy, very fatherly and gentle to me.

"Well, Roy didn't belt the guy or throw him across the room or anything. He just did like a sudden cobra squeeze on his throat, and the warped little dude sank down to his knees, gasping for breath, and then the police came and carted him away again."

Sally reflects a minute, then expels a pained sigh: "I'm grateful for one thing, though. I'm glad Mr. Peckinpah wasn't around when that happened, because there's no telling what he would've done to the poor simp. Mr. Peckinpah is like . . . King Tut, you know? A truly awesome figure. He's not all that big, really — he's sort of slight physically. I don't really know how to explain it, but he gives off such powerful vibes that you have to . . . well, fear and love him, I guess, just like little kids learn to fear and love God in Sunday school."

Sally swings her legs off the bed and hugs her arms to her breasts as if she feels a sudden chill. Outside, the sun's last purpling light is streaking across the slopes of the shadow-washed mountains to the west. "No matter how simple or foolish you are," Sally snorts wryly, "you learn real fast not to futz around with Mr. Peckinpah. That, ducks dear, is a distinct no-no — no how, no way."

Since he's done little more than hang out in the hotel bar watching daytime TV for the better part of two days, ducks dear, who, after all, is on assignment, would like nothing better than a chance to futz around with Mr. Peckinpah for a while. But the following morning when Mack Hamilton, the unit publicist, escorts him out to the *Getaway* location site — a two-lane farm road fifteen miles north of town that traverses a lush grid of irrigated strawberry fields — there's no how, no way. Several city blocks short of the camera setup, a bare-chested grip with tattooed biceps and a gravelly voice waves Hamilton's rented sedan off on the dirt shoulder. Stooping down to the window, the grip motions toward a generator truck up ahead and rasps: "Don't walk or drive past that point, you read me? You fuck up Sam's frame, it'll be the hair outta both our asses."

Shrugging helplessly to the writer, Hamilton kills the car's engine and steps out on the blacktop to survey the flotilla of vehicles strung out along the road ahead for perhaps a quarter of a mile. "Lots of local gawkers out today," he grunts. Overhead, a high cloud cover is drifting in from the mountains, and there's a metallic edge to the choppy breeze soughing through the geometrically spaced rows of strawberry plants. Squinting narrowly ahead, then jabbing his pipe stem toward three tiny stick-figures in the distance, Hamilton laughs shortly: "There's Steve and Ali and Sam up there now — can you make 'em out? No, not there — over by that old pickup truck, see? And that young guy with the beard who's walking up to them? That's Gordon Dawson, the associate producer." Standing storklike on one leg, Hamilton tamps out his pipe on the heel of his shoe, then packs the bowl with fresh tobacco. "I once asked an associate producer at Metro what his duties were," he ruminates with a lopsided grin. "He said he was the only guy on the lot who could stand to associate with the producer."

Over by the generator truck, one of the film unit's minor functionaries, a faggy, forked-tongued Lotus Land yenta, stops the writer to cadge a cigarette. "Thanks and thanks, my man," he clucks, drooping one eyelid shut in what can only be intended as a wink, though the effect is more like a neurological tic. "Oh . . . hey, wow, you smoke Players, huh? *Far out. Fan-fucking-tastic.* I'm gonna carve your face on the Mount Rushmore of my heart, my man!"

Darting his eyes around to check who's within earshot, the man lowers his voice to a conspiratorial hush: "Have you noticed how uptight everybody is today? Take a close glom at Steve McQueen, my friend, and you'll snap to what I mean. But then, Steve's always uptight, isn't he? The poor sonofabitch doesn't have any friends, you know—not a single one. He's always neck deep in greed-heads, though—'bike buddies' and creeps like that, all of them sucking up to his ass for favors. As of this instant, I'm not . . . ah, you know . . . *absolutely* certain what's going down between him and Ali McGraw"—again, he flashes that Mondo Twisto parody of a wink—"but I bet I could guess. Did you hear that Bob Evans flew in from L.A. last night?" Bob Evans, in addition to being vice-president in charge of worldwide production for Paramount Pictures, is Ali McGraw's husband and the father of her year-old son. "Yeah, Evans showed up out of the blue, so to speak, heh-heh. Oh, he was *expected*, of course, but still and all . . . Anyway, pick up on the vibe for yourself, my man—it's *heavy*. Say, listen, you haven't by any chance seen Al Lettieri out here anywhere today, have you? Al's a weird one, too, if you can dig what I mean. I guess it's no secret that he used to be a mainline armbanger—did you know that? Yeah, but he hung up the gun, or so they claim, anyway—"

The writer couldn't care less who's sticking what into who or where, and he's relieved to hear his name called from behind. Forty-odd yards away down the row of cars banked along the opposite side of the road, his massive head and shoulders bulging out the window of a Hertz station wagon, Slim Pickens is flailing the air with his grime-encrusted Stetson sombrero and whooping like a hermit line-rider ripped to the tits on vanilla extract: "*Yee-hah! Gah-dang, son, c'mon over here and climb in this ol' hoopy with me! I ain't seen you in a dawggone dawg's age!*"

Grinning toothily and swinging the car door wide, Pickens extends a meaty paw to the writer in greeting, then bellies over under the steering wheel to make room on the seat. "Sonofagun, it's been a few years, you know it?" he wheezes, mopping his brushy mustache on the sleeve of his frayed work shirt. "I recollect that time real well, though—I was out per-motin' *Dr. Strangelove*, I guess it was, and I took and drunk ever' awnery one of you citified Fort Worth boys under the table up there at that Press Club. Hah! That'us some toot, one for the durned books."

Whinnying at the recollection, Pickens hikes up his pants legs to display the cracked, discolored, and run-over-at-the-heel ruins of what once must have been a pair of ordinarily sorry cowboy boots. "Ain't that a foul spectacle, though?" he muses fondly. "Them's my workin' boots. In the pitcher I play 'Slim Kanfield,' the old feller which he helps Steve and Ali ex-scape across the border."

Clasping his hands behind his neck, Pickens lolls back comfortably in the seat, his hat slanted forward at an angle over his eyes. "Aw, shore, you bet," he bobs his head vigorously at a question, "I purely love workin' for ol' Sam Peckinpah. This here'll be my third feature with him, was you aware of that? Yesser, I done *Major Dundee*, and then a right smart later on, *The Ballad of Cable Hogue*. I also played in a coupla his TV shows years and years back. They was episodes of a series called *The Westerner*, which was real good, I thought, and years and gone ahead of its time. You recollect that show with Brian Keith and that big ol' gawky dog?

"Funny thing—I've knowed Sam and his family most alla my life. Him and me was raised up in the same country, right up around Fresno and thereabouts in the San Joaquin Valley. I knowed Sam's granddad—a long time back, he was a congressman and a superior court judge there in Madera County. Later on, Sam's dad set on the same bench, and now his brother, Denny, he's a superior court judge over in Fresno County. Shoot, Sam's dad, in fact, was my lawyer when I was just a kid of a boy.

"When we was growin' up, my brother used to hunt with Sam out around Peckinpah Mountain, and I'd go huntin' with Denny, Sam's bud. Sam and me wasn't all that close back then. But, heckfire, by now I know him well enough that we get along just like a million. Sam's a real hard-workin' feller, and he never has no problems with people who're workin' as hard as he is. The only kind of folks that he won't put up with are the ones that're goofin' off. Boy hidy, lemme tell you, I'm a hunnerd percent behind him on that. There's too many damn problems in the pitcher business today to have to jack around with people who ain't innersted in it.

"The movies, God bless 'em, has been real good to me—and japin' around in front of a camera sure beats rodeoin' all to hell." Pickens slaps his leg and guffaws explosively. "Ridin' the rodeo circuit is hard on the ol' bones, you savvy me? I rodeoed, all told, oh, about thirty years, I reckon—ridin' broncs, doin' a little bulldoggin', all such stuff as that. I worked as a clown, too, and I done a right smart of bloodless bullfightin' in them years."

Pickens takes off his Stetson, an ancient, almost napless beaver, and affectionately dusts off the crown with the heel of his hand.

"Yesser," he nods, looking reflective as he settles the hat back into place over his bald spot, "the movies has been as good to me as a man could hope to ask for. Last year, I done four features and three or four guest shots on TV, and I'll be doin' about the same again this year. Workin' along at a pace like that keeps me about as busy as I wanna be, tell you the truth. Shoot, you make any more money than that, you got to give it to the dadgum government anyhow. And me, well, I like to hunt and fish a heap better than I like actin', though I ain't knockin' it, you understand. Like this comin' fall, I got me two hunts planned awready. I'm gonna stalk elk and deer up in Wyomin', and then later on, I'll track me some bear over in Utah —"

Leaning forward, Pickens peers through the windshield at the gravel-voiced grip, who's motioning to him from up the road that he's needed at the camera setup. Waving in return, Pickens gets out of the car, yawning and stretching. "Looks like it's my time outta the chute," he calls out over his shoulder as he saunters away. "Wish me luck, hear? Maybe I'll win me the day money."

Back at the Holiday Inn–Downtown just before the noon lunch rush, John Bryson sits slope-shouldered across from the writer in a deserted corner of the first-floor coffee shop, absently trailing a spoon through a cup of coagulating coffee. Although he plays a substantial role in *The Getaway* — second-in-command to Ben Johnson's lead heavy — Bryson isn't an actor by profession, but a top-caliber freelance photographer and former picture editor of *Life* magazine. A jowly, complex, likable man who retains only faint vestiges of his native Texas accent, he is clearly bewildered, perhaps even a little troubled, about his role in the film, as well as his relationship to Sam Peckinpah. Jutting his head forward, placing his large, well-manicured hands palms down on the table, he speaks in a low, resonant voice, and his urgency to make himself understood comes across at times as an almost physical force:

"Christ, it's been incredible, man, all of it. I've never done anything like this, you know — hell, I'm a journalist. But I've known Sam for . . . oh, for years, I guess, we've been drinking companions in Malibu. Sam's very tight with Jason Robards, who's one of my closest friends. That helped us get acquainted. Then, too, they did *Cable Hogue* together, and I hung around with them while that was in the works.

"Anyway, I guess Sam saw something or other in me he figured he could put to use—my big shambling walk or something. One thing I'm certain of, though—he didn't cast me in the film out of friendship or anything like that." Bryson dismisses the notion with a knife-slicing gesture of his hand. "No sir, none of that bullshit. Sam's such a perfectionist, he wouldn't cast Jesus to play Christ if Jesus didn't look right for the part.

"No, the way it happened, I was hanging around one night while Sam was auditioning actors to play the young soldier, a bit part, three or four lines in the picture, you know? While I was there, Sam must've tried out fifteen or twenty guys. Then he looked over at me and laughed and said, 'How'd you like to be in the picture?' I said sure, great, but I thought he was kidding. Next thing I knew, though, the casting people sent me a script and I was being fitted for wardrobe. They bought me four Brooks Brothers suits, all exactly alike, in case I spilled something on myself or got run over by a truck or something.

"Then—*whoosh*—the company came to Texas. Meanwhile, Sam hadn't said much of anything to me, and I was a little puzzled by that. The first day of shooting, I was supposed to drive up to the prison at Huntsville in a chauffeured Cadillac and lay a message on McQueen, who was playing a convict getting out. By now, I was damned edgy and nervous—nobody had said do it this way or that way, nothing. Finally, McQueen, who's a very strange guy I don't like too much, he stuck his head in the window of the car and said, 'Just relax, man. Remember, in your role you're a rich, influential member of the Establishment and I'm just a little pissant convict that you couldn't care less about. Hang on to that and it'll go great.' The only thing Peckinpah had ever said to me, like two weeks earlier, was something like 'Don't act. Just react.'

"So I'm sitting there trying to think how to go about reacting when Sam walks over to the car, and the sonofabitch is wearing these mirrored glasses so that nobody can ever tell if he's really looking at them or not, and he just stands there and looks at me for about a minute and then shakes his head like, 'Jesus Christ, what have I done,' and turns and walks away without a word. I'm telling you, I could've wet my pants."

Half-rising, Bryson signals for a waiter to bring some fresh coffee. Spooning a generous portion of sugar into his cup, he grins wryly:

"Well, they shot that scene in one take—the car pulled up, I laid the line on McQueen, and that was it. And that got to be more or less the routine in the next few days. Then Bob Visciglia, the property master, a guy who's worked with Sam on a bunch of pictures, he came up to me one afternoon and said, 'Jesus, man, you know what you're doing?' I didn't get what he meant. 'You're wrapping your scenes in one take,' he said, sort of impressed. I told him I figured that since I wasn't much more than a bit player, Sam obviously wasn't going to spend as much time on my part as he would on, say, McQueen's. 'You dumb cocksucker,' Visciglia said, 'if Sam didn't like what you were doing, you'd be doing it sixty-four times in a row.'

"Around that time, I began to realize for certain that things were OK, because my part in the script was enlarged. I started getting lines from other actors, which made me pretty unpopular with a few of them." With an iodine grimace, Bryson tilts his chair back on two legs and laughs shortly.

"Then, just a few days ago, I wasn't moving right in a scene we were shooting. That was the big climactic shootout at the Laughlin Hotel. I was moving fast, but Sam wanted me to move slow, and I just couldn't seem to do it. My inclination, in the midst of all those shotguns blasting off, was to get the fuck out of the way. Sam said, 'John, move slow, very slow. You're in charge, you're the big honcho in this outfit.' Well, I understood, but I didn't understand. So he rode my ass all that day, and I was about ready to cut my throat by nightfall, because I wanted to do it right for him, because I really love the sonofabitch.

"The next day, I 'died'—got my neck broken in a elevator crash. Again, Sam didn't tell me how to do it or anything. He just said, 'You bounce up and you bounce down and you crash and your neck is broken.' Well, I did it the best way I knew how, and when I got back to my hotel room that night, there was a big bunch of roses and a note that said: 'Dear John, I loved your death scene. Your Silent Admirer.' Then, later, after Sam'd seen the rushes, I guess, up came an even larger bunch of roses—gigantic—and this time the note said, 'Now what? Now what?' Isn't that weird?

"Sam is . . . hell, I don't really know how to put it in words. He's a monster and a saint. He's the meanest, kindest, toughest, softest . . . I think he runs the whole gamut from Ying to Yang. He's all that. Good, bad, soft, hard, evil, sweet—the whole range of human emotion is at work in him, and it seems to move back and forth in his case with less complications than it does for most people. You know what I mean? He can shift his range.

"See, Sam's had some truly hard times. He was standing tall after his first two features, The Deadly Companions and Ride the High Country, but when Major Dundee was taken away from him and reedited in '64, he went on the skids for a while. He was fired off The Cincinnati Kid. He was physically barred from several studios, broke, boozing hard, shedding wives — I don't know what all. Maybe he went bankrupt, too, I'm not sure.

"But he snapped back after doing *Noon Wine* for TV in '67 and then *The Wild Bunch*, and now he's mellowed out a lot. I mean, it's apparent he's no longer the dreaded, booze-swilling wildman of yesteryear. Only a couple of people, for instance, have been fired from this production. One of them happened to be his daughter, Sharon, who was the script girl. I asked him about it, and he just grinned and said, 'She wasn't doing her job.' By comparison, he fired so many people off *Cable Hogue*, the trade unions took out ads in the Hollywood papers attacking him.

"Sam doesn't socialize with the company in the evenings much nowadays — for one thing, he just got married again a couple of weeks ago to a girl named Joie, one of his former secretaries — but somehow he still manages to keep up with everything that's going on. It's uncanny — I don't know how he does it. He always knows who's having troubles, who's sleeping with who, the whole ball of wax. It gets downright eerie. Like, in my case not long back, there was something that had to do with my personal life that nobody in the world could've known about, but then Sam said to me one evening, 'John, don't do such-and-such.' I nearly fell over dead. I said, 'Holy shit, this scares me beyond belief. How could you know anything about that?' And Sam just smiled that Jesus-like smile of his and said, 'I always know everything that happens in my company.'"

Braying out Bryson's name — "Jawhn!" "Hey, Jawhn!" — Roy Jenson and Tom Runyon come loping tipsily across the now-crowded dining room to bid him their good-byes. With their parts in the picture completed, the two bad-guy actors announce in a babble of mutual interruptions, they're setting off that afternoon for Southern California in Runyon's private plane. Awkwardly, the three men exchange handshakes and promises to keep in touch. Bryson studies Jenson and Runyon with a look of mock distaste: "God, but you assholes look bed-raggled." "Well, it's been a hard day's night," Runyon drawls with a sly grin. "You shouldn't of went to bed so early, Jawhn, and maybe thataway you wouldn't of had to go alone." "As far as I'm concerned," Jenson sneers in a slap-bass growl, "this has been one of the most unpleasant relationships on record. Personally, I'll be glad to get shut of both you fuckers." Turning to go, Jenson glances quickly from Bryson to the writer and makes a pistol with his thumb and forefinger. "Don't forget what I told you, baw-uh," he grunts, cocking the gun and carefully squeezing off a round. "Don't forget what I said about ol' Sam overlearnin' you."

Around sundown that afternoon, David Foster, one of the producers of *The Getaway*, is seated at the cluttered desk in his makeshift office cubicle at the ramshackle old Laughlin Hotel a few paces down the hall from the creaky, mesh-grilled elevator in which John Bryson simulated breaking his neck a few days previously. A paunchy, sleepy-eyed man in his early forties, wearing straight-legged jeans and a *Getaway* T-shirt, Foster is sipping Chivas Regal from a Styrofoam cup and studiedly ignoring the battery of winking lights on his console telephone.

"Oh, boy, let me tell you, we've had a sweet ride on this picture," he says to the writer, planting a red canvas tennis shoe in a wallow of papers atop the desk. "You don't have to be terrifically sharp as a producer, you know, if you've got, say, just McQueen. Or just McGraw. Or, for that matter, just Peckinpah. Somebody or other will finance a picture if you've got any one of those. But when you've got all three and — a strong property" — Foster rolls his eyes in a parody of ecstasy and enunciates each succeeding syllable distinctly — "the-stam-pede-is-not-to-be-be-lieved. Listen, you wanna little more Chivas?" Lowering his leg, Foster leans across the desk and splashes a good three inches of scotch in the writer's cup, then plops back down in his swivel chair and hoists his foot back onto the morass of papers.

"So my partner and I, Mitchell Grower, we studied all the various offers — it was like a stampede — and we decided to go with First Artists. There's one guy at First Artists — Pat Kelly — and he's literally the whole outfit. Kelly said, 'You people wanna make a picture, and you don't want any interference, you got it.' And that's the way it's been. No hassles. In three months, we've seen Kelly a total of three times. Sam got every cent of budget he asked for, upwards of $2 million. McQueen took a percentage — that's the only way he works anymore. Yeah, well, sure, Steve owns a piece of First Artists, that's right — he and Streisand and Paul Newman and Sidney Poitier are the major stockholders in the company. But there wasn't any namby-pamby, believe me. We went where the best deal was. You reach a certain point, art has to connect with business. It's art, but it's business. Business-art. Art-business. Whatever."

Swirling the scotch in his cup, Foster grins and traces a finger along the slope of his broad, waxen nose.

"Have you talked to Steve any? He's all right, a very physical guy. He and I go back a long way together. When he was first breaking into the business, I was his publicist. He was doing a TV series, *Wanted—Dead or Alive*. I remember one time the first year that was shooting, he punched a horse right in the nose. No shit. It was a Western series, and this horse was getting pretty nervous under the lights and all, so the poor dumb beast balked and stepped on Steve's foot. So Steve balled up his fist and punched the fucker right in the snoot." His wispy mustache twitching, Foster rocks back and forth with laughter, stirring up alarming waves in his Styrofoam cup.

"Steve, though, physical dude that he may be, was pretty much the key to putting the *Getaway* package together. What happened was . . . well, I bought the book. An agent gave me a copy of it—a yellowing out-of-print twenty-five-cent Signet paperback original by a guy named Jim Thompson, published one time only in 1959. I thought it was dynamite, so I sent it to Steve from Vancouver, where I was producing *McCabe and Mrs. Miller* at the time. For years, I'd been bugging Steve to play an out-and-out gangster—you know, a ruthless, cold, but ultimately redeeming baddie. So within days, Steve sent word back for me to lock it up.

"We hired a sharp young screenwriter named Walter Hill to do the script, and when he was finished, Steve and Walter and I sat around speculating about who we should try to get to direct it. Steve had just finished doing *Junior Bonner* with Peckinpah, and was very excited about it, so Sam's name naturally came up. Well, I went to pitch Sam on the idea with my heart in my throat, prepared to hype him till Kingdom Come, if necessary. Right away, he said, 'I know the story cold, for Christ's sake. I'll do it.' Turned out, he'd read the book when it first came out, and had even talked to Jim Thompson about the possibility of filming it back when Sam couldn't get arrested, much less get a job at a major studio."

Foster finishes off the scotch in his cup and purses his lips thoughtfully before reaching across the desk for the half-empty bottle.

"Sam's a bloody fuckin' genius, that's all that makes sense to say about him. In my mind, he's one of today's four or five truly original American filmmakers. Kubrick would have to rank along in there somewhere . . . hell, I can't even think who else. Sam's gut-level, you understand—totally instinctive. He does his homework at night, but he doesn't sweat it, at least not openly. I'm sure there's a lot going on inside with him, though, that nobody's conscious of . . ."

Leaning forward across the desk again, Foster smiles and poises the bottle over the writer's cup: "A little more scotch? Or maybe we could go have dinner someplace. With a little *nachtmusick*, or something. You suppose there's any *nachtmusick* in El Paso?"

Mack Hamilton, the film's publicist, is a lanky, contemplative, white-haired man who gives the impression of aristocratically failed health. Driving east from El Paso to the *Getaway* location the next morning under a lowering sky, he whiles away the miles fussing with his pipe and reminiscing about the various directors he's worked around, beginning with C. B. DeMille. "George Stevens was a singular man," he muses as the car glides through the dreary little farming hamlet of Fabens, Texas. "He despised the whole breed of studio executives — called them 'money men.' Once, on the set of *A Place in the Sun*, he peeked through a viewfinder all morning, waiting for a bunch of visiting moguls to go away. Wouldn't even call the actors while the brass was around."

Half-listening, the writer is toying with a vaguely formed notion. Something in the eye-stabbing green of the irrigated fields and orchards stretching ahead reminds him of the landscape in Peckinpah's *Straw Dogs*. He is wondering who the actual villains of the film are supposed to be — the brutish workmen who attack the farmhouse . . . or maybe the besieged couple themselves? Out the window, a road sign flashes past: PORT OF ENTRY 6 MILES.

At the location site — a newish two-lane bridge across the Rio Grande linking the tail-end of Texas and the village of Caseta, Mexico — the 120-odd members of the film crew are eating lunch at long commissary tables set out under a stand of blowy live-oak trees adjacent to the U.S. Customs station. The wind is near gale-strength, gusting hard enough to lift slices of bread off plates. In the spring, the Rio Grande is normally bone dry in this vicinity — bands of Mexican kids, trailed by yapping dogs, are wandering freely back and forth across the powdery riverbed now — but gauging by the dark cast of the sky, it might not stay dry for long. A husky extra from Fabens shovels a slab of barbecue into his mouth and jabs his fork worriedly toward the dirty yellow clouds massing over the Sierra Madre. "If it rains, you gonna wish to hell it stops," he mutters to one of the gaffers. "Shit, it come a gully-swamper here two years ago and washed the damn highway out. That baby there hits, it'll make Noah's flood look like the mornin' dew." Across the river channel, the low, earth-colored huts of Caseta look to be nailed to the leaden horizon.

"Oh, gee, *fruta*," Ali McGraw croons at one of the serving tables, ladling fresh-diced fruit onto her plate. A fragile-looking, fine-boned woman dressed in an unbecoming mustard suit — her prescribed outfit for the upcoming scene — she has eyes dark as Darjeeling tea, and she smiles indiscriminately at almost everyone.

Singly and in groups of two and three, the crew members finish their meal and stroll leisurely across the bridge to Caseta. On the main street there, ringed by barefoot kids and swaggering Mexican customs officials in scruffy uniforms, Sam Peckinpah is grinning fixedly as he poses for photographs with the town's potbellied chief of police in the boot-heel-deep dust in front of the Oficina de Población. When the photographer is finished, Peckinpah's grin goes off like a shot-out light bulb, and at a murmured word from Mack Hamilton, he turns to give the writer a sharp, raking glance and a handshake that's both perfunctory and somehow measuring. A short, wiry man with metallic blue eyes and iron-gray hair bound up in a blue bandanna, Peckinpah mutters something that's lost on the wind, then strides away to set up the scene in which Slim Pickens drives Steve McQueen and Ali McGraw across the border in a rattly old pickup truck. Peckinpah's physical bearing indicates some clue as to why he's spent so much of his career working in TV, not working at all, or piss-fighting with producers — he moves like he's stalking an animal bigger than he is. "*El es muy macho,*" a skinny-legged little girl titters in the crowd. In the gray distance, cocks crow, and the wind whips up stinging sheets of sand along the street.

Peckinpah confers briefly with the cinematographer, Lucien Ballard, then barks into a walkie-talkie to somebody stationed at the U.S. end of the bridge: "The VW camper should be just at the end of the customs building there, pointing your way. Yeah, that's right, the hippie van. Turn it around as if it had come back from Mexico to the U.S. And try to make it snappy, hear? Let's beat the fuckin' rain if we can." While the van is being maneuvered into position, Peckinpah passes the time playing liars' dice with Bob Visciglia, the property master. When Visciglia puts on a woebegone expression, Peckinpah crows in triumph: "Hah! That's three bucks I'm into you for today, chico. You better throw your bony ass into gear."

While the routine bridge-crossing scene is being shot — "*Get your fuckin' head out of the picture, goddamn you!*" Peckinpah bawls at some unfortunate during the second take — Visciglia and the writer take shelter from the wind in the lee of the paint-flaking Mexican customs shed. An intense, muscular little Italian who carries himself like a boxer, Visciglia laughs fondly and says that Peckinpah rarely wins at liars' dice or poker, either: "He loves both games, but he almost always loses. I remember when we were making *Cable Hogue* in Nevada, Sam lost around $500 playing poker, and most of it ended up in a pot won by Max Evans, the writer. Sam got so pissed off, he howled like a hyena and grabbed the money and tore all the bills into little pieces. So Max had to spend the rest of the picture putting it together like a jigsaw puzzle.

"Sam and me play another game where we both can win. Sam made it up — it's called Airport. What we do, see, is go to an airport and have a few drinks, and get on a plane and fly to the next stop, and go into another bar and have a few drinks, and then get on another plane and fly on to the next bar. And so forth. Sam and I get a lotta grins like that, you know?

"Oh, sure, he yells at me from time to time, like he does with everybody, but if he didn't, I'd think he didn't love me anymore. Sam expects from everybody else what he expects of himself, no more, no less. In other words, know your job — do it well. Sam involves himself 100 percent in a picture, and he expects all the others to do the same."

Back at the camera setup, Peckinpah wraps the scene on the third take and signals for the crew to trundle the heavy Mitchell camera equipment further along the street. When Steve McQueen climbs out of the pickup truck, wearing a threadbare old suit coat over a dingy T-shirt, somebody jokingly hands him a pair of welding goggles. Grinning, he puts them on, and looking something like an outtake from *The Blob,* wanders over to the driveway in front of the customs shed. A purple '57 Chevy filled with solemn-faced Mexican workmen pulls up for inspection. When none of the customs officials immediately pays notice — they're all huddled together over by the pickup truck ogling Ali McGraw — McQueen steps forward. "Any fruits or vegetables?" he inquires sternly. Not recognizing him, the men nod their heads no. McQueen grins hugely. "*Pase,*" he says, waving them through with a sweeping gesture. A few of the crew members whistle and applaud as the car chugs away: "Academy, Steve." "Way to go, Stevie baby."

Frowning, Peckinpah summons Visciglia and gestures toward the swelling crowd of spectators, mostly chattering kids kept in semirebellious queues by a couple of gruff Mexican cops: "Get some ice cream. Get all the goddamn ice cream in the world. Tell the *niños* they can have it if they'll keep quiet till we finish shooting." Visciglia makes the announcement to lusty cheers from the kids, and scurries off in search of a well-stocked ice cream cart.

Standing ramrod-stiff on the sagging wooden porch of the Oficina de Población, eyeing the writer's cassette machine with a dour grimace, Peckinpah responds tersely to a few questions. Taking quick, intense puffs on a Delicado, he talks like somebody hunting-and-pecking very fast on an electric typewriter.

"Hmn, you're right. That's very interesting. *Straw Dogs* is the story of a bad marriage going wrong. The married couple are the heavies. They precipitate everything. They incite and invite every single piece of action in the picture. It's a good picture, I think. But then I think all my pictures are good pictures. A lot of people don't agree. I would say that I always expect to fail with certain people and succeed with others. . . .

"Yeah, I'm very pleased with the progress on this one. We've had ten good weeks of shooting, some extraordinary performances. If you really want to learn about acting for the screen, watch McQueen's eyes. John Bryson? He's been doing his job, hitting his mark, doing very well—

"I've got three projects planned for the future. Two of them are Westerns and one is contemporary. One's for 20th, one's for MGM, and one's for United Artists. It's not certain which'll go first, so I don't want to discuss them. I've got the rights to Max Evans' book *My Pardner*. One of the three screenplays is my own I'm happy to say. . . .

"Who do I like to work with? That's a stupid question. This crew I have right here. And I like to work with any talented actor who's professional. Everybody I've worked with more than once obviously is a favorite. I look forward to doing other pictures with Bill Holden. I certainly want to work with Bob Ryan again, and Brian Keith. This is the second picture I've had with Steve—*Junior Bonner* will be out this summer, and then this one around Christmas—and we're already talking about doing a third. Ben Johnson's been in most of my pictures. After this, I can't afford him, though. Thanks to his Oscar, his price has gone too high. I got him this time around, the last dying quiver. . . .

"*Major Dundee* was my absolute best film until the producer, Jerry Wexler, edited it into a piece of worthless trash. Then I got involved with a character named Martin Ransohoff, another producer, and got fired off *The Cincinnati Kid*. Why? I wouldn't let Ransohoff on the set, for one reason. He had no idea of what filming is all about, or the story, or anything else. He was involved in his own ego problems, and I can't waste time with people like that. I'm not sure what he's up to now—peddling garments, maybe. . . .

"Yeah, I've had my share of headaches with producers. Phil Feldman was another one. I had great difficulties bringing in *The Wild Bunch*—it took eighty-one days of shooting—and then Feldman let those rotten sonsofbitches at Warners chop out twenty minutes so they could hustle more popcorn. I'm suing them on three separate counts. Uh-huh, a guy named Walon Green wrote the script for *The Wild Bunch* about five years before the picture was made, and I rewrote it. . . . Walon's OK. He's a tough motherfucker. . . .

"I haven't seen many films for a while. The last year and a half, the only thing I've had time for was my own dailies. I did catch *Two-Lane Blacktop*, and loved it. I thought *The Last Picture Show* was a piece of shit, except for Ben Johnson. Apparently, I'm in a minority on both opinions. . . .

"That's correct. I did fire my daughter off the production. Her attitude was punk. She wasn't doing her work. So I canned her and she went off to Acapulco with some longhaired guy."

Hearing his name called, Peckinpah strides off briskly toward the customs shed, where the next setup is ready. Within minutes, the shot is secured, and everybody concerned looks pleased. Then the first quarter-sized patters of rain begin to streak the dust. "Jesus God," Peckinpah groans and heads off for the cantina across the street, trailed by Steve McQueen, Ali McGraw, Slim Pickens, the writer, and Kathy Blondell, Ali's hairdresser.

A typically dingy border-town bar, the Gardea has Formica-topped booths ringing a dance floor, a fading mural showing an Indian maiden paddling a canoe, and a jukebox that features accordion and trumpet music. Peckinpah looks the place over, then bellies up to the long wooden bar and orders tequila neat. The others ask for the same, except for Pickens. "Make mine a *cerveza*, will ya, hon?" he asks the dark, pretty woman tending bar. "A Dose Ekkis, if you please. Shoot, it's too durned early in the day for me to be drinkin' hard liquor." Down the bar, Kathy Blondell kibbitzes with one of the company's drivers, and McQueen and Ali touch hands and smile at each other a lot.

Peckinpah barks out a laugh and lifts his glass to the writer in a sardonic toast: "Well, cheers, doctor. This is the way to make a Peckinpah movie, right? The genuine article—belting back tequila in some fuckin' dive in Mexico. Hah!" Laughing, the writer returns the toast and rummages around in his shoulder bag for a newspaper clipping. The AP story, datelined New York, announces that Peckinpah has recently been voted one of the Pussycat League's annual Sourpuss Awards—the Kinky Machismo Trophy "for making films which instruct men to prove their masculinity by killing instead of kissing."

Peckinpah squints at the article, then whacks his palm on the bar and guffaws: "Shit, I showed a guy eating pussy in *Straw Dogs*—what do they think about that? What in hell is the Pussycat League, anyway? Sounds to me like some bunch of dumb cunts. I'll bet Judith Crist belongs to that outfit. Hah!

Well, believe me, I'm not gonna get weepy or despondent or anything. Who could ruin a day like this? I'm stuck in the middle of a dust and rain storm, I'm lost somewhere in Mexico, I'm all fucked up, if I don't get the next shot, my ass is dead—I ask you, who could fuck up a day like that?"

Grinning ruefully, Peckinpah nudges his glass forward. "*Otra, por favor, mi alma*," he says pleasantly to the woman behind the bar. When she refills the glass, he drains it off in one swallow and contemplates Slim Pickens, who grins and raises his bottle of Dos Equis in salute. "Good ol' boy, Slim is," Peckinpah muses. "Gentlest soul in the world. You don't want to ever cross him, though. You get out of line, Slim'll set you straight right quick. Tough as a boot full of bobwire."

Standing up, Peckinpah hitches up his baggy corduroy pants and leers at Kathy Blondell. "Hey, c'mere, girl," he growls, "I want to play with your privates, I want to gobble your box." A fetching, willowy young woman, Kathy grins crookedly. "Up yours, Peckinpah," she says.

Peckinpah lights a Delicado and cocks his head at the writer with an appraising look. "I don't much go for reporters, ordinarily," he murmurs softly. "They haven't been too kind to me, and I don't trust them as a breed. Rex Reed, for example, published a byline piece about the making of *The Getaway*, but he never even showed up down here—he sent some woman who works for him instead. And there was that dreary dame from *Esquire*. . . ."

With a shrug, Peckinpah wheels and strides away, and the writer, feeling maybe a shade overlearned, moves over to one of the booths to scribble some notes.

Outside, the blacktop street is slick with rain, but the downpour has ceased for the moment. Swarms of mosquitoes buzz around the gaffers and grips as they roll the massive camera equipment, shrouded under huge green umbrellas now, along the street to the front of the Cine Estrella, the next setup. An ugly blue wooden structure with rusty signs on the front that read TOME COCA-COLA—BIEN FRIA, the theater looks near collapse. "Man, that's the Last Picture Show if there ever was one," Stacy Newton cackles, popping the joints of his fingers. Peckinpah's personal driver, Newton is a lean, knobby-faced cowboy wearing boots sharp-toed enough to open a beer can.

Hands jammed in his coat pockets, looking red-eyed, McQueen comes out of the bar and stands a little unsteadily alongside the writer while Peckinpah sets up the next shot. "Sam is straight," McQueen says with a slight slur. "That's a rare quality out in my town, you know? People in Hollywood will hem and haw and fuck around playing all kinds of cute little games, and then you'll finally realize they want something from you. And eventually you'll have to ask, 'You want something from me, don't you?' But Sam's not like that. He's straight as they come." McQueen grins and shakes his head woozily. "Whew, that fuckin' tequila, I tell you. I'm bombed, man. I think maybe everybody's bombed." From behind the camera, Peckinpah motions for McQueen to get in the pickup truck with Ali and Pickens. "Well," McQueen mutters, moving away with a funny little wave, "another shitty day in Paradise, I guess."

A light patter of rain resumes, causing a slight delay. Ali and McQueen both quickly doze off in the truck, but Pickens climbs out of the cab to search for a restroom. "That danged Dose Ekkis runs right through a feller," he grumbles. Not meaning to, a couple of shirtless boys stray into camera range. "*Al otro lado, ándale, ándale!*" one of the cops screeches, flailing his arms and shooing them to the other side of the street. "I never even knew this town was out here before today," one of the extras from Texas remarks to Peckinpah. "The folks who live here probably didn't, either," Peckinpah sniffs. Turning, he gazes off toward the mountains to the south. "When I was a lot of years younger and considerably more foolish," he muses to no one in particular, "I was married to a Mexican woman. I asked her one time to tell me all about Mexico. 'Don't be silly,' she said. 'Nobody knows all about Mexico.' She was right, of course."

When the rain dies away, Peckinpah wraps the shot, the last of the day, in one quick take. Then Bob Visciglia wheels out a homemade pushcart with bicycle tires. "*Helado!* Ice cream for everybody!" he bawls, and he's virtually trampled in the human assault wave of kids who race to surround him, laughing and snatching Popsicles and howling with glee. One of the swiftest kids, a scabby-kneed boy with enormous eyes, clambers with his chocolate bar to the top of a stunted tree. Standing close by, about eye-to-eye with him, Peckinpah laughs and tells the kid he looks just like Emiliano Zapata, the national folk hero every kid in Mexico wants to look just like. The boy in the tree ducks his head. "Who are you?" he asks shyly. Squaring his shoulders, Peckinpah strikes a haughty stance like a matador. "Who am I?" he asks sternly. "You inquire of my identity, *viejo?*" Slowly, Peckinpah plays out an imaginary cape in a flawless veronica. "I am *el jefe!*" he thunders. "I am the chief!"

The weather clears that evening, and the next day's shooting site—a barren, sunstruck stretch of highway in the desert near Anapra, Texas—looks as if it hasn't seen rain this century and maybe the last. By mid-morning, Peckinpah is wearing his shirt tied around his waist, and there's sweat glistening in the thatch of wiry gray hair on his chest. The dizzying heat mounts as the hours pass, but the cast and crew stay in high spirits. With luck, they might be able to wrap the picture by nightfall, and it looks to be a good film. Between takes, Ali playfully dabs patchouli oil on anybody in reach, and McQueen follows Peckinpah around with an umbrella, claiming that it's part of his job. "Yeah, it's in my contract," he complains with a droll grimace. "I got to hold this fuckin' umbrella over Sam all day long. Ain't that the shits? Ain't it terrible what you gotta do to put together a few nickels and dimes these days?" Peckinpah grins thinly at McQueen's clowning, but he's busy talking to the first assistant director. "That's right, Newt," he agrees, nodding his head rapidly, "blood on the handkerchief, blood on the shirt, goddamn right, lots of blood."

Noticing the writer wandering around in search of a patch of shade, Lucien Ballard, the cinematographer, invites him to sit under one of the green equipment umbrellas. An urbane, dapper little man who looks substantially younger than his sixty-four years, Ballard began his film career as an assistant to the Austrian director Josef von Sternberg, which perhaps accounts for Ballard's vaguely Germanic burr.

"Sam is the most talented director in Hollywood," he says with a delicate cough. "Excuse me. I've worked with Sam, you see, on all of his pictures except *Major Dundee* and *Straw Dogs*. I'd like to have done *Straw Dogs*, too — I thought it was a beautiful film. Sam's tough to work with, obviously, and we have our beefs, but no one directs a scene the way he does. He's so intense, and he misses nothing. I've worked with most of the directors of the last forty years who're considered to be great, and I put Sam at the top of the list, no question about it.

"No, no, Sam and I don't collaborate in any strict sense. We worked most closely together, I suppose, on *Ride the High Country* and *The Wild Bunch*. We spent months of preparation on each of those. For *The Wild Bunch*, we had an idea about shooting it a certain way in a certain color, so we ran a lot of old films of Mexico. We ran them over and over, and tried to get that vintage look. We wanted to get a washed-out backlight-brown effect, and it took some effort, but we got it.

"As I say, Sam and I have our differences, but deep down he's one of the nicest men in the world. I respect him, and I enjoy working with him. I really do — I wouldn't just say it."

By noon, the crew has dressed a scene in which McQueen, Ali, and Pickens are to exchange almost three pages of dialogue in a bar ditch beside the parked pickup truck. "All right, let's stand by, please," one of the assistant directors calls out over a bullhorn. Toeing her mark, Ali leans over to flick a smudge of dust off one of her boxy, plain-Jane shoes. "I don't know what's come over me," she murmurs, straightening up and smoothing her skirt with little pats, "but I'm beginning to like these tacky damn shoes." Pickens peers down at her feet and blinks: "It's the cut of 'em, probly. They look real sturdy." Ali titters: "Oh, Slim, you're such a dear. Where in the world did you get that godawful hat?" Shrugging bashfully, Pickens touches his grimy hat brim and grins: "Aw, I stoled it off a ol' boy 'bout thirty years ago. Used to be a hunnerd dollars worth of Stutson, but it's kiley a sorry sight now, ain't it?" "OK, people," Peckinpah booms out tersely, "let's get it over with." "Rolling," the camera operator intones. "Take one, master shot 581," a grip with a slapstick recites. Halfway through the take, the shot is ruined by a car full of rubbernecking locals. "Oh shit—*cut, cut.* Tell those goddamn sonsofbitches to go home," Peckinpah snarls. The action starts again from the top.

The scene, which is tight and funny and well-written, plays well enough to stir heated applause from the crew at the conclusion. Peckinpah's voice carries over the clamor: "Very good, everybody, excellent. Print it. We'll get to the angles and close-ups after lunch."

Pickens eases a leg up on the pickup's fender, looking pleased with himself. "Gahdamn," he beams, "it ain't ever day you get a good scene. Looks like they'll be tyin' the ol' can to my tail right quick, though. I've went and worked my way out of another good job, I reckon." Over the bullhorn, the assistant director announces the location of the commissary setup. With their arms twined around each other's waists, Ali and McQueen stroll off along the apron of the highway in that direction, McQueen trilling a James Taylor lick: "*Highway, yeah, yeah, yeah.*"

Eyes to the ground, cradling his script in the crook of an elbow, Peckinpah strides away alone, but in a few minutes he relays an unexpected invitation to the writer to have a drink with him. Crouched over the overflowing sink in his air-conditioned live-in trailer, stirring together an unholy mixture of gin and wine favored in the vilest Mexican whorehouses, Peckinpah motions his visitor to a seat on the carpeted floor and sinks down on the sheet-tangled bunk with an expiring sigh. "I remembered another movie I liked," he mumbles. "*The French Connection*, a good movie-movie."

Raising up on one elbow, Peckinpah fixes the writer with a chilly, probing stare: "What do you want to know, anyway? You must have all the poop on my pictures or you wouldn't be here in the first place." Scowling darkly, he takes a long swallow of his drink and lies back on the bunk, his arms crossed behind his head.

"Well, my grandfolks pioneered up around Fresno, to begin with," he mutters in a faint, ruminative voice. "I grew up hunting and fishing on Peckinpah Mountain with guys like Slim Pickens. Most of the men on my father's side of the family were lawyers, and I was supposed to be one, too, but I had no stomach for it, so I joined the Marines when I was still a kid. I served for twenty-eight months around the end of World War II. No, I never saw any combat, but I was ready to. I was pretty gung-ho.

"After the shooting was over, I served some time in China, and eventually I tried to get mustered out there. Why? Are you kidding? That's a dumb question. Anyway, the Marine Corps shipped me back to the States for discharge, and I began to spend a lot of time in Mexico.

"Went to Fresno State College, started directing plays. Got a master's in drama at USC. Worked for the Huntington Park Theater, did a season of summer stock in Albuquerque, then joined the crew at KLAC-TV in Los Angeles as an actor-director.

"It was around then that I started writing. One of my first film jobs was a rewrite of *Invasion of the Body Snatchers*. Then, a lot of TV—*Gunsmoke*, *The Rifleman*, *Klondike*, *Zane Grey Theater*, I don't remember what all—and the rest is common history.

"What do I like to do besides making films? What do you mean by that? You mean like smoking dope and fucking upside down? Who doesn't? Who doesn't? That was a dumb question."

Hearing a commotion outside, Peckinpah draws back the curtains and peers out at Steve McQueen, who's whizzing hell-for-leather through the sagebrush on a sleek Japanese motorbike. Grinning, Peckinpah stands up, scratching the hair on his belly. Something in the set of his shoulders reminds the writer of the character "Pike" in *The Wild Bunch*. "Let's go," Peckinpah growls. "I've got a fuckin' movie to make."

Stockton, Calif.—The Memorial Civic Auditorium, located not far from the central ganglia of this crumby hick town, is old, cavernous, sweltering hot, and overripe with the stink of vintage sweat and piss. The litter-strewn floors are coated sticky with spittle and worse. The gallery semicircling the glaringly lit prizefight ring in the middle of the hall is packed with cretins and worse—San Joaquin Valley fruit bums, rheumy-eyed winos, Right Guard dropouts, mean-faced pachuca-chicks swilling Oly from cans.

Occasionally, as the furious action in the ring prompts them, this mob of six-hundred-odd tank-town lames roars its bloodthirsty approval. And the action going on in the ring is . . . wait a second here . . . just what in the name of Christ's sweet body is a nice, classically trained actor like Stacy Keach doing in a creep joint like this?

Making a movie called *Fat City*, of course—and at this precise instant, that means he's getting the living firk wailed out of him by one Sixto Rodriguez, an honest-to-god light heavy bruiser who once clobbered Bobo Olson to a viscous pulp and battled both Von Clay and Piro del Pappa to bruising draws.

It's all in the script, understand, but try explaining that to Judy Collins, Keach's special lady. Out of camera range, she's standing with director John Huston and the film's producer, Ray Stark, and she winces fretfully every time she hears leather slam into meat. Huston, a big, loose-limbed man in a tan gabardine safari outfit and penny loafers, lights a panatela and pats her on the shoulder in commiseration before she wanders away, looking stricken. "It's only a movie, my dear," he calls after her softly. Nearby, a bored grip man grips a fog gun which emits an acrid shmaze resembling tobacco smoke; Leonard Gardner, the author of *Fat City* in both novel and film version, stumbles through the nose-stinging vapor, looking tiny, frail, and maybe lost.

While cinematographer Conrad Hall (*Cool Hand Luke, In Cold Blood*) calls a sotto voce consultation with Huston and Stark, Keach and Rodriguez continue to spar. "Christ," an electrician mutters, "those guys been at that shit for seven hours now. You'd think they'd take a load off." Stark, a slight man wearing a knit shirt and an expensive imitation of Levis, shakes his head violently at Hall: "No, no, no, no, *no*," he says, raking an exasperated hand through his longish, ginger-colored hair.

The action resumes. Up in the squared circle, Rodriguez quickly knocks Keach to his hands and knees. "Oof," Keach says, looking as if he means it. "Kill the bum!" some demented honky-tonk woman cries from the balcony. Keach wobbles to his feet, snakes out a weak feint, and this time Rodriguez nails him but good. Back down to the canvas on his hands and knees, hair matted with sweat, nose and eyes streaming, Keach says over and over, "Ooof, ooof, ooof."

That evening, at the suburban ranch-style house he's sharing with Judy Collins during *Fat City's* location shooting, Keach proves to be much more articulate. Wearing a tie-dyed jean jacket and Army surplus pants with a U.S. flag stitched on the hip pocket, he introduces some visitors to his friend and aide-de-camp, Billy Comstock, explains that Judy has driven into San Francisco for a recording session, and leads the way to a big, pleasant sitting room. "What can I offer you?" he asks with an expansive gesture of his balloon-swollen hands. "Wine, beer, grass?"

While Comstock adjusts the volume downward on a James Taylor album and fetches the refreshments, Keach sprawls in an overstuffed chair, gingerly caressing one raw hand with the other.

"Yeah, Judy's my old lady," he says in a musing tone, "that's no secret. We're not married, if that's what you mean. De facto, yes, legally, no. We've been together, lessee, I guess over two years now. Even my family pretty much accepts the situation by now, although that's not to say there haven't been some pretty hairy moments. . . .

"Judy makes me a happy man—it's that simple. We share a lot of things, and we're not intimidated by one another as we were at the beginning. We work together and we talk everything out, and we try to be as open and honest with each other as we possibly can. So we've talked about marriage from time to time, and tried to figure out what use it is as an Institution outside of a legal means of protecting children. We're just cooling it for a while, waiting to see what happens, trying to psych out what's right. See, I was married once, quite unhappily, as it turned out. I was much too young for it—twenty-two, twenty-three.

"What's really important to me, and becoming more important all the time, is intimate relationships with people, trying to open up and be less defensive to people, more genuinely interested in the experiences you're sharing with them. You know, without bullshitting, or some kind of ulterior motive. I think people, a lot of people, are trying hard to get into a new thing, trying to achieve a kind of breakthrough to an achievement of personal dreams and goals without impinging or presuming on others. I've just been reading *The Greening of America*, and Reich touches on what I mean, to an extent. His book is important, I think, because it articulates a point of view that's been in need of being put together for a long time — not so much for the people it describes as for the larger middle-class audience that doesn't know, doesn't grasp what's going on. . . .

"I think as I come to understand more of myself and the people around me, my life gets . . . simpler. Judy and I have a house in Connecticut, and when I'm not working, I like to just loaf around there, hang out, you know, read, listen to music, get stoned . . . L.A. totally turns me off. Every time I have to go there, I get traumatized — I actually start getting catatonic. I grew up there, you know, and then went to U.C.-Berkeley and after that the Yale Drama School. As a kid, I spent most of the summers down in Taft, Texas, with my grandparents. Those summers saved me, in a way. There was a freedom and a reality in Texas that I never knew in L.A. I guess it was always that vacuousness, you know — the need to reach out and touch something real, but there was nothing real there, even less that's real there now. I don't know — the kids, maybe. But even the kids don't seem real down there. The Los Angeles-ization of the planet."

Keach scowls morosely and takes a deep swallow of wine. Outside, a backfiring hot rod barrels down the otherwise still street with a sound like a fusillade of gunshots.

"The Los Angeles-ization of the planet," he repeats, looking glum and pained and slumping further down in the chair.

"See, like a lot of people, I don't like most things that're going on in America nowadays. The injustices that've gone down and are *still* going down. I mean, I *hate* Nixon — at least the things he stands for. But when I stop and reason it out, I realize those kind of negative vibrations aren't ultimately doing me any good. My politics are . . . liberal, I guess. I don't dig violence in any form, whether it's throwing rocks or offing the cops. It sounds like a cliché from in front, but I feel the only way the people are going to get together at this point is through a new consciousness. And it seems to me that it's developing. I mean, just in my own experience, I know I don't have to look too far anymore to find somebody who shares my views and interests. It sure as hell wasn't that way five, six years ago."

Keach leans forward intently, frowning in concentration. "So where does that leave somebody like me? With the people I love and my work, as far as I can figure it. I've been lucky in both respects. The films I've made so far—*The Heart Is a Lonely Hunter, End of the Road, The Traveling Executioner, Doc*—haven't been uniformly successful, but they were all interesting and offbeat, and each of them was a challenge for me. In a way, *Fat City* is my favorite. Part of it has to do with working with John Huston and Connie Hall. Huston is incredible, man—larger than life. He's a kind, brilliant guy, and I mean, he sees *everything.* He knows *exactly* what the finished film is going to look like. And Hall—goddamn, what a talent! He reacts to the emotion of a scene with light, and the results are fantastic. He's better than any two other cameramen I've ever heard of."

Keach tosses off the rest of his wine and excuses himself; he's got a 5 A.M. makeup call. On the drive back to the Holiday Inn, where the film troupe is quartered, one of the visitors asks Billy Comstock what he principally does, working for Keach. Comstock flashes a lopsided grin. "Drive," he says.

Round about midnight, Leonard Gardner weaves to a corner table in the hotel's cocktail lounge, looking definitely lost by now. Stirring his drink with a doleful finger, he launches into a morose recitative to his drinking companion about the recent split-up of his long-standing love affair with a lady novelist in San Francisco. "Well, I lost her, goddamn it," he concludes with a bitter grimace, "and now I'm back down here in Fat City choppin' weeds." What he's said is a paraphrase of a line in his book, which is more about losers than it is about boxers, and an affecting one.

"Am I mad?" he growls rhetorically. "You goddamn right I'm mad, man. All this bullshit Hollywood stuff is getting to me. I want to *strangle* somebody. How about a self-destruct movie? Why not? I'd like to *bomb* somebody, but I'd need an accomplice. Somebody who can run slower than I can."

Early the next morning, Keach and Sixto Rodriguez are going to Fist City again in the auditorium ring, the fog gun man is busily squirting puffs of smoke like benign CS gas up toward the plug-ugly extras in the gallery, and

John Huston is taking a break while Conrad Hall edges in close to the boxers, shooting handhold. Perched on a high canvas stool with his name lettered on the back, Huston sips from a paper container of coffee and confirms the scuttlebutt on the set that there'll have to be some retakes on the picture. "Not all that much, though. Some of the stuff's too dark for drive-in showings, is all. I fucked up on a few things."

Laughing in a booming basso, he fishes through the pockets of his bush jacket for a panatela. "I haven't made a picture in America since *The Misfits*, you see," he says, clipping off the end of the cigar, "and that was eleven years ago. Oh, no, the fact of my having taken out Irish citizenship doesn't mean I'm in exile from America. Far from it. I follow events here very closely, and for the first time in a long time, I think I see some light at the end of the tunnel. The country's response, for instance, to the Pentagon Papers. Older people are belatedly but surely waking up to the reality the young have been aware of for years.

"*The Misfits*, yes . . . Gable was in it, of course, Monroe, Montgomery Clift, all gone now, as many of my close colleagues are gone . . . James Agee, Bogart. Agee was, I think, essentially a poet. He was perhaps the finest writer I've ever worked with. He had great sensitivity, and he was one of those rare people who was completely aware of the complexity of life around him. He was the most modest and dearest of men, and very strong, too, within himself.

"Bogart was another type of person entirely. I was personally very fond of him. We did some six or seven pictures together, and over the years a friendship developed between us that is uncommon in this business. Bogart loved a good time, loved to celebrate his successes. He had a certain worldliness that I imagine would've made him laugh at the present 'Bogart cult.'

"Monroe, umn. I must confess I didn't recognize her potentialities when I first worked with her. I only did two films with her—her first, and, as it turned out, her last. I had a sense during the filming of *The Misfits*—and I think all of us did—that she was headed for the rocks and disaster.

"Monty Clift was, in a sense, the male counterpart of Marilyn in my life. Again, I did only two films with him—*The Misfits* and *Freud*. In his last years, he was far from well, either physically or emotionally. Monty was on his last legs, too, during the making of *Freud*. Among an assortment of ailments, he was going blind from cataracts. A pathetic figure.

"By way of contrast, it's a joy to work with someone as strong and stable as Keach.

"My plans after the filming? Vague. Inchoate. Except to go back to Ireland and get on a horse's back."

Ray Stark strolls by to tell Huston good-bye before leaving for New York. He pats his briefcase significantly and winks: "Well, it's time to take the money and run, John baby. The picture looks good so I might as well finance it myself. Take good care of the store." Nearby, a grip bites into a breakfast roll and winces: "Jeez, this tastes like a Frisbee with grease on it."

Up in the ring, Rodriguez challenges Keach with mock ferocity: "Hey, gringo!" Keach assumes an awkward crouch-and-advance stance a little like the young Gene Fulmer. After the two trade a few tentative feints, some intangible tension that's built up between them all morning abruptly blows, and there's a moment of joyous, anarchic release. Howling with glee, they spontaneously fall into each other's arms and begin waltzing. *Waltzing in Fat City*. The goons in the gallery eat it alive as Keach and Rodriguez swing-and-sway around the ring.

But at a signal from Conrad Hall, the two retire to their respective corners, and when the bell clangs, rush toward each other, swinging savagely. Head down, chin in, Keach furiously windmills Rodriguez's midsection until Rodriguez gets a clear shot at his temple. Then, stunned and glassy-eyed, Keach goes down to the canvas on his hands and knees, hair matted with sweat, nose and eyes streaming, saying over and over, "Ooof, ooof, ooof."

One Step Over the Fucked-Up Line with Robert Mitchum

Rolling Stone, 1973

After twenty years of playing a comic strip character called Super-stud, Mitchum at last is being recognized as the gifted actor he has always been. He is a master of stillness. Other actors act. Mitchum is. He has true delicacy and expressiveness, but his forte is his in-delible identity. Simply by being there, Mitchum can make almost any other actor look like a hole in the screen.

— Director DAVID LEAN to a reporter

"What I mean by that certain thing is . . . like . . . it's like you be a certain way, when you ain't crossed over that line yet. . . . I call it . . . I call it . . . that old fucked-up line, y'understand? . . . It was a time back before I'd done crossed that old fucked-up line I'm talking 'bout — and I guess it's somethin' like a bringdown. . . . Time pass and pretty soon I woke up one day and I didn't have that certain thing no more."

— AL YOUNG in the novel *Snakes*

On a clear, bone-cold morning in early November — the same day the nation is opting for four more years — the news flashes across Boston's church-encircled Commons with the speed of a virus ravaging an old-folks' home. Among the cast and crew assembled in the park to film George Higgins' street-savvy study of New England hoodlum folk-ways, *The Friends of Eddie Coyle,* the surprise announcement causes near-pandemonium. The gaffers and grips, the electricians and soundmen, all the technicians begin to mill about briskly on the thick-sodded grass adjacent to the ice-rimmed children's wading pool. Peter Boyle and Richard Jordan, both principals in the film, exchange mock-significant glances. Peter Yates, the director, flashes a contagious grin which the writer-producer, Paul Monash, promptly catches. Soon, even the park's casual strollers, walking their diarrheic poodles and mastiffs, begin to form small, excited queues, because the word has it that Robert Mitchum . . . fabled wild boy of the road, myth-dripping bête noire of more than a hundred movies . . . is arising . . . and coming to the location site . . . before noon!

Yates, swaddled to his stringy gray helicopter hairdo in a bulky, fur-collared parka, flashes the V sign to a writer from San Francisco. "It's a tribute to Bob's professionalism, rayly," the Scottish-born director drawls out of the corner of his mouth in a characteristically clipped mid-Atlantic brogue. "Bob's only tahsk will be to feed lines to Richard Jordan off-camera, you see, which could be done by anyone here. But contrary to common myth, Bob takes filmmaking very seriously. And I've been absolutely astounded by his performance so far. This will be the finest role of his career, I assure you."

"It'll be his *Zorba*," the local publicist chimes in nervously. The local publicist—let us call him Portnoy in deference to his concordance of real and imagined complaints—is a thick-bodied, prematurely graying gnome who is not without interest. For one thing, he is mortally terrified of Mitchum, and with comprehensible reason. The week before, during a filming sequence at the Boston Garden, Big Bad Bob had hurled a Styrofoam cup of beer at Portnoy's photographer. The photographer had been too zealous in his work, that was all—"He got in too close and made Mitchum's shit hot." Since that incident, as Portnoy had confided to the writer earlier, he had kept his safe and discreet distance. This morning, hopping from foot to foot to keep warm, Portnoy looks visibly relieved when Yates hospitably offers to introduce the writer to Mitchum.

A blue-jowled Irish cop is controlling the queues of spectators massing along the park's main path. "Can youse step back dere, lady? Dey're fixin' to take some movie heah."

A snaggle-toothed little man in a twill hat asks the cop when Mitchum is supposed to arrive. The cop shrugs. "Zowie!" the little guy yodels, shadow-boxing in the air. "I wouldn't want ol' Mitchum to belt me one, you know what I mean? That guy, he's as tough as John Wayne—tougher, maybe."

Peter Boyle, his bald pate gleaming in the heatless autumn sun, is standing near one of the monster Panavision cameras, his big-knuckled hands jammed into the pockets of his seedy-looking suit coat. "It's so boring," he complains to Richard Jordan. "No wonder there's always an outburst of wild fucking around your typical household movie set."

A papaya-bazoomed teenybopper crossing the green with an Airedale on a leash hesitates, then approaches Boyle and taps him on the shoulder: "I saw you in *Joe*," she blurts with a shy smile, "but I can't remember your name."

Boyle instantly goes into a Groucho-like crouch, ogling her breasts: "You saw me in *Joe*, eh? Well, that's your story, dear. Actually, I'm dubious — Lawrence W. Dubious. And in this magnificent picture that's r-r-rolling here, I play the role of a sensitive Cherokee teenager torn between the white man's world and his own desire to escape into fantasy."

The girl titters: "Who else is in the picture besides you?"

"Nobody much. Some kid starlet named Mitchell, Mitchum — some dubious hick name like that. No, seriously, my name is Peter Boyle, and I'm playing the role of a bartender named Dillon who is into, let's say, the incredible algebra of betrayal. And my costar — I should say my *esteemed* costar — is Robert Mitchum. Working with Bob has been a great pleasure, one of my most prized experiences as a professional actor. Bob's a very kind, a very easygoing man, and he tells a lot of great stories. Besides, I get to kill him at the end of the picture. What're you doing for dinner tonight, my dear? Have you ever slept with a world-famous movie star before? Or schlepped with one? Do you object to oral sex during the *Johnny Carson Show?* Will you marry me? Somehow I think I'm being used."

Seated in the stork-legged leather director's chair Steve McQueen gave him during the filming of *Bullitt*, Peter Yates is studying his script when a tiny, bird-featured old lady ventures near. "You give us a lot of plesha, sir, bein' heah in the Commons and all," she coos in a voice to match her face. "What do you do in the movie?"

Yates coughs delicately into his mitten: "I'm the, uh, director, madam."

"Oh. Well, I don't keep up with many directors since we lost Cecil B. DeMille."

"My name is Yates, madam. But I don't fire enough people or curse foully enough to be well known."

Over at the Beacon Street boundary of the Commons, a sleek black limo driven by a bullet-headed Teamster named Harry docks at the curb, and Mitchum alights, wearing pitch-black shades and a dark topcoat. There's a hush as he walks leisurely down the grassy glade toward the camera setup, moving in the loose, powerful stride that's known in the trade as the Mitchum Ramble. On the way, squaring his doorwide shoulders, he surveys the park's gnarled trees, the coveys of pigeons wheeling overhead, the State House dome glowing gold in the distance, the crowd of hushed onlookers in their orange-lined Styrofoam parkas. Mitchum is a massive hulk of a man, with a jowly face battered as a used VW bus. Silently, he shakes hands with Yates. "Where we at, Dad?" he asks.

As Yates smiles and begins to explain the setup, Mitchum glances around at the individual members of the crew, nodding, counting heads. Portnoy flashes him a sickly smile. Mitchum looks at Portnoy and doesn't see him. Does not see him. Mitchum, it turns out, looks at a lot of people that way.

Mitchum's gaze moves on. He regards the writer as if he doesn't necessarily approve of what he sees. By now, the writer is eyeing Portnoy in much the same way, and keeping his distance.

Mitchum studies the spectators, paying particular notice to several fetching college-age girls showing tantalizing expanses of panty-hosed shank and thigh between boot tops and coat hems. "Hot damn, Dad, it's great to get up durin' the day," he deadpans to Yates in a bass rumble. "I get to see some ladies with clothes on for a change."

An hour or so later, after Mitchum has spoon-fed his lines to Richard Jordan and departed for the day, Peter Boyle, Jordan, Portnoy, and the writer are taking lunch together at the Beauchamp, a small French restaurant a few blocks up the slope of Beacon Hill. Stabbing a fork into his tossed salad, Boyle throws back his head and laughs raucously when Portnoy asks what effect the success of *Joe* has had on him.

"Oh, it's been unbelievable. My life's just fallen apart. Believe me, I don't recommend stardom to anybody. If this is stardom, I'm in the wrong movie. Where's that waiter? *Garçon? Garçon?* Ah, yes — red wine for the three of us, please, and a bottle of beer for this scumbag scribbler. Do you have Kronenberg beer? Yes, make it Kronenberg. Make it a six-pack, in fact. The man's thirsty."

"*Un paque de seis,*" Jordan, a young, good-looking New York actor, murmurs with a smile.

Boyle feigns a double take: "Oh, you speak fluent and mellifluous frog, too, eh? Well, you're fired."

"As a matter of fact, I do speak fluent frog. I acted in French in my last picture, opposite Genevieve Bujold, which was fun. Before that, I made three Westerns" — Jordan makes a sour face — "all of them bad. *Valdez Is Coming, Lawman,* and *Chato's Land,* directed by Michael Winner, whom I despise, I might add."

"Winner is a loser, eh? I saw *Chato's Land.* I was driving across the country stoned on several strange substances. I stopped to see the movie—I was too stoned to drive any further. I remember that Charles Bronson spoke only a few lines, and I was struck by that, because I was once into that silence trip myself. I've noticed that there's a silence revival lately, and I can really understand that."

"When were you into a silence trip?" Portnoy asks curiously.

Boyle droops his head toward his vichyssoise in mock-penitence: "Back in the Fifties. I was an early-Fifties Jesus Freak. I did it for about a year—I never spoke when I wasn't supposed to speak. I was an acolyte in the Order of the Christian Brothers. Yeah, yeah, I know—the Friends of the Winos. But I took it very seriously at the time. I pursued, you know, God, somewhat unsuccessfully for several years as a professional religious person, and then I forsook that life and took myself back to the world and, through a series of incredibly stupid errors, became an actor. And after many hard, bitter years of struggle, I've achieved the immense fame I have now. Wealth. Happiness. Beautiful women throwing themselves at me. Believe me, it's not all it's cracked up to be. Ahead of me I can see only more stardom with liberal doses of obscurity."

Everybody laughs, Boyle included, but Portnoy's curiosity is further piqued—why had Boyle departed the religious order?

"The world, the flesh, and the devil," Boyle leers, gulping down a dollop of wine. "And not necessarily in that order, believe me. I don't know—I just wanted to, you know, maintain my sanity. At first I actually thought a thunderbolt from the sky was gonna snuff me out."

"An acute case of the Manichean heresy," Jordan diagnoses with a fiendish cackle.

"Yeah? Well, listen, doc—is it serious? Will my wang fall off? Am I terminal? Ah, I don't know from heresies, but I was pretty fucked-up for a while. I think I carry a good deal of residual guilt from those days. Sometimes I think I'm a deeply immoral man."

"Amoral?" Jordan asks, intrigued.

"No, not amoral. Immoral, I don't know what it is. I just don't seem to have the stamina for any of those long-distance spiritual trips. I tend to be swayed by fads. I'm fickle. You know—like this year it's Buddhism, say. So what'll it be next year—nuts and vegetables? I don't do it consciously. My latest venture has been to sort of dabble in Reichian philosophy and bioenergetic therapy."

Planting his elbows on either side of his plate, Jordan clasps his hands under his chin and leans forward intently: "Listen, there was a show on TV about books that're popular on campus, and Reich is being read by everyone, which I think is just terrific."

"I read a book of his," Portnoy puts in. "It was called, um, let's see, *The Function of the Orgasm*."

"Right on!" Boyle growls, thumping the table with an open palm. "Let's hear it for more orgasms, and more functional ones, too! No, seriously, I relied on Reich in doing *Joe*. I used *The Mass Psychology of Fascism* because that was what the character of Joe represented to me — the perfect prefascist man. Terrific book."

"That guy who directed *Joe*, John Avildsen," Jordan muses, "I went to school with him. I always thought he was basically a crook."

Boyle wiggles his eyebrows Groucho-style. "Why do you think he's a successful director? It's certainly not his looks — his mother dresses him too tacky. You like my Groucho impression, eh, Jordan? If I can be so bold as to inquire, what is your position on sex? Veet-veet now."

"I always like to stay on top," Jordan ripostes with a cool smile.

"I see. Hmn. A very unusual case. Tell me, when you masturbate, do you use different instruments?"

"Just the usual deviled eggs and turkey salad."

Suppressing a guffaw, Boyle swings around to Portnoy: "And what're your strange kinks, my boy? Like a taste of the old birch rod, is that it? Go for those tasty little starlets, do you?"

Portnoy feigns a morose look: "Yeah, but the ones I get are the ones who've been cut out of the picture." Portnoy pauses with the timing of a paid assassin. "You know — the cutlets."

"Jesus," Boyle hoots, turning red in the face with laughter, "I'm in fuckin' *trouble*, I'm gettin' *out* of here. *I'm* supposed to be the comedian, right? Christ, I'm goin' back to off-off-off-Broadway. I'm goin' back to off-Hoboken. I'm goin' back to *FTA*, where things are distinctly not so funny."

Laughing along, Portnoy capsizes a chunk of bread in the pool of orange sauce on his plate. "About that *FTA* thing, Pete," he asks, "why did you leave that show, anyway? Was that another fickle-fad impulse?"

Boyle grimaces theatrically. "Strictly speaking . . . um, possibly. No, I don't know. I felt the show hadn't become a kind of satirists' cooperative, which I'd thought it was going to be. I just sort of got out of it. I didn't feel free enough to . . . satire and revolution don't really go together. I mean, if I want to do a bit about a dumb cunt — well, you see the problem. Fonda and Sutherland are a little serious, yeah. So-o-o . . . I've just been making a lot of pictures and breaking, you know, a few hearts. Christ, counting this one, I've got four unreleased pictures, did you know that? I played in *Slither* with James Caan, *Steelyard Blues* with Jane and Don, and I went down to Durango to make *Dime Box, Texas* with Dennis Hopper."

"I read a long article somewhere about the making of *Dime Box*," Jordan recalls. "Weird piece — all kinds of dopey goings-on. Was all that true?"

Boyle nods emphatically: "Jap Cartwright's piece in the *Rip-Off Review*. Jap also wrote the screenplay with Bud Shrake. They're both crazies — old-style Texas crazies that make the hippies and the zippies look like a kiddie matinee. Not to mention Dennis, who's stone crazy. Oh, yeah, the article was all true. Understated, in fact. I wasn't down there that long, fortunately. Probably why I'm still alive today. I thought Durango was really great. I had all this incredible energy. Seems like you can get higher, you know, at 10,000 feet —"

"Than at sea level!" Portnoy whoops.

"I mean that in the way I mean that, young fella. I'll stand foursquare behind all my heathen crimes, except those against old ladies and young boys. And . . . where was I? Oh, yeah — I haven't seen the final cut of *Dime Box* yet, but I have the sneaky suspicion that my part has been cut a lot. Well, I enjoyed doing it, so I don't really regret that. Actors just don't have that much control over a picture. You can give a part all you've got, you know, but it doesn't necessarily mean anything."

"I have a funny feeling about this picture," Jordan says hesitantly. "I mean, I think we're moving along on it awfully fast."

Boyle drains off the last of his wine and nods in agreement: "Yup. Could be a lot of reshooting on this baby. No way to know, really."

"Mitchum's great, though," Portnoy ventures optimistically. "I keep telling people *Eddie Coyle* will be Mitchum's *Zorba*, and I really believe that."

Boyle yawns and stretches and pats his belly with an air of satisfaction: "Yeah, you could be right, I really like Mitchum. The thing about him is that he's so fantastically hyperkinetic. I mean, questions of tolerance and energy and all that stuff — he's just not quite human."

"The elemental male," Jordan muses.

"Yeah, all that stuff. The broads and the booze — I don't understand how he keeps up the pace. The guy's incredible in a lot of ways. He and I were talkin' one time and he was describing to me how you can bite somebody's nose off, you know? How if you bite a guy's nose off, he'll bleed to death, choke in his own blood. I asked him if you had to bite hard, and he said no, you just go" — Boyle acts out a savage crunching of the jaws — "and that's it, that's all she wrote. It's apparently a favorite form of homicide among primitive people. Ever since then, when I've been around Mitchum, I've been a *lit-tle* careful. I don't want him to get any sudden nipping notions."

"The sexy reactions Mitchum gets from women are just incredible," Jordan says, pushing away his plate. "Watch him in a restaurant or anyplace like that sometime. It's like he's dirty, but it's OK."

"Vic Ramos — you know, the casting director — Vic claims that Mitchum has seven balls, like a cluster of grapes," Portnoy snickers.

Boyle claps his hand dramatically to his forehead: "And a brace of Sabines to hold them out of the dust — Fruit of the Loom won't do! My God, lady, what're you doing to me down there? Oops, she's dead . . . and her eyes rolled just like a teenager. Long live the queen! But enough of this balderdash — what time is it?"

Portnoy peers at his watch and looks apprehensive: "Uh-oh, it's three o'clock. We were supposed to be back twenty minutes ago."

Gesturing expansively, Boyle rises from the table. "Ah, don't worry about it, pal. Yates was late this morning — we can be late this afternoon. We get any flak, I'll just say fuck you or somethin' cool like that. You know — 'Up your giggy with a meathook, Mary.' Jeez, it just struck me — wouldn't it be fun to be a real movie star and get to act like one? 'A round for the house, waiter.' Get shitfaced, get snockered. Wow! Just like Robert Mitchum. That'd be somethin', friend — that'd be somethin' else."

Back on the Commons late that afternoon, a cacophony of church bells peal vespers. Paul Monash, the writer-producer, is huddled deep inside his topcoat on a park bench, watching over the film technicians as they pack up the unit's cumbersome equipment for the night. A slight, clear-eyed man wearing Beverly Hills denim and a McGovern button on his coat lapel, Monash has the odd habit of raking a hand quickly through his long, thick salt-and-pepper hair to emphasize his points.

"Boston is a splendid city. I always relish being here. I'm in flight from Los Angeles, among other things. I find it a very deadening place. I just wrote my wife a letter saying one of the things I will not do is live there, in California, at least not for a while. It took me years of playing tennis to realize that I was getting tennis head instead of tennis elbow.

Grover Lewis (left) autographs Jann Wenner's arm in one of the happier moments during Lewis's tenure at Rolling Stone. Photo © Annie Leibovitz.

"Yes, that's correct, I began by writing novels. You've *read* one of them? Incredible. Which one? Ah yes—*How Brave We Live*. How brave you are. Well, that book swiftly passed into, um, literary history. And there was another one, too—*The Ambassadors*. I rather hoped readers would mistake it for a work by Henry James. No such luck, of course. There's probably a warehouse full of remaindered copies of that book somewhere.

"Then or now, I never found any consistent theme or emphasis in my work. I was always like a crazed hunter in the woods shooting anything that moved. No, I don't contemplate writing any more novels, because I'd write some dreary story about a middle-aged producer getting divorced, you know, and falling in love with nubile young girls or something like that. The prospect doesn't enrapture me.

"*Eddie Coyle* is what might be called an old-fashioned film, except that there's nothing old-fashioned about it because it's creating its own technique. It's a film about crime and criminals in which the emphasis is not on the action but on the people involved. The screenplay is very faithful to George Higgins' novel, which I consider a work of true brilliancy. My main task in writing the screenplay consisted of organizing the material already at hand. The dialogue in the book, which the critics praised so lavishly, is the dialogue in the film.

One Step Over the Line with Robert Mitchum   85

"My feeling about the picture so far is generally more than affirmative. I have an extraordinarily good feel about it that scares me a little bit. I guess I would say that the whole test of the film is going to be in the first scene, in which we have two men—Mitchum and a young actor named Steven Keats—sitting down in a dingy cafeteria and talking to each other for several minutes about stolen guns. Mitchum plays a character called Eddie 'Fingers' Coyle—Eddie got the nickname after some hoods he was working for broke all his knuckles for some minor indiscretion. Eddie is a hood himself, a freelancer—one of the so-called blue-collar workers of the underworld. And Keats plays a cold-blooded, no-nonsense gun dealer. And for several minutes, the two of them talk very seriously about guns. If at the end of that time, the audience feels that Mitchum really is Eddie Coyle and that what he's doing or about to do is interesting, then we've got a hugely successful picture.

"And it's happening—I can sense it building. Mitchum fits into the role amazingly well. We'd originally picked him to play Peter Boyle's role, which shows you what foresight and cunning we had. I suppose we felt that Mitchum was too strong and, in a way, too good-looking. I wouldn't say handsome. Too prepossessing, too forceful.

"But we were wrong. I have to say I really don't understand how Mitchum acts, what his techniques and resources are. It just happens. It's kind of an event. It's up there on the screen before you know it. He simply does it. It's like Willie Mays, you know—running back to the wall and catching the ball over his shoulder. Mitchum's a natural.

"Eddie Coyle is a small-time loser at the end of his rope, but the marvelous thing about Mitchum is that he doesn't play him as a groveling, uncourageous man. He imparts to the role a quiet dignity the character in the book lacked, I think. Mitchum radiates a genuine presence. Above all, you can say about Mitchum that he *is*.

"Oh, yes, it's true that he has a reputation for outrageous behavior, but I haven't experienced it personally. We haven't had many direct dealings, but the contacts we've had have been more than cordial. Still, you have to re-member that Robert Mitchum is a star. He's starred in 115-odd films, and be-ing a star marks you somewhat. A star is a nut. Just as Fitzgerald said, the rich are different from you and me, and so are stars different from you and me. Mitchum is definitely different. No, I won't attempt to itemize the particulars.

"As you're certainly aware, stars in general tend to be . . . difficult. For in-stance, I understand that Mitchum rarely, if ever, talks to reporters. Oh, yeah, sure, for whatever it's worth, I'll put in a good word for you. I'll even lick his boots if it'll help. If he's wearing boots, that is. I wouldn't lick his bare feet."

The next morning a cold, salt rain drenches Boston, and the film troupe sets up shop inside Pier Five, a high-vaulted and echoing warehouse that juts out over the slate-colored waters of Boston Harbor. Clammy as a tomb, the municipally owned building is blocks long, and its interior light is a perpetual dusky gloom because of its opaqued windows and skylights.

The troupe's objective for the day is to shoot two key scenes. The first shows Mitchum delivering a cache of hot guns to a bank robber and his mistress, played by Alex Rocco and Jane House. The location of the delivery is a Trotwood trailer, the long, unwieldy kind that takes the mobile out of home. At mid-morning, while Yates rehearses the actors, electricians and soundmen scurry in and out of the trailer, masking its windows with black gauze. The second scene, to be shot behind a canvas scrim a few yards from the trailer, shows Peter Boyle blowing Mitchum's brains out in a parked car. The weapon to be used is a long-barreled .22 caliber Magnum revolver loaded with live ammunition, but the brains are only putatively Mitchum's. A ghastly wax effigy of him has been prepared for the scene, which everyone carefully avoids looking at.

Just before noon, Trina Mitchum arrives on the set. Mitchum's only daughter, she's a willowy, twenty-year-old aspiring writer, pretty in a hesitant way, wearing two-toned sunglasses, a tan greatcoat, and crepe-soled boots.

"Dad has kind of an aversion to reporters these days," she reflects, expelling a long blue spume of mingled cigarette smoke and cold breath. "Mainly, that's because of a single guy, a writer named Brad Darrach. Darrach trailed Dad around for months in order to do a piece about him for *Life*. And Dad treated him like a friend—the whole family did. Well, for one reason or another, *Life* wouldn't take the piece, and Darrach rewrote it for *Penthouse*, and it turned into something else, if you understand what I'm saying. *Penthouse* wanted stuff that *Life* wouldn't have ever printed. You know, about Mom and Dad squabbling, and Dad's various women, and Dad fighting with my brothers, Christopher and Jimmy, and me being some kind of acid crawlback or something like that. Well, sure, I went through that routine a little bit, I guess. Just as much as anybody my age growing up in California and being exposed to those things. But not very heavily, you know.

"The thing is, it was all so *private*. It hurt Dad, and made him mad, too. It did all of us. Oh, it was a fairly accurate story, sure, but I don't think it was a fair story. I just don't believe in invading people's privacy to the point where you expose their family fights and stuff like that. I think, personally, if you can't say something good about somebody, there's no point in writing at all.

"My dad's a pretty fair man, actually. Difficult to understand, but he's a pretty fair man. He really is. When I was growing up, he wasn't around too much, so I had a lot of freedom. When I was between eight and fourteen, we had a farm, and I spent a lot of time there. I ran around a lot and did whatever I wanted. There were no big rules or anything — no strict church training or any regimentation like that. The only thing Dad would get upset about was if one of us did something stupid. Then he got mad. Dad has a very low tolerance for stupidity. But that's worked out for my benefit, really.

"My mother's much the same way. She's a great lady. Don't ask me how she puts up with Dad — I don't know. I don't know if I could put up with him for thirty-some years. She's a very strong lady, though. She's stood by him through everything, and I guess she's put up with a lot and suffered a lot, but she keeps on going. She's a beautiful lady, very stable, very steadfast. My mother's always been there — for me, too, and very steady. I haven't just been tossed around like a lot of Hollywood brats.

"Mom and Dad and I live in Bel Air. But Dad also has a seventy-five-acre ranch out in the country. He usually keeps thirty-odd quarter horses there. Yeah, they're raced professionally, but I think Dad's real interest is in improving their breed. Mom works all the business end of that. And she's also very active in a charity called SHARE, which is a group of show business wives for mentally retarded children. She used to paint very well, but she hasn't done anything like that for quite a few years. She keeps pretty busy with the horses and keeping the house together and everything. She's quite domestic. She's a Taurus. She just hangs in there.

"Dad's pictures? No, I haven't seen them all. A lot of them I have. I never saw *Night of the Hunter,* which I've heard is his best performance. That's the one where he's the murderous preacher with L-O-V-E and H-A-T-E tattooed on his fingers. I saw *Ryan's Daughter,* though, and it was great. I walked out of the premiere with tears streaming down my face. I was very touched by that.

"Dad's always had the reputation of being an outrageous oddball — the last of the iron-assed loners, blah-blah-blah — but he's always been pretty straight with me. One time when I was a little kid, though . . . Oh, it was funny, it cracked me up. Back then, he used to take me out for a drive every Sunday morning before everybody else was up. We'd stop at Schwab's and buy the paper, and he'd always buy me a hand puppet. I had this great collection of hand puppets. So one morning, we drove down to Venice, a crazy little town south of L.A. We were driving along and suddenly a policeman stopped us. We were driving on the sidewalk, and Dad hadn't even noticed. He just got a little reprimand, but it was pretty embarrassing for him. Pretty embarrassing."

Despite the fact that Mitchum has been married to his wife, Dorothy, for thirty-two years, he has the reputation of running through women like a stray dog through tall cane, and sure enough, when Mitchum emerges from his two-room camper, he's trailed by two pretty admirers—"Girl A and Girl B," as Peter Boyle snickeringly dubs them. "Gah-damn, man," Boyle mutters, ogling the two women in a parody of lust. "Ol' Bob's entourage is swelling. I had either one of those babies, I'd die of terminal euphoria. Zowie! You know what the 2001 theme is? That's the sound of Mitchum *waking up.*"

Girl A is a leggy United Airlines stewardess named Dawn, who looks as dumb and sweet as her name. Girl B, no girl at all, really, is an aging, elfin beauty named Sascha, who speaks with a heavy Scandinavian accent. Both women cling closely to Mitchum, but he more or less ignores them, breaking away first to greet and embrace Trina, then to banter with a circle of Teamsters that includes the boss of the teamos, Howie Winter, a dapper-dressed, pinch-faced little man whose thin smile bears no connection to mirth.

The Teamsters pose a constant and calculatedly deliberate menace to the picture's successful completion. Any infringement of the union's rules, and the picture shuts all the way down, that's it. Most of the drivers are self-acknowledged heavies associated either now or in the past with the notorious Bunker Hill Gang, which has been linked to seventy-five-odd gangland killings in the last decade. Characteristically, the teamos swagger around the set as if they themselves were the stars, chattering casually about warehouse shortages, last month's murder, and the gamier particulars of barnyard sex. Driving for the stars is lucrative, too. Billy Wynn, Mitchum's pug-jawed Irish attendant, receives a full day's pay for sitting in Mitchum's camper, emptying an occasional ashtray, and keeping the fridge well-stocked with beer. At the union's base rate, that amounts to upwards of sixty dollars a day. Harry, Mitchum's limo driver, draws the same for driving the actor to the set, then out to lunch somewhere, then back to his hotel.

The teamos guffaw and pound Alex Rocco on the back when he saunters up and joins the group. Interestingly enough, Rocco was a Boston Teamster before he trekked west to play the role of Moe Green in *The Godfather.* While he was a teamo, Rocco was indicted for one of those gangland-type slayings linked to the Bunker Hill Gang. The case was dismissed for lack of evidence after Rocco retained F. Lee Bailey as counsel. The teamos affectionately refer to Rocco as "Bobo."

Glancing around at the loud clatter of a grip's ladder overturning, Mitchum's gaze chances to fall on Portnoy, who's standing nearby shivering in his mittens and parka. Mitchum's smile shuts off like a shade being permanently drawn, and he mutters something about a lost ball in the far weeds that sets the teamos to horse-laughing. Portnoy tries to play it cool and composed, but he's been on the picture for weeks now, and he's developed a noticeable twitch in his right cheek.

During the delay before his scene is shot, Boyle grows increasingly manic. He says he wants to do a film with "lots of laughs and pretty broads with greasy DA's." Boyle does the twist to show what he means. Peter Yates summons Boyle for the murder scene in the car. Boyle rubs his palms together and cackles evilly: "Well, little girl, time to splatter yo' daddeh's blood all over that windshield."

"Ugh," Trina shudders, "that sounds worse than a T. Rex concert."

Behind the canvas scrim, Yates regards the wax effigy, his hands on his hips. "The only thing that alarms me is that we may set fire to the thing," he murmurs to no one in particular.

"For this scene," Boyle leers, "I need a combo of speed, cocaine, and *dope.*" Handling the Magnum pistol gingerly, Boyle clambers into the backseat of the car behind the dummy, and when the cameras begin to roll, fires seven deafening shots into the fake head.

"Cut," Yates calls out. "That's a print. Excellent, Petah."

"Sure makes you feel like a man," Boyle grimaces.

Boyle gets out of the car, hitches up his pants, and winks at the writer: "Well, that's it, lad — my last scene in the picture. Now I'll have to find a whole new set of neurotic problems. Thirty minutes from now, you know, I won't be able to bum carfare outta this joint."

As a farewell gesture to Boyle, Mitchum gets together a luncheon party for fifteen at Jimmy's Restaurant on the Fish Pier. As the host, Mitchum sits at the head of the table, flanked by Yates and Trina. The writer, oddly enough, ends up at the far end of the table, adjacent to Girl A and Girl B. Girl A — Dawn, the airline stewardess—says that she's on a diet, and not much more except that she "admires" Mitchum. Girl B—Sascha—turns out to be an advertising photographer who works in Spain, and she tells an amusing story about Sal Mineo's reputed predilection for nuns. She also says at one point that she can't abide men under the age of forty-five. "They're useless," she declares emphatically. Mitchum's bio says he is fifty-four.

After the meal, as the party is straggling out to the lobby in two's and three's, somebody points out Mitchum's signed photo on a wall decorated in pointillist style with framed pictures of celebrities: "Hey, look—Kirk Douglas!" Mitchum, who has belted back four or five doubles during the meal, regards the picture with a flat, baleful stare. "Would you believe that fucker was hanging down at the bottom when we came in here? No shit."

Outside, the teamos are impatiently waiting in a convoy of cars at the curb. One of the neckless ones gestures angrily to Peter Boyle. "Wheh's Peter Yates?"

"He said he was looking for his smother," Boyle tells him.

"What in hell's that?"

"His coat, I think."

"Well, fuck 'im—let 'im walk back," the driver snorts in a gunmetal voice, and accelerates away into the traffic.

Late that afternoon, George Higgins is seated at the desk in his office on the eleventh floor of the Post Office Square Building in downtown Boston. The day's bone-chilling rain hasn't let up, and the office is starkly lit and furnished, anonymous except for colored snapshots of Higgins' young children on the wall and a stack of out-of-date *New York* magazines on the windowsill. Higgins is the author of *The Friends of Eddie Coyle*, his first published novel and a bestseller of 1972. Higgins is also a cop—specifically, a practicing assistant U.S. district attorney for Massachusetts specializing in bank and postal fraud, and bank robbery. The fact wasn't lost to Norman Mailer in his jacket blurb for the book: "What I can't get over is that so good a first novel was written by the fuzz."

Higgins is delighted with the way his book is being filmed. "The script—I like it very much. I also like the people who're in it very much. I particularly hit it off with Peter Boyle. He's been over to my house a couple of times late at night looking for something to swallow, and I generally have something. I must admit I've swallowed a little myself from time to time. But Peter's gotten deeply into his part, and understands the character of Dillon as well as anybody, including myself.

"See, I'm no judge of acting—at least, not that kind of acting. I'm a trial lawyer, and that's acting of a different league. But Jane House certainly looks good, and the same applies to Mitchum. He really looks right for Eddie Coyle, which surprised me. When he was first being considered for the part, I was a little taken aback. I just hadn't thought of him. I don't know who I had in mind, if anybody, but it wasn't Mitchum.

"Once you see Mitchum in the part, though, it's amazing. He's just perfect, his mannerisms and everything. I've watched only four or five minutes of the rushes, but he's remarkable. I've been pretty busy here lately, so I've been on the set no more than a total of maybe four hours. My contact with Mitchum, so far, has been very slight. He's a great raconteur, I'll say that. In fact, I think he got into the wrong line of work. He should get himself a typewriter and stop fooling around with movie acting. He's a natural-born storyteller.

"*Eddie Coyle* germinated as a short story called 'Dillon Explained That He Was Frightened,' which was accepted by the *North American Review* in the spring of '70. A friend on the West Coast asked me if it was part of a novel. I honestly hadn't realized until he asked that it was. I write from the first sentence. If I get that first sentence right, the whole book's in it. I think it took me about four tries to get 'Jackie Brown, at twenty-six, with no expression on his face, said that he could get some guns.' Then I had the whole thing. I wrote the book in six weeks.

"I can't articulate yet how its success has affected me. I'm just getting it sorted out. I'll have a new book out in March, called *The Digger's Game*. The Digger is Digger Dougherty. It's probably fair to say that Digger is what Eddie Coyle could have been if Eddie had been more successful.

"I don't know for certain whether I'll continue on with my legal work. The truth is, I don't know what I want to be when I grow up. The likelihood is extremely strong that, yes, I will. I need the collision that I get with other human beings. I'm not a gregarious fellow. If left to myself, I'd go down to Nantucket and walk the beach. I do not initiate human contacts. This is something I've learned about myself. I need to have it forced upon me. I need collisions."

That evening, over cocktails with the writer in the bar at the Holiday Inn on Blossom Street, Portnoy complains, long and loud. Robert Mitchum, Portnoy is firmly convinced, has every intention of driving the publicist smack into the clutches of a rubber room.

"I'm supposed to write forty-odd press handouts about him, and the guy won't even *talk* to me," Portnoy moans with the look of a burnt-out tank fighter contemplating a dive. "I can't even get close to him. I mean, what am I gonna do?

"Uh-huh, yeah — movie stars are different than you and me. Right. Thanks a lot, pal. OK, so Mitchum's a superstar, he's made 115 pictures, he's worth five mill, blah-blah-blah. The point is, he's a *legend*. I've heard wild stories about him all my life in New York and Hollywood.

"Did you know he once dropped a professional fighter in a bar with one shot? It's true. The fighter later went three rounds with Marciano. And some director once told Mitchum at the start of a picture, 'I've got a hot temper. When I get rattled, I shout at actors. But don't let it worry you — next day I've forgotten all about it.' Mitchum said he understood — 'I've got a temper, too. When a director yells at me, I flatten him. But don't let it worry you — next day I've forgotten all about it.' And some other director got salty with him another time, so I've heard, and Mitchum tied the guy's shoelaces together and hung him upside down from a lamppost.

"A *weird* cat. Somebody told me he once gave away a new car to a stranger in a bar. And do you recall those famous pictures with the topless actress at Cannes in '54? Mitchum's wife was looking on while he squeezed around on that babe's knockers. That actress, by the way — Simone Silva, her name was — later tried to crash into movies in New York, and she was rejected everywhere because of those pictures, so she ended up snuffing herself. *Pffft*.

"I mean, Mitchum has been the whole route. Even that dope bust back in '48 — my God, man, nobody but gangsters and *shvartzes* smoked dope back then! Jesus, I don't know where to begin. Forty stories, hah! God, I've tried to figure it from every angle, and I just can't understand why he dislikes me so."

Portnoy, bless him, is virtually quaking with anxiety, but the writer can't resist the observation that even paranoids have real enemies. Portnoy grips both arms of his chair and juts his chin forward. "Whaddya mean by that?" he blurts suspiciously.

The next morning, while Mitchum, Alex Rocco, and Jane House are getting ready to resume their scene in the Trotwood trailer at Pier Five, Trina invites the writer into the warmth of her father's camper, where she, Girl B — Sascha — the teamo Billy Wynn, and a mod-coiffed Connecticut restaurateur named Fred are passing around a hash pipe and listening to *Sticky Fingers* on a cassette machine. Everyone is crowded around a built-in Formica table, on which lie a freshly opened pack of Pall Malls, an ancient copy of *Reader's Digest*, and eight or ten tightly rolled joints. Through the camper's curtained window, Mitchum can be seen standing over near one of the pier's open portals, silhouetted against a background of seagulls circling low over the rainy-day harbor. Wearing a pale yellow windbreaker and ink-black sunglasses, he's standing abreast of Tim Wallace, his longtime stand-in and constant crony, and the two of them are chousing with Girl C and Girl D, a redhead and a blonde. Girl A, it seems, has gone back to the friendly skies of United.

Gazing anxiously out the window at Mitchum, Wallace, and the two women, Sascha is in a sulky mood, too. "Zat Tim Vallace," she pouts in a poisonous little hiss, "he iss not a nize man at all. Vhy, last night, he tried to tell me vhere to sleep. I think he iss hor-rible."

With a wave to the two new ladies, Mitchum strides across the pier and clambers up into the camper, trailed by Howie Winter, the head-honcho Teamster. "Desperado time," Mitchum growls and heads for the john, where he pisses splashily without bothering to close the door.

Winter declines a seat at the table, but eyes the stockpile of joints hungrily. "Here, take some home with you," somebody says, scooping him up a handful.

Zipping up his fly, Mitchum strolls up to the table, and noticing the burnt-out pipe, hurriedly empties it. "You children left a *hod*," he rumbles in a mock-scolding tone, "and we can't have that. Never leave a *hod* layin' around, children."

"How's the scene going?" Fred asks with a grin.

Mitchum pulls a tall can of Budweiser out of the refrigerator, tosses the tab in the sink, and drains half the beer away in a gulp. "No fuckin' way will we ever make it," Mitchum grunts. "Like the pope says, no fuckin' way. That damned trailer's too crowded."

"Sounds like you need some midget propmen."

"Yeah, well, we got one. He's only this high, but he's this wide. Can't get the fucker through the door." Mitchum smiles at Trina. "You seen any of the rushes yet, Treen?"

"Saw that scene with the gal who plays your wife. She's a pretty thing."

"Oh, yeah—Helena Carroll. She's built just like a Belgian mare."

Mitchum acknowledges the writer's presence with an amiable nod: "You met my friend Fred here? The first time I ran into Fred I asked him what he did, and he said, 'fuck you.' Nice guy, Fred. Just like a high-steppin' dog. He goes to parties out on Long Island, Fred does. He's family. Uhm . . . you gonna be around awhile? Maybe we can talk a little, later on."

One of the assistant directors raps on the windshield to announce the lunch break. Everybody hurries off to the waiting cars—all except the writer. No fucking way is he going to leave that camper. Remaining seated at the table, he whiles away the next three hours staring at those joints a lot, and re-fusing to touch the *Reader's Digest*.

When Mitchum returns from lunch, he has clearly been exercising his el-bow, perhaps both of them. His gait is unsteady, his speech is thickly burred, and he is, in fact, distinctly one step over the fucked-up line as he draws two cans of Bud from the fridge, waggles a beckoning finger at the writer, and sags onto a clothing-strewn couch at the rear of the camper.

"Very seldom have I a trailer," he mutters darkly. "On most locations, there is one, usually, yes. But there's rarely room for me. Rarely room for me. People crowd in—friends, strangers. I try to tell 'em, but they won't listen. 'Stand back, jack. No? Ka-whap!'" Laughing mirthlessly, Mitchum swigs a lug of beer and lets one eyelid droop toward a brooding wink.

Perching on a tiny edge of the couch, the writer relays Tom Wolfe's admi-ration and curiosity about *Thunder Road*, filmed and released in 1958 but still a perennial favorite with the hot-rodding drive-in audiences of the South.

Mitchum nods gravely: "Yeah, it was received for true, for real. Still is. That was my original design, and I figured it that way. I wrote the story—the origi-nal story—and the title song. The screenplay I felt neither ambitious enough nor qualified to do, because those dissolve-cuts and all that kind of shit are largely technical. Beyond me, and boring, too.

"How come I haven't done more of that sort of thing? How come I'm not out diggin' a ditch between takes, you know? I choose not to work. I've got a gig goin' that's probably not the most satisfactory expression in the world—nor is anyone's—but it's the course of least resistance. It does me well, and every-one else well, so why should I belabor myself? I mean, I do my good works qui-etly and elsewhere, and I can't make a profession of it. It's denied me. I can't make a profession out of doing better because I learned early on that if you do better, you do well, you don't get to do better—you just get to do *more*. You know—'while you're resting, would you mind carryin' this anvil upstairs?' Like that shot. So, for me, it's no strain—just the course of least resistance. Do it until it poops out, you know, and then maybe wheel in once a year like

Lionel Barrymore and play Scrooge—wrap it up and go back to the Bahamas or whatever happens. Cure my arthritis and spike myself out—whatever . . .

"Yeah, it's true, I work a lot of pictures. I guess I do. I guess I do because we've gone through a period of some flux and change in our industry, and the effect has become somewhat boring. The effect per se — just that, you know. The innovative or innovative effect has become boring because it's so obviously designed as effect. Those anal shots up through somebody's wisdom teeth and all that whirling-light jazz, you know, is not too much fun. The main thing that we lack now is writers. We've developed some really serious current speakers as actors, mainly because of the import of British slum morality into this country and the reawakening of the children to the fact of what goes on beneath the Victorian collar and bosom. Not so with writers, though. They're mostly still hung up on the tickity-pop-poop kick.

"Sure, I like George Higgins as a reportorial writer — actually, as a novelist, too. I was impressed by his book largely because I think that work like his is necessary. I think it's necessary for people to understand something about the humors of the criminal mentality. I know a little something about the criminal mentality. I think I comprehend the freakers, too, and very well. I know enough about the criminal mentality to know that it is so designed only by the strictures of the statutes. I mean, if a certain act wasn't illegal those guys wouldn't be criminals, dig? Like that. But they get away with it or don't, right? Or they bargain for it or don't. Now, Mr. Higgins is a very ambitious fellow, a man of very strong opinions, and he's on the staff of public protection. He warns Peter Yates that I'm associating with known criminals, warns him that I'm going to get busted or tainted or something. Well, fuck, there's hardly anyone you can talk to in Boston without—you know. Anyway, it's a two-way street, because the guys Higgins means are associating with a known criminal in talking to me. A point is a point. If somebody wants to cock his finger and rap on the table in a court of law, the point remains. So if they want to bust you for a faulty taillight, Daddy, you're busted."

Mitchum laughs, this time with genuine amusement, and rises to fetch two more cans of beer. Sprawling back on the couch, he rumples a hand through his already tousled hair and lights one Pall Mall from the butt of another.

"I don't know. I've known a lot of cops. When I was in Vietnam, I met a lot of cops—fighting cops. They were humanists — actually humanists, and they died for it, didn't they? A lot of them died for it. They felt that people really deserved a chance, that everyone deserves to live, and they were going to fight for that. But then they died, a lot of them.

"I went to Nam in '67, I guess it was. To find out what was happening. Some people in the Defense Department kept nudgin' me — 'Why don't you go find out?' Next thing I knew, I was fallin' off an airplane at Ton So Nhut — February 3rd and it's 117 degrees. I went *waughhh*, and they said, 'wait'll summertime, man. It gets *hot*.' It was hot all the time, and I was very impressed. I was very encouraged, enormously encouraged by what I saw. You get semisophisticated or cynical, you know, and it's quite humbling to find that there are still people of high purpose and straight direction.

"I dealt mostly with Special Forces — the Green Beanie. I saw people teaching people — trying to teach them, oh, the legend about the chicken and the egg, and not to drink out of toilets — all kinds of very basic things. They were truly concerned, totally concerned. They'd come back from long search or battle stretches and immediately check into the village to see how the school was progressing. No, sir, it definitely wasn't set up for my benefit. *No way.* No way for my benefit. I came in hot. They didn't know who was comin' in. I ended up thinking — well, they still make good people. Good, honest people who give of themselves for other people. Like somebody's grandmother, like that.

"Sure, they were over there to fight a war, which is wrong in principle maybe, but that wasn't their doing, was it? Not their doing at all. There are always the advantagists, the opportunists who make a lot of money out of other people's misery. Then, of course, there's that French combine which controls the rights to the rice supply which feeds five-eighths of the whole world, which is the main reason for the whole caper anyway, why everybody's hassling. And there are all the individual people who wake up in the morning and say, 'Hey, a war's on — let's go get a piece of the action.' Same way on both sides. Little slant-eyed people wake up and say, 'Let's grab something. Why not, as long as it's happening.' Get a bicycle or something. And ultimately, of course, there're all the manufacturers who build battleships and airplanes and stuff like that. All of which is not wasteful, because it employs people — it's just a different form of commerce. It's a form that I don't endorse, but there it is.

"The single thing that I'm grateful for that's come out of the whole war mess has been some recognition of the need for communication. I've gone sometimes on dangerous waters in the interest of communication, because I believe in it. I believe that everyone in the world should have at least the privilege of knowing what's happening all at the same time. One thing I've learned is that the greatest fuckin' slavery is ignorance, and the biggest commodity is ignorance — the dissemination of ignorance, the sale and burgeoning marketing of ignorance.

"Nah, I didn't bother to vote yesterday. I'm an anarchist, anyway. I haven't really been interested in voting since they took Norman Thomas off the ticket. I don't think it makes any difference who has his duke in the till, really. I mean, you can bring on Liberace or somebody simpering about the idealism of the hardworking miners, and, 'My brother George who plays the violin is a Jew,' and so forth and so on. Well, the idea is marvelous — really marvelous. And as I say, people go out and fight and die for it. But life is life, you know, so the new leader of Bangladesh goes to London to have his gall bladder removed and takes over a whole floor at Claridge's and has an entourage of two hundred people — two private jets he flies on. His attitude is fuck those starvers. *Fuck those starvers.* Wise up, cranapple — right? Take your best shot. Well, what you do about it is do something about it. You put one brick on top of another — make it better. If you come to get it, get it. Like the Incas did to the conquistadores — when the Spaniards came for the Incas' gold, the Incas pried open the Spaniards' mouths and poured 'em full of the shit — all the molten gold they could fuckin' hold."

Mitchum drains his beer and gets another. He makes a wincing face when the writer asks about the writing he's rumored to have done over the years.

"I don't write. Nah. Yeah, there was a play at one point. Yeah, it was called *Fellow Traveler*, and, yeah, it was optioned by the Theater Guild. How'd you know about that? I thought you looked like a persistent motherfucker. Whatever happened to the play? Nothin'. I put it back in a drawer. There were so many critical notes on it. . . . Eugene O'Neill read it, and his notes were longer than the play. I'd done it hastily when I was about eighteen or nineteen years old. . . .

"It was about Harry Bridges bein' deported. He's shipped out of the country because of his union activities, and he organizes the ship in transit. When there's a fire in the hold, Bridges is suspected of sabotage, so they put him ashore on a cannibal island in the South Pacific. There's nobody there but a little toothless Barry Fitzgerald Englishman who's married to a giant Negress native. Umn . . . then the next visitor is a sort of Peter Ustinov–bearded member of the OGPO. Finally, there's a wedding ceremony, and Bridges is given the biggest — always the biggest, the biggest, fattest broad on the island. And he's also awarded a trophy—the shrunken head of the OGPO guy. The play winds up with a minstrel song. It was nothin', really. It was written before the war, and it did prognosticate the forthcoming Japanese situation. Those honchos at the Theater Guild thought it was somethin' remarkable, though.

"I really don't remember how O'Neill got involved. Somebody sent the manuscript to him, I guess. And I got summoned into the sacrosanct inner sanctorum of the esoteric Theater Guild, and I thought, *oh, shit.* The whole time I was there, I was tryin' to suppress an erection.

"The play was just a piece of shit. Looked like it was written by a left-handed retarded child in crayon. Maybe there were one or two good sections in it. What I should do, really, is sit down and write it right, just for the hell of it. Or burn it up. That's what I should do—burn it up. I don't know—it all tied together. I suppose I could've pursued it. The choice came down to workin' with little theater groups in Ontario or bein' a movie queen here in Boston. Which was the best way to go?

"Writing—I don't know. When I first got to Hollywood, I wrote night club routines and song lyrics, which paid very well. The only thing is, I got married, and workin' at home you have to spend all your time around this one broad, and I said fuck it, no way. I was a fuckin' ferret-faced twenty-two-year-old, fuckin' broken-nosed—"

One of the technicians sticks his head in the camper door: "Pardon the interruption, Bob, but it's a wrap for today. You can change your clothes if you want to."

With a woozy wave of the hand, Mitchum sways to his feet and fumblingly strips to his jockey shorts. When he's changed to canary-yellow bell-bottoms and a jersey pullover, he sinks back down on the couch and gropes around on the floor for his beer can. He grimaces again when the writer inquires about the poetry he's written.

"I quit writin' the stuff, you know, because you throw it in the wastebasket and somebody picks it up and your mother thinks it's precious or something. One time here in Boston, I was on the radio with a disk jockey named Robert Kennedy and he suddenly started reading something I'd written. Yeah, suddenly. Suddenly in the middle of a conversation, he *suddenly* read this poem on the air. I thought, how fuckin' *dare* he?

"Barnaby—you know, the bullfighter—Barnaby Conrad had a place in San Francisco where you were sort of encouraged to write on the shithouse wall. I wrote somethin' or other on there and Herb Caen reported it verbatim.

At least I hope he knew what he was talkin' about, because—well, that's why I had to quit. I didn't know what the fuck I was talkin' about. I ran into Dylan Thomas one time and I told him, 'You lost me with this and that.' And Dylan said"—Mitchum mimics Thomas' rich Welsh basso—"'Christ, I lost me fuckin' self. I'll have to get Caitlin to explain to me what I was talkin' about.' And that happens, you know. You become so fuckin' secret and abstract that you can't interpret your own stuff.

"I haven't done anything, really. I wasn't doin' anything, really. It was all very private and personal, and I really wasn't doin' anything. Fuckin' horrible junk. But I guess it was the only way I could speak. And I found myself either desperately inarticulate, seeking scan and rhythm, or hopelessly, esoterically overarticulate—and either way it was hopeless. I guess I thought I would become the darling of the ladies' literary society and they'd pat me on the ass and endow me with profound meanings that I really never had and knew nothing about.

"I used to spend some time with William Faulkner, and Bill told me about his total bewilderment and frustration on that score. They always credit you for the wrong thing, for the wrong reasons. I remember when Bill got the Pulitzer Prize or whatever the hell it was, and he said, no, he couldn't make it, he was gonna be drunk for another four weeks. I first met him when he came to California to write movies. He said he was there to write a treatment of something. We went all through it—I was a movie expert, see, a starlet. What, Bill finally asked me, was a treatment?

"A similar thing happened to me with [A. B.] Bud Guthrie. I picked him up one morning goin' to work and he said, 'You had your breakfast?' I told him no, and he poured me a glass of whiskey. I asked him what he was doin' and he said, 'Well, I'm doin' this treatment for Paramount,' blah-blah-blah. Stopped for a red light and he says, 'What the fuck is a treatment, anyway?' Hah!

"The secret of writin' for the studios was to get yourself a hat and hang it up in some prominent place. I learned that when I was a studio writer. Just get a hat and hang it up, so when somebody asks, 'Where is he?'—well, he's gotta be here somewhere, his hat's here. Handy little trick of the trade, you know."

Mitchum rises and steers a swaying course to the john, again relieving himself noisily with the door ajar. Trina is entertaining some friends in the front of the camper. "Can I offer these guys a beer, Dad?" she calls out.

"Sure. What are we—Chinamen?"

When Mitchum returns to his seat on the couch with a fresh beer, the writer asks him if he was set up for his sensationally publicized dope bust in 1948. Mitchum gingerly massages his jaw.

"I was. So what? Stranger things have happened. Listen, one night I was takin' a leak in a restaurant in New York, and a guy walked up next to me at the urinal and—*whap!*—he hit me. I took his best shot, but I didn't fall down. So I went upstairs and I was havin' dinner with Bob Preston. This was like five minutes later, and I had a kind of weal on my cheek. Bob asked me what had happened. I told him I was standin' there pissin' and some guy hit me in the head. The maître d' came up and said, 'You still talkin' about that?' Meanwhile, the guy who belted me was on his head in a garbage can outside.

"Yeah . . . the bust was a setup. I don't know all the details. I really don't. I learned all the names later. I paid for it—took the hank. Man, what's the difference? I had a bug in my chimney for six months. I was at the scene of the bust exactly seven minutes. At that time, there was a big war on between the L.A. Police Department and the L.A. County Sheriff's Department. I got two years. Big deal, you know? I got off with six months. Served only sixty days. Any more time than that, they'd have had to pay a lot of travelers across the stage. They got what they wanted—a three-ring circus for a few weeks. Television cameras.

"Real strange, you know. The charge was conspiring to possess. I don't know—if somebody had handed me a joint to take with me on the road, I might have taken it, so it makes little difference if I was actually guilty or not guilty. Not guilty—I don't know. Anything to get the hell out of the joint, because the minute I walked in I went sniff-sniff, and the place was *hot*, man. I walked over to pick up the phone and somebody said, 'Where you goin'?' I said, 'Ah-hah, a lotta heat in this joint. What're those two faces at the window?' And those goddamn dogs—*bam!* Down came the door and I went *uh-oh*. One of the cops yelled, 'Mitchum is raising his arm in a threatening manner.' I said, 'Hang me up, boys—I been had.' Slightly *yentzed*. Roundly fucked."

Mitchum throws back his massive head and guffaws uproariously.

"Yeah, that's right. I got a ration of shit in the County Jail, but so what? I wasn't like a virgin, you know. As a matter of fact, they tried to set me up again in there. They wanted to make me for the whole deuce. They didn't want to be wrong. I didn't know which side of the fuzz it was, but somebody told me, 'Watch it. They're tryin' to make you, rack you up in the joint.' I said fuck it, put me in an individual cell. The food was better, anyway, and the security was better—better for me, better for them. A cell where they locked the doors every night—clang, clang, clang. That way I couldn't bust out and hurt anybody. Hah!

"Well, it was the only thing to do when I found out they were maneuverin' against me, plantin' me with stoolies and all that kind of shit. Man, they can do anything they want, you know—charge you with some minor infraction of the rules, and you end up doin' two big ones in Quentin. *No fuckin' way.* I couldn't hack that. And for nothin', really. Fortunately, there were enough guys on my side who said, 'Wait a minute—what're you doin' to this asshole? Why're you tryin' to break his balls?' Really, I didn't give a fuck. I didn't try to hurt anybody. One or two cops made a move on me, but I said, 'Look, enough of that shit. You want to go that route, I'll meet you after school at the Y.'

"I get along with people very well, really. I do. I do. Really. Every now and then, some guy gets the hots and figures to go home and tell his old lady he just decked that motherfucker Mitchum. Why, she'll shoot him, man! She'll shoot him! 'Robert Mitchum? You stomped his ass? Why, you dirty motherfucker!' Me, I'm easy. I don't go through red lights. I don't steal.

"Yeah, sure, I'd been busted before. When I was a kid, I was hitchin' a ride on a freight and a fuzz batted me with his club. That was in Georgia, and I was sentenced to a chain gang. I worked for a while repairin' rocks, then I took a walk and never went back. OK, so I was a bum. I was busted for the simple crime of poverty, that's all. No big deal. Back at that time, there were no champions of poor people. But I didn't consider myself particularly victimized. I didn't think of myself as a baby. I was fifteen, and I chose to go to a flat joint instead of a punk farm.

"Nah, it wasn't particularly hard to take. I got fed, you know. I guess it was depressing. The first night, I slept on the floor and the guy next to me was dyin' of a tubercular hemorrhage. They kept him alive and turned him out on the road the next day so he wouldn't die inside. They didn't want the fuckin' book work and all that shit. They didn't want to dig him a hole.

"After my fugitive status began to be publicized, that county, Chatham County in Georgia, wrote that bust off for me. They said they'd dismissed me after five days. Actually, I'd been there thirty days when I ran off. The sentence was 180 days. An indeterminate, really. For being a 'dangerous and suspicious character with no visible means of support'—the common charge of begging or vagrancy, you know. A leech on society. Well, it was quite a system. If you did good work, they could rent you out for two bucks a day, and it only cost them thirty-six cents a day to feed you. Fuck it. I didn't do too good work. And I couldn't handle so much shit, really. I was barely fifteen, you know, and listening all the time. The fellows who were kind to me were the murderers, you know, the long-timers. They were handlin' my case, and they weren't fuckin' me. They handled my case. They wouldn't let anybody take advantage of me.

"Like if I sold a bunk that didn't belong to me or to anybody to a fish for two bits and somebody else threw the guy out of the bunk, the fish would corner me and say, 'Listen, you little asshole, I paid you a quarter. What's the fuckin' deal?' When that happened, some fuckin' murderer would come up to him and say, 'I'm Ebo City Pete,' and that's all it took. Those murderers helped me with my clothes and everything when I split.

"No, I don't identify in my mind with criminals, but my exposure to them has helped my understanding. Oh, sure, sure, sure, sure. Sure. I know the freakers, you know—the burglars, the uptighters, those creeps who puke or jerk off or something every time they make a score so you can pick up on their modus operandi.

"I tell ladies, I say, look—for protection, go to a sporting goods store and get one of those ship horns that comes in an aerosol can and makes a loud noise. A freaker breaks in, that's all. Just trip that thing and he'll spook out. But don't ever try to face one down, because they'll fuckin' kill you. They will fuckin' *kill* you.

"They're crazy, right? Oh, I met 'em in fuckin' jail, man. I've seem 'em fight with a razor blade on the end of a pencil—fight over some fuckin' boy office burglar, slashin' away at each other, kickin' each other in the cunt. I always steered a wide berth. I want no part of people like that. No fuckin' way."

Mitchum swallows the dregs of his beer, stands erect, and hitches up his trousers. "Better go round up Miss Sascha and hit the road, I guess," he mutters, yawning hugely. With a crooked grin, he points at the couch. "Maybe I'll bed her down here tonight. Check her out tomorrow after all those warehousemen get at her. She told you she was what? She's naïve? Uh-huh. Oh, boy. Well, I'll tell the man. I'll tell the man when he comes in."

Early the next morning, the weather is still chill and drizzly at the pier, so Tim Wallace, Mitchum's stand-in, and the writer commandeer one of the teamos' cars for shelter. A hulking porterhouse of a man, Wallace is a kind of physical parody of Mitchum. He has essentially the same facial dimensions, but his nose, mouth, and chin appear to have fallen in the oven. Snuggling deep into his horse blanket topcoat, Wallace jams his blue toboggan cap down over his ears and says that he's been with Mitchum for twenty-four years now.

"Yeah, we started out together on a Western called *Blood on the Moon*, and I been with 'im ever since. Dozens of pictures, yeah—I don't know how many. I did a picture with 'im in Rome, one in Canada. We did several down in Mexico. One in Africa—hah! When we were flyin' back from Africa, this fat old black guy wearin' a jelly bean hat got on the plane, and he had a whole string of wives and servants with 'im. He musta been a king or somethin'. So this guy give Bob the once-over and said, 'I know who you are—I've seen your movies. Do you know who I am?' Bob looked the guy up and down and said, 'No, but you must be the head nigger around these parts.' Hah!

"Bob and me, we get along real well, usually. Aw, we argue and squabble sometimes, just like anybody else. Over trivial things, you know. I look on 'im like my brother, and we've had a lotta laughs together. Bob, he's got a temper, though. Did you hear about 'im dousin' that photographer with beer last week at the Garden? It's a good thing the fucker ran, man. Bob woulda threw 'im outta the balcony.

"You gotta treat Bob with respect or—*whap!* Left to hisself, Bob's a pretty easygoin' guy. He loves his quarter horses—that's his big hobby. That and readin'. He reads alla time. He calls himself a 'street intellectual,' you know? He can recite lotsa that stuff, too—whole pages of Shakespeare and all those old guys like that.

"Yeah, I remember the dope bust. Fact is, I told 'im—I'm not braggin' or anything—I told 'im please don't go out with that big fellow. Bob Ford, his name was—he was a bartender around. I said don't go out with 'im because he's no good—he's a rat. The next morning, I wake up and look at the paper and there's a picture of Bob and two girls and another fellow walkin' into the Hollywood police station. Well, it was a setup, see—Ford was tradin' Bob to the cops to clear a bust of his own.

"My own self, I think it was good that Bob served his time. By doin' that sixty days, that made him bigger than ever. It made him a bigger man, and it made the public respect him. If he'd of got some creep-o shyster to squash the case for 'im, I don't think he ever would've amounted to anything. As it turned out, his career just blossomed like a flower."

After a late lunch, Mitchum is visibly sloshed again, and clowning around outside his camper with Alex Rocco, Peter Yates, Tim Wallace, and a couple of the Teamsters. Mitchum belly-laughs at the multicolored beanie Yates is wearing, and swings around to Wallace: "We're gonna get you a hat, too. Made out of fuckin' *wood.*"

"What kinda wood?"

"*Stinkwood*, you cocksucker."

Laughing, Mitchum chances to notice Portnoy and the writer, who're standing a discreet distance away. "Hah! There's two cocksuckers!"

"One cock and one sucker," Portnoy mutters plaintively under his breath.

Mitchum turns back to the two Teamsters. One of them, Harry, claims to have once transported Howard Hughes into the Ritz Hotel in a wooden packing crate. "Some very talented thieves around this town," Mitchum drawls, "but some of 'em suck, too."

Harry makes a leering face at the accusation and pretends to be masturbating and jabbing a thumb up his ass simultaneously. It's the kind of bawdy, two-handed divertissement that Mitchum enjoys, and he hoots with harsh laughter.

Alex Rocco seizes the moment to make some teasing comment about Mitchum's bulging bay section. "Yeah, I'm gettin' a gut," Mitchum concedes with a philosophic shrug. "I'm lucky if I can stay under 190."

"Well, you eat a lotta cunt," Wallace puts in. "Plenty pro-teen in that."

"Nah, you're lyin'—I just *breathe* on it a lot. You ever see me doin' any of that stuff? That's against the *law,* man."

"You want me to tell the truth?"

"No."

"Listen, you guys. I gotta tell this story on Bob here. He was ballin' this babe one time, see. He was in the saddle, see, and his nuts was swingin' back and forth in the air, see. And this babe's dog jumps up on the bed and takes his nuts in its mouth, see. *Big* sonofabitch—"

"The dog was like half Great Dane and half bull mastiff," Mitchum muses. "Like a pony."

"*Huge* sonofabitch."

Mitchum nods. "Yeah, big yellow-eyed mother."

"So I walk into the room by accident, see, and this dog has hold of Bob's nuts like a retriever would hold a bird. I couldn't help it—I started laughin'—"

Mitchum grins. "I told him, *don't laugh.* I *very slowly* got, uh . . . disengaged. And I smacked that motherin' dog—*whap!*—clear across the room. I woulda shot it if I'd had a gun."

"I tellya, I had water in my eyes from laughin' so hard at 'im. There was water all over the place, in fact. The bed was wet, you can bet your sweet ass on that." Wallace cackles shrilly, then fixes the writer with a stern glare. "Don't put that in your fuckin' story, friend. It's a true fuckin' story, but jeez — Bob's wife, you know . . ."

Mitchum yawns and stretches and strolls over to one of the pier's open bays to look out across the harbor. It's nearing dusk and bobbing blue buoys are already flashing and reflecting on the slate gray water. After a minute's hesitation, the writer follows. He has one final question: Did Mitchum, as legend had it, once actually piss on David O. Selznick's immaculate white rug?

Mitchum sniffs and kisses a knuckle and then laughs hoarsely: "I did that, I did that, yeah, but it wasn't an immaculate white rug, necessarily. I was in New York, and David called me up and said, 'Bawb, how long've you been here?' I said whatever it was — couple of weeks, two days or whatever. He said, 'I've been here for some extended length of time and you haven't called me.' He was one of those sort of sybaritic, wet-mouthed Jews, you know, so I said, well, I'm sorry about that. He said, 'Why don't you come up and see me?' He was staying up in a floor-and-a-half penthouse suite at the Hampshire House, so I told him fine, sure.

"My wife was gone off somewhere, so I had to leave a note for her. I went down to the bar of the hotel and I was writin' the note and I had a couple of belts — I don't think I've ordered anything less than a double since I was fifteen years old.

"And I was walkin' up the street past the Drake Hotel, and I saw Herman Mankewicz standin' apart from his wife and her sister or his sister, whatever, neither of whom had any use for Herman at all. He was just standin' huddled up, and they were glaring and *righteous*, you know — waitin' for a cab or something. I said, 'Hello, Herman,' and I walked about thirty feet past, and he came after me and clutched me and dragged me back and said, 'How about a drink?' And those two women sighed heavily and followed him into the bar, and he ordered a double scotch for him and a double scotch for me. The ladies ordered a ladylike champagne cocktail and sat somewhat apart from us. By the time the bartender served the first round, Herman ordered another one. OK, now I've got like four double scotches goin' for me, right?

"So I walked on up to the Hampshire House in a good, steady, manful stride, because I like to walk. As I go in the lobby, Barney Ross, the fighter, is just gettin' off the elevator. He says, 'Hey, man, I just made a score. How about a drink?' I said, 'Man . . .' He says, 'C'mon, c'mon.' So we went in the bar and I had two more double scotches. That made it . . . how many? Whatever. Whatever. That's eight now. Six straights, at least.

"So I go upstairs, and it's the thirty-something floor in the Hampshire House. Private elevator. I remember there was a piano, and a little reception office as you walked in. There're four or five guys sittin' around up there, and everybody is sort of lookin' each at the other and wondering what's to be done. And they say, 'Are you waiting to see David?' And I said, 'Well, you know—yeah. He called me.' Well, these guys had all flown in from somewhere on business. They just came in from the Coast, like they say, and they had to fly back and report to their wives or production managers or whatever their problems were. I had nothin' going, really. I mean, David owned half of my contract at that time, but mine was just a social visit as far as I was concerned.

"So David came in just as someone was being ushered out. David says, '*Bawb*, my God, it's difficult to catch up with you. Why don't you have a drink?' I said, 'Uh, I don't think so, really.' 'C'mon, why don't you? I'll have one with you.' Well, OK, fine. So David has whatever he has, and I ask the girl for a double scotch and water. She handed it to me, and by this time I was sort of thirsting and hungover and dry, so I just drank it down and ordered another one.

"Finally, David's last conquest or victim was shown out, and I walked into his office and sat down, and I was stoned out of my *bird*. David started talking, and he crossed his legs, you know, and he talked and he picked his lip, and he was rather dignified, and he kept talking. Me, I was feeling a weird sense of urgency that I couldn't quite locate. I took my trench coat off. I had a hat somewhere. I'd left a hat in the office. I never wore one, but for some reason, I had a hat that day. So I took off my trench coat, and I took off my jacket, and David kept on talking. I finally put my jacket on again, and I put my trench coat on again, and he kept right on talking. He was the genius and I was the boy, see, so I just sat there and it finally dawned on me that my sense of urgency was the simple need to piss. So I finally just hunkered myself off to the side and sat there in the chair and pissed on the rug. And that shut him right down. That shut him down flat.

"So I got up—'Thank you very much'—and I walked out. As I was leaving, I hadn't really finished pissing, you know, so I was waitin' for the elevator, and they had a sandbox there, so I was pissin' in the sandbox and the door opened and the lady receptionist stuck her hand out and said, 'Your hat—you forgot your hat.'

"That was it. Hah! You can imagine David's version of the story—'This degenerate sonofabitch comes and pisses all over my wife's *wig*.' Oh, man, I tell you."

After dark falls, the company is still at work, and Sascha is saying her good-byes before departing for New York and her flight home to Spain. Fussily patting at her hair and smoothing her skirt as she poses with Mitchum for pictures by the set photographer, she looks to be close to tears. Mitchum looks thirsting and hungover and dry.

Impulsively, Sascha hugs Trina, and Trina, visibly touched, responds with a kiss to Sascha's cheek. Mitchum endures Sascha's parting embrace without discernible expression, then shrugs as she hurries away with the teamo who'll drive her to the airport. "Sweet lady," Trina remarks with a tentative little laugh. Mitchum sighs heavily. "Uh-huh. Built just like a Belgian mare," he grunts, and walks away.

Who's the Bull Goose Loony Here?

Playboy, 1975

The mid-morning sky over the Oregon State Hospital in Salem looks liverish, quiverish, ready to collapse with torrential rain at any second. On the crew-cut lawn behind the main building, an orderly shoos his excursion troupe of exercising patients back to shelter past a charter bus disgorging a troupe of Hollywood film technicians.

The two lines of shuffling men pay scarce attention to each other, even when one of the patients — a spindly Latino in a Hawaiian shirt — suffers some sort of convulsive seizure and slams face first to the ground. The orderly quickly kneels beside the victim, clawing for his tongue, while the other patients stand around in a frieze of distracted inattention. "*Momma, momma, ayúdame,*" the stricken man manages to cry in a wet strangle. "Crazy," one of the film technicians clucks, then cuts his eyes away uneasily.

A rush of wind blows a hole in the overcast. The squall begins.

A few minutes later, wearing $35 squeakless sneakers and somebody else's awning-sized windbreaker, Jack Nicholson comes barreling down the Oregon asylum's ground-floor corridor. His gait would be arresting anywhere — a speeded-up version of the moneymaker-shaking street strut he choreographed to near-squeakless perfection in *The Last Detail.* Nicholson walks like Martin Balsam sounds — solid, chunky, chock full of cod-liver oil.

Strolling along the drab-linoleumed institutional corridor in the opposite direction, Michael Douglas is escorting a visiting writer through the archaic, all-too-grossly authentic mad wards where Milos Forman is directing Fantasy Films' $3,000,000 production of *One Flew over the Cuckoo's Nest.* Douglas is Kirk's kid — the one who plays Inspector Steve Keller in the TV series *The Streets of San Francisco.* Michael Douglas is also the coproducer of *Cuckoo's Nest* and right now, without all that much visible effort, he is being charming, courteous, even voluble when called upon. He has, in fact, just introduced into the conversation the pleasant fiction that he and the writer had met "years before . . . in San Francisco, wasn't it?" Michael Douglas is a smooth-rising young biscuit in all respects except that he wears hideously disfigured cowboy boots the writer figures he must have copped from some dying wino in Stockton.

The writer is trying his mightiest to stay attentive, but his mind is blipping into erratic wigwags and test patterns. He has a root-canal case of the fantods. His sphincter is fluttering, he is breaking out in a sour sweat, and he is wishing to hell he had an amyl or something harder to bite on.

What's queering the writer's internal wiring isn't Douglas's pleasant fiction nor Nicholson's abrupt, looming presence—which in itself registers about a 6.5 on the Richter scale. N-o-o-o, the germ of the trouble lies in this rotten, overwhelmingly oppressive and repulsive *place*. At long last, lunacy—the funny farm, the loony bin, Rubber Room Inn. For years, assorted editors and ex-wives have been predicting the writer will wind up in just such a cuckoo's nest and—well, he's been here now for half an hour and he's wondering queasily if he will be allowed to leave when it's time to go. He is also wondering about *his notebook*. Has he mislaid it somewhere? That notebook is too goddamned important to lose—it's an Efficiency Reporter's Note Book No. 176, and scribbled among its two hundred leaves and four hundred pages are the liver and lights for two unwritten stories, plus an itemized list of business expenses totaling over $1,300—*God have mercy, where is that slippery fucker?*

The notebook, of course, is securely glued to the viscous resin bubbling out of the writer's swampy palm. When he discovers this, the writer executes a jerky, agitated little flamenco of relief and gratitude.

Passing abreast of Douglas and his visiting charge by now, Nicholson instantly registers the dysfunction. The actor flashes Douglas a high-caloric high sign in greeting, then swivels his gaze to zero in on the writer's sagging knee action. Unsmiling but not unsympathetic, he notices the man's small, panicky dance of distress and release, the jittering aftershock of wrenching visceral trauma. He files it all away for future reference. Nicholson notices things like that and no doubt uses them to flesh out his riveting film performances.

Without irony, the writer regards Nicholson as a national treasure. This literalist view of the actor will get in the way of the substantive story waiting to be perceived here, but not for long. Meanwhile, Nicholson whips past in his squeakless sneakers, vanishing soundlessly down the institutional corridor.

With the writer in tow, Douglas advances a kilometer or so into the bowels of the fortresslike asylum, pulling up short at a point in the corridor where the color of the walls abruptly changes from scabrous green to shit brindle. In his voluble register, Douglas is explaining—no, *proving*—that this is no gypo movie of the week they're engaged in here; nosirreebob, this is the quality goods, all AAA feature of the caliber that's rarely indulged in anymore for all your ersatz disaster operas and *Godfather* begats. Standing near the wire-mesh entrance to Ward Four, the film's principal set, Douglas ticks off *Cuckoo's* championship qualities on his pale, pencil-thin fingers:

"Our daily nut is $35,000, see, so with that kind of dough at stake, we're not chintzing around about *anything*. When Saul and I decided to do the picture"—Saul Zaentz is the Main Man at Fantasy Records/Films in Berkeley and *Cuckoo's* other producer—"we agreed first off that we'd only settle for the best. I mean, screw it, across the board, whatever the field of talent, whatever the cost. And we got it all, man—everybody and everything we wanted—bam, bam, bam! Nicholson was our first and only choice for McMurphy. Nicholson is the 'bull goose loony'—watch his stuff this afternoon and you'll understand what I mean."

Nicholson as McMurphy—a dead-solid ringer. Back in the Sixties, before the bliss ninnies began slouching toward Hesse and Tolkien, McMurphy was a kind of fictive national treasure in his own right. Everybody—everybody who could read, anyway—copped a hint of style and character from the hell-raising drifter who feigned insanity to escape a penal farm, who locked horns in the mental slammer with the tyrannical Big Nurse, who both won and lost the battle and in between gave life-to-life resuscitation to the Chronics and Acutes on his ward.

"And Milos," Douglas goes on, "he's just goddamn marvelous—one of the finest directors in the world. It's a wild thing to watch happen. We've got a great cast, down to the tiniest walk-on, and probably the best crew in the business. Jack Nitzsche is composing the score . . . Bill Butler's our cinematographer—he just did *Jaws*. And, lessee—yeah, the sound man, Larry Jost? He's up for an Oscar for *Chinatown*—like Jack. But come on, let's go take a run around the set. Brace yourself, though. I warn you, man, it's terrible—it's *ghastly*."

Yes, exactly. Ward Four would gag a maggot. It is a cagelike enclosure furnished in the brutal paraphernalia of shrink-tank pathology run absolutely amuck: cramped rows of hospital cots with rumpled gray sheets and matted blankets . . . obscenely stained bed tables littered with puke pans and hot-water bottles . . . a scattered fleet of decrepit, cane-backed wheelchairs . . . framed calendar portraits of dogs and wild geese hung uniformly awry . . . and perched above all this mess, on a high, centrally located shelf, a smeary-windowed TV set bearing the brand name of its manufacturer, one "Madman" Muntz.

An immaculate, glassed-in nurses' station controlling egress to the ward cage rounds out the picture. Big Nurse's Orders of the Day are posted there on slot cards in a wallboard. The slot cards read:

> THE YEAR IS 1963
> TO DAY IS WEDNESDAY
> THE DATE IS DECEMBER 11
> THENEXTHOLIDAY
> CHRISTMAS
> THE NEXT MEAL IS BREAKFAST
> THE WEATHER IS CLOUDY

Ye gods, The Compleat Toilet — "Ol' Mother Ratched's Therapeutic Nursery," in the phrase of the book's author, Ken Kesey. Which prompts the writer to clutch his sweat-slick notebook all the tighter and wonder aloud about Kesey's connection with the film.

Douglas takes on the expression of a man who's just been put on hold during a transoceanic call. He motions vaguely toward the ward's rails-blurred windows. "I can't say for sure," he mutters, "but I've heard he's out there in the hills somewhere muttering rip-off. We hired him — paid him over $10,000 — to write a first-draft screenplay. We found out pretty quick that he couldn't write screenplays to suit our standards, and he couldn't get along with the people involved, and he couldn't or wouldn't show up for production meetings. From what I hear, he's been spreading the word that the movie version distorts his book. Well, fuck it — I just have to disagree, that's all. We've taken some liberties with the basic material, sure, but all of us expect the picture will come very close to the spirit, the wallop of the book. Milos thinks it will, and Nicholson thinks so, too, and so, in fact, do I."

Douglas dismisses the subject with a short shrug and points along the corridor, grinning. "See that place where the color of the walls changes? That's Milos for you — a stickler to the teeth. He made us repaint the whole ward —

dirty beige, I guess you'd call it. I asked him, 'Why, Milos?' And he said, 'Vy? Because ve cahn't chute an entire comedy against *green*, dot's vy.'"

By this time, members of the technical crew have started work around the nurses' station, hammering and sawing and wheeling around bulky film equipment on dollies. Wandering among the electricians and gaffers and grips are a dozen or so other men — odd-looking spooks dressed in ratty old hospital robes and felt slippers. These, presumably, are some of the actors who portray Kesey's Chronics and Acutes. Uh-huh . . . and where, uh, are the real patients, the certified dafts?

"Everywhere," Douglas crows with a gleeful sweep of his arms. "Well, no . . . let me qualify that. The patients committed here are quartered on the third floor. Oregon, you understand, like a lot of other states, is releasing a high percentage of its mental patients to so-called local responsibility.

"But, see, the director of this hospital — a terrific guy named Dean Brooks — has very advanced and, I believe, civilized ideas about what constitutes good therapy, and the distance from the third to the first floor is just two flights of stairs. In other words, there's an amazing crossover between the film troupe and the patients. Everybody visits back and forth, plays pool, plays cards, horses around together. A couple or three of the patients are even working for us in various small jobs — and you can actually see the effect on their spirit, their morale. After a while, they start to blend in and — hell, at times there's *no way* to tell the patients from the crew. Look over there — see the little fellow with the broom? He's on the payroll — Ronnie the Patient — interesting guy, as I'm sure you'll discover. Two months ago, Ronnie was classified as a catatonic mute."

Douglas indicates a frail, stoop-shouldered boy-man, perhaps twenty-five, who is abstractedly sweeping sawdust into a pile near the entrance to the nurses' station. He is wearing vague, Permaprest civvies and a vague, Permaprest smile that disappears into a brush mustache and no chin at all. He is clearly crazy at a glance, but just as clearly harmless.

The writer stares toward the nurses' station, scanning the individual faces of tile workers and actors congregated there. Sure, he nods numbly. Crazy.

The lingering insane of Oregon — some of them the criminally insane — are upstairs on the third floor. Well, except for the ones fraternizing down here on the first floor. The writer considers this awhile and searches out a hidey-hole where he can repair unobserved. There, in crying need of repair himself, he hikes up his coattails and jams his Efficiency Reporter's Note Book No. 176 deep into the rear waistband of his trousers, snug between belt and bum. The writer feels immensely better for this, although he has somehow lost track of his Sony TC-126 tape recorder.

The hospital's Tub Room looks like a used-bathtub lot washed up the coast from the psychic environs of L.A.'s Pico and Western. A few minutes before noon, Forman is in there having a heart-to-heart with Scatman Crothers and Louisa Moritz. The two are about to play a seduction scene involving a drunken ward attendant and a flagged-out semipro whore. Roughly three dozen technicians and onlookers are shoe-boxed into the sweltering, seedy-tiled hydrotherapy facility where Oregon's crazies used to assemble faithfully for the purpose of undergoing water torture. The writer is huddled spine down in one of the enamel-peeling tubs, keeping an eye on as much of the elbow-to-ass action as he can follow. "Quiet, please — let's get it *very* quiet in here," one of the assistant directors bawls.

Forman concludes his huddle with Crothers and Ms. Moritz, nods curtly, and strides off a few paces to fire up his pipe. A human path peels open for him wherever he chances to move. The Czech-born director is hairy on the head, arms, and chest and built like a lunch box wrapped in a pair of old San Pedro–style dungarees. He is prone to yelling a lot when he gets excited.

Louisa Moritz, with the face of a zonked china doll, scratches a lank flank through her grungy pedal pushers and puts on what could be interpreted as a pensive look. In a glissando croak, she allows to Scatman that she doesn't much care for one of her lines. "Say anything you want to, honey," he urges, patting her hand comfortingly. "Don't worry about it, you hear what I'm tellin' you? Fuck it." "Oh, I know!" Louisa crows in inspiration. "I'll say — at the end? — I'll say, 'Oh, well, what the hell — any old fart in a storm.' Isn't that better?" Scatman cackles and claps his hands on his slick black pate in delight: "Yeah, yeah, crazy, that's fine, that's awright! Listen, I tell you what, girl — why'n't we just wing it? Hell, let's have us some *fun!* Shoo-be-dop! Jabba-dee-boom! Skee-doop! Zack!" Louisa giggles into her fingers and crosses to her toe mark.

"*Everybody quiet!*" another assistant thunders. Forman raises and lowers a hand in the hanging silence. "Roll, please," Bill Butler murmurs to his camera operators. Two grips with slapsticks spring before the massive Panavision cameras. "A and V 107, take one, A camera." "B camera."

The cameras begin to whir with a faint ta-pocketa-pocketa, and the scene flows like water. Scatman, playing an orderly named Turkle, entices Louisa, a dim-witted mattressback, into a deserted corner of the Tub Room, where he plies her for a taste of strange with Smirnoff, Tokay, and generous doses of speedy sweet talk. She responds by covering her head with a brown paper bag—that's her impression of a fish—and prattling off a long, disjointed story about a dead boyfriend who got that way by gobbling light bulbs. During this synapse-rattling recitative, Turkle is steadily stroking his way up her pedal pushers, but just as he is about to lay hands on her trade goods, a prearranged KAW-BLONG! off-camera propels him to his feet in petrified consternation. *What the fuck—those goddamn Chronics and Acutes—they're stagin' a midnight insurrection out yonder in Ward Four! Holy fuckin' doomsday—Big Nurse will mess her whites!*

Scatman and Louisa play the scene five times, five different ways. They play it fast and slow, sweet and sour, mournful and manic. They play it fey and lyric—every way but poorly or backward. For one take, Scatman improvises the line, "Let's get drunk and *be* somebody." For the next take, he rephrases it. "Let's get drunk and be somebody *else*." Louisa fields all of Scatman's wild tumeling and burns back a few swifties of her own. The two are natural foils, the Lunt and Fontanne of bull goose loonydom.

Forman watches the good times roll with tooth-sucking detachment. His response to all but the final take is unvarying: "Cut, cut, cut, cut. Very good, very perfect. Ve will chute it again, please."

As the crew begins to strike the set, Scatman and Louisa wink, embrace, and take their leave of Bathtub City. Entranced, the writer flexes out of his porcelain squat and trails them to a makeshift dressing room furnished in rump-sprung rattan. Plopped down beside Louisa on a litter-strewn settee, Scatman airily waves the writer toward a chair positioned beneath a Lenny Bruce poster. "Set down, friend," Scatman croons, "you look like you come from about halfway decent stock."

Scatman produces a tenor guitar from somewhere, an age-burnished Martin, and begins whanging hell out of its four strings: "'Who's sorry now / Who's sorry now.' . . . Jahba-dee-wop! Dee-onk, dee-onk! Ain't that tasty, though? Listen, you ever watch *Chico and the Man?* I'm Louie the garbage man on that mutha—I'm the man who empties your can! Can you dig it? 'Cause never forget, you are what you throw out!"

Louisa has a guitar, too, a Japanese job, and she starts singing something that goes "Da-da-da-dee-da-da." The effect is singular — comparable, maybe, to the death rattle of a squeegee. Scatman tries his best to harmonize with her. "Ain't she pretty?" he beams. "I love this lady — I'm *crazy* 'bout her. She's the *real* Divine Miss M!"

Louisa segues into "Behind Closed Doors," but she hits a clinker that makes her stamp her foot and hiss, "Oh, for the luvva shit!" She winks conspiratorially at the writer and asks, "Did you see our little scene just now? . . . Oh, I'm so *glad*. It was supposed to make you laugh. Did you see my Alka-Seltzer commercial last night? It was supposed to make you buy Alka-Seltzer. . . . I do a lot of commercials, uh-huh, but I also do the Carson show, and I'm doing more movie roles lately. Some pulp men's magazine ran a story on me last month, but they didn't get my credits right for the last four years. *Truly.* I just did the second lead in a picture with David Carradine called *Death Race 2000*, and they didn't even mention it. I mean, you would think people would do their jobs or something."

"There's a man does his job — the head nigger of this joint!" Scatman cries, racing to the door and tugging Dean Brooks into the room by a tweed sleeve. An affable, gracefully graying man, the director of the hospital shakes hands all around and murmurs something sympathetic about Louisa's chord-strumming ability. "Oh, well, thank you," she chirrups, "I only started playing, lessee, oh, about three hours ago." "Dr. Brooks here is one *helluva* doctor," Scatman assures the writer, "one *helluva* shrink. And you know what? He plays that same part in the movie — a shrink. Ain't that weird? Wobba-dee-doo-bop! Pa-hoochas-matoochas! Merf!" "I've got one more scene to go," Brooks mock-sighs, "but right now I'm on my way back up to the third floor, where it's safe."

Scatman follows the doctor away, seeking, as he says in a braying aside, "free medical advice — all I can get. Hell, babies, I'm sixty-four." Louisa waves toodle-oo to the two and commits murder one on the intro to "Sounds of Silence." She snuffs the rest of the song, too, chord by chord, line by line. "Isn't that pretty?" she asks at the end. She laughs at the writer's poleaxed expression and pokes a good-natured finger at his midsection: "Don't forget to put it in about *Death Race 2000*."

The commissary is another recycled mad ward where the *Cuckoo* troupe assembles en masse at four P.M. daily to be served up mess (yes) by a local catering outfit. In the early afternoon, the place is virtually deserted. Saul Zaentz, the picture's coproducer, is in there noshing a fast bear claw. . . . The brawny kid with the purple birthmark who tends to the coffee urn is tending to the coffee urn. . . . An actor named Danny DeVito is escorting his kinky-haired lady friend fresh from da Bronx on a tour of the dingy dining area. *Kind of a neat-o place, once you get the drag of it. Tablecloths. Funny pictures and shtick on the walls. Almost like the old Village, sort of.* . . . The lady has the drag of the place at a glance and she is rolling her eyes in speechless revulsion. She is scanning all visible surfaces for—who knows?—cockroaches, spirochetes. . . . *God, and she flew all the way across the country to break bread in this Dachau of the stomach?*

The writer enters the mess hall in search of anything wet and he tunes in a sound. *Rrr, rrr.* Low but distinct, the sound reminds him of—he can't immediately think what. Zaentz strolls across the tatty linoleum and pokes out a family-sized paw in greeting. "Good to see you again," the shmoo-shaped producer says with a benign show of teeth. "We met years ago, if I'm not mistaken—in Berkeley, wasn't it?"

That pleasant fiction again. The writer puzzles over it briefly, but it doesn't yield up much of a mystery. In plain-vanilla usage, it's a mode of status shorthand that is commonplace among film folk. It's Gollywood's way of saying: *I'm OK—you're OK. If you're here among the Somebodies, then you must be a Somebody, too. But I already know all the Somebodies, so we must have met somewhere before. . . . Sure, we met before . . . Berkeley . . . Barcelona . . . some fucking place . . .*

Rrr, rrr—that sound again—sinister.

"Been a lot of yelling around the set recently," Zaentz muses as he munches the heel of his bear claw, "but that's par for the course, a deal like this. I mean, this has been a goddamn long location. We got here the first week in January and we're halfway into what now—March? That's ten weeks—lots of long hours, tough setups. And we've got two, three more weeks to go, so naturally everybody's getting a little edgy . . . you know how it goes. Hell, I'm a little edgy myself. But in my estimation, it's all been worth it. We've put together one classy picture—everybody connected swears it's a killer. Who'd stoop to shitting about a thing like that?"

"Lemme tell you about this picture," Danny DeVito chimes in. The actor stands about four feet nothing, and from the hairline down, he is built like a potbellied stove. He chooses his words with excruciating care. "This—picture — is — the — weirdest — experience — of — my — entire — existence — as — a — human — bean.

"Lemme explain, OK? I'm from New York City, see, so naturally I was figurin' on seein' the famous, gorgeous countryside around here — Oregon, you know, the Pacific Northwest, all that shit. Well, I end up workin' straight through for the first nine weeks I'm here, and then finally I get a couple of days off. Terrific, I think — fan-fuckin'-tastic! — and so I run downtown, I rent a car, I score some deli for a picnic and . . . I couldn't leave. I drove out here from the hotel for lunch. So help me, I came out here and peeked in the ward at my *bed!*"

The writer turns at a tiny tug on his sleeve. It is Ronnie the Patient — surprise, surprise — clutching that errant Sony TC-126. Without explanation, Ronnie shoves the tape machine forward and bolts off into the corridor. The *rrr, rrr* clicks off like a radio in a distant room.

An hour later, a Chautauqua of dementia is rampaging around the nurses' station. Every crazy in showbiz except Dub Taylor and Sam Peckinpah is queuing up on the set for A and V 108, take one. In ensemble, the actors who portray *Cuckoo's* gallery of lames are shatteringly convincing. They hobble around on crutches, carom around in wheelchairs. They wander the ward in flapping hospital gowns, mismatched pajamas, piss-stained Jockey shorts. They belch, fart, scratch their scruffy asses. They call up visions of creatures out of Dante, or the crowd at Spec's in North Beach.

Nicholson doesn't look as bombed and strafed as the rest, nor is he supposed to, but he bounds around the set with demonic energy, all snap and brio. He whomps William Redfield on the shoulder, feints punches at Brad Dourif and Vincent Schiavelli. He tickles fingers with Sidney Lassick and Will Sampson, whispers something obscene to DeVito, laughs aloud at the sight of Michael Berryman and Delos V. Smith Jr. Skidding to a halt, he waggles his fanny at Phil Roth and puts the arm on Scatman for a cigarette.

"C'mon, B. S., a nail — *a nail.*"

"Nothin' but tobacco in that, Jack. Need a light, too, do you?"

"Naw, I got this here little Cricket —"

"I could fan your ass. You need a little suction. Just say the word —"

"Not necessary at all, B. S., but it's a real pleasure to see you here. Welcome to the stairway-to-heaven party."

Scatman squinches his eyes shut, flings his head back, croons. "We'll—build—a—freeway—to—the—stahs . . ."

"Ah, B. S., you're a rock to me—a rock to me. The Louis Armstrong of the tenor guitar."

"Say what?"

"And—I sometimes suspect this—the father of black comedy. Am I correct?"

"Yeah, that's correck, Jack. In both senses. Ah-hah, that was your faithful Scatman in the original woodpile. Jobba-dee-wop! So-cony mo-beel! Zoop!"

Nicholson and Scatman continue poppin' their chops until Forman stalks across the set and positions them firmly in front of the cameras. Both assistant directors bellow the babbling company to order. "Shot—shot!" "This'll be picture, people. Quiet—shut up!"

The scene shows Nicholson, aka the bad-ass McMurphy, dispensing illicit pills and Jim Beam to his fellow Chronics and Acutes in a spontaneous-combustion midnight revel. Midway through the caper, Scatman/Turkle bursts in on the group, sputtering, outraged: *What the shit's goin' on here? Mc-Murphy, you motherfucker, get outta here—alla you motherfuckers! G'wan, I don't wanna hear none of your crazy shit! Get your asses outta here! Pron-toe!*

The dramaturgy goes dit-dit-dit, but a light bank blows and Forman blows with it: "No, no, no, NO!" Two more scuttled takes and everybody is yelling—Nicholson, Scatman, Forman, the Chronics and Acutes, even a grip or two.

During the interminable delays, Scatman entertains the idlers on the sidelines: "Gentlemen, I'll show you a tough one. Ver-ry difficult, so watch closely. My impression . . . of a lighthouse in the middle of an ocean." Slowly, he pivots in a circle, flapping his mouth open and shut at ten-second intervals. When the cackles hit high C, Scatman mock-scowls and snaps his fingers impatiently: "Awright, cut the shit and levity—who's got a cigafoo around here? I'm in need of a nail! I need a nail *bad.*" Grinning, he accepts one of Nicholson's filter tips.

Nicholson starts hopping up and down on one leg. "Give us some kind of move over here, will ya?" he catcalls to Forman.

"HEY, MY-LOS!" Scatman brays. "You remember ol' King Solomon? Man said there's a time to dance and a time to grieve . . . a time to harvest . . . and a time to GET THIS MOTHERFUCKER ON THE ROAD."

"Yeah," Nicholson yowls, "*let's shoot this turkey!*"

"Wait a minute, though," Scatman mutters with a frown, "have I got time to go wet? I got to go wet."

Nicholson continues to hop in place, but he shifts to the other leg. "B. S. . . . Benjamin Sherman 'Scatman' Crothers. By God, you look like the real thing, B. S. What number is this for us?"

"Our third masterpiece together, Jack. The first was *The King of Marvin Gardens*, and then came *The Fortune*—"

"Hmm . . . number three it is. You got a great memory, B. S. You're a great American."

"That's right. FA-ROOK! ZA-GOOF!"

In the commissary, the writer is toying queasily with a serving of vulcanized chicken when Nicholson straddles a chair opposite him. "What's Hefner like?" the actor asks abruptly. The writer blinks a few times and confesses he's never had the pleasure. Nicholson seems disappointed at the reply, but he continues unloading his overfreighted lunch tray.

Two salads. Four buttered rolls. Three side orders of vegetables. Mashed potatoes and gravy. Half a chicken. A glass of iced tea. Two half pints of milk. A double wedge of fruit pie. When Nicholson has all this archipelago of nourishment arrayed in front of him, he sprinkles hot sauce over vast geographic portions of it. Scanning the faces at the surrounding tables, Nicholson spots Scatman. "Hey, B. S.," he calls out, "you want some *speed?*" Scatman fields the lobbed bottle of salsa in a chamois-colored palm.

Nicholson makes some amiable small talk, but food is what figures most precious in his life at the moment and he bends to it with wolfish gusto. "Jesus," he groans, "I haven't been this hungry"—gnawing relentlessly on a drumstick—"since breakfast." The writer laughs, feels at ease for the first time since—breakfast. Nicholson talks and eats and turns out to be exactly what he looks like: a personable black Irishman from Pickup Truck America—a stand-up guy who played schoolboy sports in New Jersey, who got smart, who got out, who got to be a star. No, make that a national treasure. Any dumbass can be a star.

Forman resumes shouting and shooting after the dinner hour, but the writer retreats to the downtown hotel where most of the film troupe is quartered. Holed up with a stash of scotch in handy reach, he studies his notes—fast-draw impressions of the asylum, the movie people, the eerily unsettling *rrr, rrr* phenomenon. He goes through the material three times and stares for a long while out a window at the rain sweeping the swimming pool.

Around midnight, the writer pulls on his boots and wanders down to the hotel bar to join B. S. Crothers and Will Sampson for some pro-am elbow calisthenics. Sampson is a butter-hearted lad, but he looks like the toughest, rottenest seven-foot Indian in the world, and he savors the part on and off the screen. "I'm mean as hell when I drank," he growls, "and I drank a little all the time." "Cheers," Scatman toasts, "and Roebuck."

The bar is a sort of color-coordinated bull pen, one of those places where people order things like Salty Dogs. A trash band plays moldy show tunes to scattered bursts of apathy from a table occupied by four or five of the film folk. The *Cuckoo* hands—a couple of actors, a couple of technicians—are nuzzling close to a round robin of local belles, licking the ladies' ears and such. "Stunt fucking," Scatman explains succinctly. "All them cats are married, see—got families and mortgages back in Beverly Hills, but they been up here for three months now and . . . well, you know. Stunt fucking."

The band cranks for dear life: "Life is a cab-o-ray, old chum, life is a cab-o-ray. . . ."

"You looked around Salem any?" Sampson asks. "Bah God, it's *weird*, I tell you. The city buses all got big signs on 'em that say CHEERIOT, and the suckers shut down runnin' for the night about seven. Yessir, *seven fuckin' o'clock*. And there's a joint down yonder just off Court Street? Got live midgets rasslin' in there, and people just streamin' in to see it. Christamighty, three and a half a head. I call that *flat-out purr-verted*."

Scatman gargles egregiously of the grape and pretty soon sinks face down in the sea of glasses on the tabletop. This doesn't inhibit some tub-butted dentist and his harpy wife from force-feeding their way into the booth beside him, gabbling like loons.

The harpy says she's a member of some civic committee that brings in chamber quartets and Henry Fonda as Clarence Darrow (a last-minute cancellation, that one, and God bless Pacemakers), and she enjoys celebrities just ever so much—they "tone up little old Salem." In light of his present assignment, she regards the writer, even, as a sort of crypto-Somebody, so she snaps her beringed fingers at the hot dog who's dispensing the busthead—she's *buying this round, by jingo, for the glory of Greater Salem!*

The writer shrinks away, trying to shun the frumious bandersnatch, but she can't or won't dry up. "Why do you use That Word?" she snaps at him sharply.

"I would think it would be far beneath someone of your education." The writer explains in some clinical detail. Calling on all his vast educational resources. The harpy grows pale and rises to depart in fairly steep dudgeon. The dentist trails along behind her like a strand of floating dental floss.

Scatman snores on, the band chugs on. Sampson removes a burning cigarette from Scat's fingers. He grins fondly. "I've drank many a merciful cup of Christian whiskey with this little gentleman," the big Indian reflects softly.

At the hospital early the next morning, the troupe from the bus troops to the nurses' station, but nobody exactly stampedes to work. The young honey of a blonde who serves as stand-in for the actresses takes up a sitting-Shiva position by a window, staring gloomily out at the gusting rain. "I feel crummy," she wails. "I woke up in the wrong crummy room."

Several of the technicians whip together a card game, others nurse on coffee mugs or take turns bashing a soggy punching bag. "Umm, umm," Scatman clucks, "if Brother Zaentz was up to see all this big-bucks talent fuckin' off out here, he'd weep like a limbless orphan."

Bill Butler, the cinematographer, arrives on the set seconds in advance of Forman, and the crew heaves to lustily. Butler is silent, bearded, monkish in appearance. He talks to nobody except his camera operators, and then in tones so low that no one can overhear. The workmen give him a wide berth.

Scatman is wearing dark glasses and Michael Douglas cackles fiendishly at the sight. "Fell in the vinegar again, huh? How long you plan to wear the blinders, Scat?" "Till my eyes congeal, man."

The actors on call for the morning's routine pickup shots labor in ten-minute bursts, then dawdle for a couple of hours. They doze in chairs, bull-shit one another outrageously, pass around the Hollywood trade papers. They gab endlessly about the stars ("Raquel got famous by inventing this zipper that wouldn't close, see") and in chorus they rattle off more household names than the Yellow Pages, but their gossip isn't meant to be smart or, in most cases, even unkind—it's just all they know, all they care about. It's like reading the trades. The damn things appear there in front of them—they didn't plan it that way.

"Bright little turn there, turkey. Take a load off."

"Make that *Mister* Turkey, if you please."

"And I told that broad and her mother both, I says, 'Don't let the door hit you where the dog bit you.' It got real quiet after that. You could've heard pissants walkin' on ice cream—"

"Shit, yeah, I done time in the Service, sonny. I worked for Standard Oil for ten years. Scobba-dee-zoot!"

"Ah, the Scatman cometh—never quiteth, in fact. I thought he was a dream of my youth, you know—like J. D. Stringer—"

"Would you believe I saw Roy Rogers on the box last night?"

"Sure, the singing cowboy's always with us. Look at Dennis Weaver."

"I wonder if Nixon ever ran off a print of *Save the Tiger*."

Somebody arrives with the news that Aristotle Onassis is dead.

"Christ, too bad, too bad . . . but that leaves Jackie in line for half a billion."

"BOO!"

"So what's to crab about, chum? That's just takin' poon and makin' it pay."

Ronnie the Patient sidles up to the writer in the corridor, offering to show some snapshots of his fiancee. The girl in the photos is sweet-faced, chubby, having fun on a picnic. Ronnie says she is a fellow patient over in the Women's Facility and he loved her the first instant he saw her.

Rain peppers the windows in the commissary. The writer is bent over his Efficiency Reporter's Note Book No. 176, recording some notes at one of the long tables. He block prints:

> First met Kesey in '62, Menlo Park. Savored his book but put off by The Author. Figured him for a benign Manson, although didn't know the term back then. Neal Cassady also present that afternoon, chasing Stanford girls through the underbrush. Didn't catch any.
>
> Reminded of this by brief encounter with Louise Fletcher, who plays Big Nurse. Inspired casting. Not a big-ba-zoomed hag but a young, petite hag, chillier than a blue norther. Had no impulse to linger with her beyond bare amenities.
>
> Crazy factor here is strong enough to siphon gas. Take Delos V. Smith, Jr. (Puh-leeze!) Smith was friends with Monroe at Actors Studio, intimates he has loads of skinny on her—tapes, letters, etc. Politely evasive about it, though. Maybe if I—

The dining hall is empty except for the writer and the coffee attendant—

and here comes that *rrr, rrr* again, higher pitched than before, quantum scarier, too—a sound full of blood rage and murder foul. It clicks this time: It's Lawrence Talbot turning into the Wolfman . . . *rrr, rrr* . . . and here comes that brawny kid with the purple birthmark banzai-charging across the tatty linoleum with a wet mop raised high above his head like an ax, and *whop!*—he flails it down slosh on the writer's instep.

The writer glances up only long enough to see too much white in the kid's eyes, then resumes block printing. He block prints the word help seventy-three times. Man flop a wet mop on your boot down where the writer grew up, you generally jump on his bones. But this is different. This is the Oregon State Playpen for Bent Yo-Yos & Mauled Merchandise.

Five minutes later, the *rrr, rrr* has leveled off to a sullen drone and the kid has mopped his way to the far side of the room. The writer rises, measures his steps to the door. Out in the corridor, he takes a deep breath. Another.

Out of a mixed sense of protocol and craven dread of underachieving, the writer braves the commissary again an hour later. Nicholson is in the chow line, bellying up to the steam tables like a famished wolverine. The actor smacks his chops over the shit-and-shucks cuisine, orders a little of this, a whole lot of that, and pauses undecided before a vile-looking vat of boiled okra. The writer glides up behind him, coughs discreetly, and says for openers:

Hiya, Jack. . . . Gee, listen, we're going to have to meet stopping like this.

Inexplicably, it comes out that way. Nicholson half-turns and cocks his head to one side, his expression hang gliding somewhere between disbelief and morbid curiosity. He picks up two dishes of the boiled okra and moves along. The writer trails Nicholson into the dining area and asks the actor if he might be available to sit and talk seriously sometime.

"Can't say, pal," Nicholson says around a quarter-pound chaw of Swiss steak. "Why don't you ask my agent about it?" He mentions a name and number in Beverly Hills.

The writer goes back to the hotel in the rain and experiences a mild epiphany in the bathtub. Up to his glottis in Mr. Bubble, he realizes he can't think of anything more he wants to know about Nicholson—nothing at all. It occurs to him that madness upstages all creatures great and small, and maybe in its wicked varieties of mystery, it, too, is a national treasure—purr-verted, of course. *Rrr, rrr. . . .*

The writer dresses, shit-cans the Beverly Hills agent's phone number, makes reservations for a flight home, and journeys down to the bar, where he immediately encounters the harpy. She is sans dentist tonight and all gussied up to party in a $300 pants suit the color of kitty litter. "*My dear*," she exclaims, "how *marvelous* to see you again. How's your little story coming along? I've never read anything of yours, but I'll bet you're right up there with Miss Rona. Oh, I've always been a sucker for talent. A sucker, know what I mean?"

Her name is . . . should be . . . Bambi. Late in the evening, she is sitting in the hotel saloon with an actor escort, the writer, and a roustabout from the film company. Bambi is a sleek sloop of a girl with an ozone-charged voice and an original face. The writer takes her for an actress or maybe a model.

Bambi's actor companion is drunk, has been for hours. Pretty soon, he can't see past his glasses. He wobbles away into the cab-o-ray darkness without explanation—none needed. Bambi shrugs and slides around next to the roustabout. "I'm Shelley Winters' daughter," she announces theatrically. "Well, not really. I mean, I don't believe that, but my mother does. What can I say?"

When the Mixmaster band unplugs for a break, Bambi is on her feet. "Come on," she urges, "I know a boîte just down the block." A *boîte*? "You, too," she says to the writer.

A boîte. You bet. A poured-concrete bunker with dime-store Modiglianis on the walls and a singer who knows all of Neil Young's gelatinous repertoire. "Far out," the roustabout whoops, hanging on every quavery verse during a millennium-long set. Facing away from the others, the writer noodles in his Efficiency Reporter's Note Book No. 176—fantasizes that he is on the verge of grasping something momentous about the lunatic tropisms of Hollywood, of America . . .

The Neil Young manqué takes his bows to the sound of two or three hands clapping and the house lights flash up. A waiter bends near and asks the roustabout and the writer to please remove their goddamned lady friend from the goddamned premises. Bambi, as it happens, is juiced to the tits—knee-walking blotto. She has been downing double gins on the sly for the past hour, the waiter says, and the tab comes to $23.80.

The roustabout and the writer steer Bambi out onto the rain-slick sidewalk and clumsily maneuver her toward a steakhouse where the roustabout says she works. "Yeah, she's a waitress, man," the roustabout grunts, sucking for breath. "I thought you knew her in front. Shit, what a deal."

Two blocks of towing a rudderless sloop through choppy weather and Bambi's boss spots the approaching convoy. He tears out of the steakhouse, his face changing colors, his arms flailing. "I'll take the cunt home," he snaps, "but don't bring her in the gah-dam ca-fay." The man drives away with Bambi unconscious beside him in a mud-spattered Datsun.

"Sonofabitch, I could've scored, too," the roustabout complains. He does a couple of quick knee bends, to ease the kinks, then shrugs philosophically. "Well, that's stunt fucking for you. Always chancy."

The Teamster who drives the writer to the airport the next morning chews tobacco and lives in mortal fear of the patients at the state hospital. "Lots of folks are fucked, you know, but especially our nuts. I mean, makin' a movie with all them basket cases hangin' around—what kind of nigger riggin' is that? Listen, my friend, I've personally known a bunch of them creepos out there since I was in first grade, and you can take my word for it, they ain't fit to be runnin' loose. You notice that beefy kid in the commissary, the one got the birthmark? Wonderful guy, swell guy—the mayor oughta give him a kiss and a medal. Fucker killed four people with his bare hands."

About two hundred miles into the Rockies, the writer's fantods stop vibrating and over a healing beaker of brandy he monitors a cassette tape of B. S. Crothers spritzing, clowning, blowing the shit.

> You ever smoke these things? Lord, we used to smoke this stuff back in '29— smoked it on the street and nobody ever bothered us. Ace leaf was common as dirt down yonder in Texas. We used to go into them fuckin' Mexican joints where they sold hot dogs and shit? They'd say, "You want some mmm-mmm?" I'd say, "Yeah, lemme have a quarter's worth." Guy'd give me a penny matchbox full, already manicured, and a few papers, and it would roll out to about ten things. For a quarter. Godamighty, man, it was good . . .

Ah, that Scatman—shee-zack! Another of your basic national treasures.

Excerpt from *The Code of the West*

Unfinished novel, about 1985

L yle Bailey had lived in the Hotel Sam Clemens since the year before sound, the same three-and-a-half rooms filled mostly with the same horsehair and leather bunkhouse-style furniture. In the summer of 1927, polishing his sidekick act, he had come into some unexpected chink performing bumpkin spills in the Art Acord series at Action Pathé, and he used the windfall to set up pots of his own away from the boarding-house district.

Smoke moved into George Raft's "harem suite" at the Hotel Sam Clemens the same weekend Raft decamped to David Selznick's "ultramoderne" Chateau des Fleurs co-op over on Franklin Place. The scent of Raft's sweet cologne lingered in the apartment for months, and Smoke's friends in the Western picture business hoorawed him about it mercilessly. He took the gibes in stride, feathering his fourth-floor nest overlooking Cahuenga Boulevard to suit his taste, taking long soapings in the zinc-walled shower he didn't have to share with anyone and lolling about in the sun that flooded the big, airy rooms nine months at a stretch. The place fit him like a shirt and it was reasonable to boot; the rent ran to sixty dollars a month, less than that on a lease.

The Western crowd came around to visit and then came around to stay. After Smoke pioneered the territory, Charley King took a bedroom on the ground floor to be "the closest drunk to the Stage Stop." Johnny Tyke moved in and doubled up with Jerome "Blackjack" Ward until the two had a rank falling-out over Johnny's dog, Widder; the bitch chow chewed up Blackjack's best pair of boots.

Cloud Smith, Vinegar Roan, Hank "Handlebar" Bell, Kansas Mooring, and Morgan Flowers all set up separate camps in singles attached to kitchenettes. In time, dozens of flash riders, bit players, and movie-struck drifters came and went, along with a few genuine stars going up or down or sideways. Andy Clyde registered under a false name while the scandal tainting him and destroying his cousin "Fatty" Arbuckle wound through the courts. Wally Wales lived in a tight cranny on the second floor in between comebacks, and even Art Acord was a tenant for a while before he packed off to Mexico gold-hunting and got himself knifed to death in a Chihuahua *pulquería*. The papers said Art Acord took poison after his career turned sour, but it was a lie. Art threw a big party at the Stage Stop the night before he took the train south. He was in good spirits, able to laugh about his ups and downs as a matinee hero. "In Hollywood," he said, "you can strike it rich or wear out your pick. I guess I've done a little of both."

The movie cowboys staked out a home for themselves at the Sam Clemens, or at least a way station, but not everybody welcomed them. Robert Benchley, the Eastern wit, was a next-door neighbor of Smoke's for a brief period in the early days when the waddies were edging out the dudes. Benchley's genius as a writer had played out, and he had forsaken New York book society to gargle martinis at Pickfair and bluff out a hand for himself in the studio game. Benchley slipper-footed into the lobby to collect his mail one morning, hungover as usual. The size and extent of the cowboy invasion must have hit him all at once. "Who *are* these hillbillies?" he squeaked to the desk clerk. Maybe somebody at one of the domino tables cocked a pistol in his direction, maybe not, but without stopping to gather up his traps, Benchley juned out for the Garden of Allah, where he drank himself to death in the comfort of tonier company.

Harry Joe Hatton took over Benchley's vacant rooms. A few times in his younger days, Harry Joe had tried matrimony, never with any success, but he always kept a string on the apartment at the hotel and moved back when domesticity had passed him by again.

It was a good place to live back then, back when Hollywood was just a shirt-tail country town on the interurban line. The surrounding neighborhood was full of family bungalows, and almost every family counted a member or two involved in making pictures or supplying the needs of those who did. The skyline was still given over mainly to the sky, and the Hotel Sam Clemens reared up as a landmark midway between Sunset and Hollywood Boulevard, a rose-colored stucco manor taller than the young plume palms lining Cahuenga. The hotel grounds were maintained like a garden, and the cowboys soon found better use for the dichondra fairways than batting around croquet balls; they ran footraces and pitched horseshoes across the fern-shaded lawns.

Most of the casting offices and studio lots were clustered in walking distance from the center of town, a stroll the length of a good cigar. The Big Red Cars ran on all the principal thoroughfares, and great, spreading pepper trees formed arbors over the sidewalks. The Sam Clemens wranglers stabled their riding stock at O. K. Coombs's Sunset Livery and spread their bunkrolls there when day checks got scarce. They traded for dry goods and new rigging at Tony the Greaser's boot shop, half a block up Cahuenga from the Stage Stop bar. If a man was flush, he could cut into the choicest T-bone west of Denver at Al Levy's Restaurant near Hollywood and Vine. In famine times, a can of Vienna sausages and a handful of crackers served the same need, and the croupy Hoosier lungers who owned most of the corner groceries often threw in a heel of cheese for goodwill.

To satisfy coarser hungers, Hollywood Boulevard was chockablock with sporting houses and fleshpots, jostling for trade with the movie palaces, one-arm arcades, and mystic parlors that stretched from LaBrea Avenue on the west to the Sunset junction on the east, where D. W. Griffith's ten-story sets for *Intolerance* stood until shanty-builders tore them down in the middle of the Depression. The cowboys frequented doxies almost to a man, and even Mr. Griffith squired around "soiled doves" to speakeasies and premieres. Smoke was never much of a hand for whores himself, preferring courtship in the privacy of his own rooms, playing Jimmie Rodgers' blue yodels on the Victrola for the occasional contract girls he favored. Smoke didn't fall in love until relatively late in life and he married even later. The fact that the woman he loved and the woman he married were not the same woman still flayed his soul and fed the spectral flames of his nightmares . . .

It was a loosely alcoholic life, and the Stage Stop bar was the cowboys' true hearth and private preserve, a barrel with the bung open for members only. The regulars woke up over spiked coffee at the Stage Stop and gathered there again at night to bend their elbows and stretch the truth. Fighting was discouraged indoors, but Johnny Tyke and Blackjack Ward deepened their grudge to hatred in another set-to over Johnny's dog. Widder peed on Blackjack's pants leg this time out, and Blackjack crowned the animal with a barstool. Johnny and Blackjack rushed together in a fury, punching and wrestling out onto the sidewalk and into the street. When the scrap was over, Johnny and his chow gimped off in search of a vet. Blackjack came back inside to stand a round, one ear hanging by a string, calling for "monkey blood and a roll of gaffer's tape" to mend it. The brawl cost both men a week's wages because they were too barked up to face the camera.

The cowboys put in hard, dirty days, ten hours or more of falling off horses and various moving vehicles. After breakfast, they gathered in a body at Sunset and Cahuenga—"Go-Hungry Corner," they called it. Until the mid-1930s, studio "standby" trucks picked up the day's quota of riders and hauled them to and from the Hollywood back lots and various San Fernando Valley locations. Later, when Central Casting came in, the cowboy pool moved to Sunset and Gower so the men could conduct their job-hunting on the pay phones in the Columbia Drugstore. By then, Wally Wales had given up on the notion of a comeback and rejoined the pack of bit players as Hal Taliaferro, which was his real name. Andy Clyde inched back into pictures, but from then on he competed for parts with Smoke instead of Charlie Chaplin.

Johnny Tyke and Blackjack Ward pawed the ground wherever they met, and their feud came to an end at the new corner. Following the usual cuss fight, Blackjack drew a six-shooter from his warbag and shot Johnny five times at point-blank range. Blackjack saved his last shell for Widder, but missed as far as anyone could tell. The dog ran off howling and vanished forever.

The papers played up the killing as a "Wild West" diversion the summer before Pearl Harbor. Writing about Blackjack's trial and eventual acquittal, some smart-aleck reporter tagged the scene of the crime "Gower Gulch," and the nickname stuck. The Gower Gulch Shopping Center stood over there now, across from the Columbia Drugstore where the cowboys once stood waiting for a call. . . .

Guinn "Big Boy" Williams took drunk celebrating the Allied invasion of Normandy and toppled off Smoke's balcony onto the one below belonging to Foy Riddle, busting up an ankle and both balcony railings and old Foy's planned seduction of a twenty-year-old wardrobe girl from Paramount. Big Boy Williams, an ox, mended without a scratch after the fall, but the Hotel Sam Clemens never fully recovered. The management used the occasion to seal off all the building's balconies as unsafe, putting an end to the cost of maintaining them. Since most of the cowboy tenants slept part of the year in cots on the outdoor porches, the clamor of protest was almost as loud as the squall of backhoes uprooting the plume palms and curbing along Cahuenga. During World War II, the city had begun to widen the boulevard in an ongoing series of expansions that eventually swallowed up the hotel's frontage grounds. The management lost no time in selling off the remaining side gardens while simultaneously doubling and then tripling the rents. By the war's end, the leftover palms flagged above Cahuenga's four new lanes of traffic in sickly isolation and the last pepper trees had vanished from the avenues, cut down because tourists kept tripping on the fallen berries.

Everybody had jobs and a little change to jingle, but in the midst of prosperity, the neighborhood slipped a notch at a time. O. K. Coombs's stable service foundered, brought low by new zoning rules and a steady decline in trade. The customers who could afford to ride for pleasure had all migrated to Beverly Hills or the Valley in the land boom after the war, and only a handful of the Sam Clemens crowd bothered to keep personal mounts by then. Another nail sealing the barn door shut was the fact that the studios were cutting back on the production of "B" programmers. O. K. Coombs, who had outfitted Westerns since the days of Bronco Billy, was forced to sell out for a song. At the auction, the old liveryman threw his own saddle on the sale pile and offered to whip anybody who entered a bid on it. He retired to his daughter's apartment across from the fairgrounds in Dallas and died within a year.

The shrinking "B" market was a touchy subject among the cowboys. "I don't care how many of the suckers they make," Roy Barcroft announced at the Stage Stop, "as long as I'm in every single goddamn one of the ones they do make."

Up past Go-Hungry Corner, Tony the Greaser's boot shop and half a dozen other storefronts fell under the wrecker's ball, to be replaced by a Greyhound bus station. Smoke witnessed the demolition and often reflected about the eerie chill of the event in the time afterward.

Between pictures at Producers Releasing Corporation, where he was under six months' contract, Smoke strolled over to the shop from the hotel. He shook hands self-consciously with Tony, who was, after all, a greaser, and took up a position on the sidewalk to watch the donkey cranes move into place for the destruction. A small throng gathered, and D. W. Griffith drove up alongside the crowd in a dusty prewar LaSalle roadster. Smoke had played an unbilled walk-on in Griffith's *Abraham Lincoln* and worked three days on *One Million B.C.* in 1940, so he raised his hat in respect to the director, one of his heroes. Griffith nodded in recognition and beckoned him over beside the car, saying little at first.

Griffith's face was half-hidden under his usual crush fedora, but his eyes looked rheumy, starred with fever, and his dark suit hung on him in folds. The director searched through his pockets for a cigar tin and selected a black Havana without moving to offer the box to Smoke. Rolling the cigar between his palms, Griffith sat in edgy silence, watching the slide of plaster and crossbeams as the storefronts tumbled down. When he spoke, Smoke had to strain to hear him.

"—broad daylight"—something, something else—"works like worms on the chosen—"

"Sir?"

"The catch is, she soils and despoils—" Griffith conducted an arm, indicating more than the doomed block, maybe the town or the world or possibly the passing of time. "The price is, she rubs the fresh off everything . . ."

"Yessir—"

Griffith lit the Havana, squinting past the hood of the car at the accumulating pyramids of rubble. "The striking of sets should always be carried out under the cover of darkness, son. Never let in daylight upon magic. Mystery is her only hope of renewal." Another baton sweep of the arm. "But try telling that to the absquatulating sons of Hollywood bitches and their mongoloid nephews."

Griffith shifted gears, ready to drive on, but his gaze strayed back to the leveled buildings. "I hear our Brother Coombs has departed for other pastures. A sleeping davenport in Big D, and no doubt a grave o'er the gurgling Trinity before long. Where do you plan to go, Lyle?"

"Why, I don't know, sir. Figure on staying around here, I guess—"

"You can't troupe any further west, or you'll get your britches wet." The director sucked a tooth and spat out the window. "More's the pity."

"I hope you'll save a place for me in your next special, Mr. Griffith," Smoke heard himself say, leaning down close.

"Hah!" Griffith snorted. He flung back his head and gave a mocking laugh at both of them, but he tossed his cigar tin to Smoke before he drove away.

It was one of Griffith's final excursions on the boulevard. The old man withdrew to his bachelor rooms at the Garden Court, projecting his silent spectacles on a bedsheet for wetback chambermaids and dying three months sooner than O. K. Coombs. Hollywood's mighty pinned on weeds to honor the master, the same men who had closed ranks to break him in his prime. Sidekick had marveled, as always, at the sight of the studio nabobs, massed to follow Griffith's coffin. If sifted by natural selection, one or two of them might have risen to a corporalcy in the post office. Louis B. Mayer and Cecil DeMille led the processional, followed by Sam Goldwyn, Carl Laemmle, and Jesse Lasky, with Harry Cohn trailing a step or two behind David Selznick and his senile father. They marched in solemn file like alien emissaries, sanctified in power and breathing the rare air of sugar mountains Smoke and his kind never expected to climb.

Lesser knobs in the industry jostled for footing in the rear of the mourning line, "the mice trying to become rats," as Harry Joe Hatton called them. Smoke dealt with some of the producers bringing up the drag at the memorial on a day-to-day, penny-to-penny basis. Herbert J. Yates, head of Republic, was a thick country sod who never forsook his cud of Brown Mule tobacco, even in the Masonic Temple. Junior Gold of Grand Slam Pictures slyly peeked at the faces in the pews, hunting for somebody fresh to exploit, man, woman, or child. The King brothers were slot-machine racketeers from Chicago, meaty and pinstriped. The Jews who ran PRC had faces like lamb chops, but they were lions of ledger-book thievery when they weren't blackmailing and scheming to murder one another.

Smoke and Harry Joe slipped out of the services early, unable to stomach a peroration by the stooge son of a studio owner who had stolen Griffith's credit on *One Million B.C.*, dreary hokum that it was. Smoke put away D. W. Griffith's Havana box in a cedar drawer among things too private and dear to examine very often. . . .

The Stage Stop bar went out of business for reasons nobody ever bothered to explain. Lucky Hoops, the bartender, disappeared without a trace like the Mexican bootmaker, and a coin laundry moved in at the site. Feeling gulled, the cowboys fanned out to drink among dudes in unfriendly "TV lounges," or worse still, drink alone in their rooms. The younger men strayed into savage scrapes with sailors and zoot-suiters along Hollywood Boulevard, while the old-timers slipped into bourbon fogs for distraction against the news that small-town theaters had started to go dark all across the country. The ground was shifting and nobody knew which way to jump, least of all the "B" riders. One by one, the Sam Clemens hands dropped away, cut down by death, sickness, money problems, or a combination of plagues.

Smoke started putting up their pictures in his apartment. Always offended by the hotel's razing of the balconies, he papered over the ghost of the balcony door in his living room with some old publicity stills of William S. Hart and Colonel Tim McCoy. Pleased with the effect, he rummaged up enough lobby cards to obliterate the plaster outline of the door completely with tinted likenesses of Harry Carey, Fred Thomson, and Reb Russell. He framed a good many of the first batch, but when the cost started mounting up, he made do with thumbtacks and tape.

The free mix of faces and scenes caught Smoke's fancy, and he prospected around for more pictures. Harry Joe's collection of press books panned out as a major strike. Smoke located wayward shots of riding actors he knew or admired in out-of-date magazines, and some of his cowboy neighbors kicked in Central Casting portraits of themselves obscenely inscribed. When PRC folded, leaving everybody but the lamb-chop Jews grabbing for hind teat, Smoke spirited away cartons of eight-by-ten glossies. Under cover of stealth or sheer bluff, he ransacked the publicity files at other studios when he found a chance.

Display stills for series Westerns were doled out by the Poverty Row producers in meager numbers and used continually until they fell apart or wound up in the hands of collectors — "film buffs," they were called. Smoke engaged in a few tentative trades with the flock of collectors who pecked around the Larry Edmunds bookshop up on Hollywood Boulevard, but he soon learned to avoid the contact. The film buffs bought and bartered nostalgia items, anything from "dirty dupes" of five-reelers to Sonja Henie's cast-off ice skates. If a "B"-picture actor specialized in falling on his butt in horseshit, as Smoke did, the buffs hovered around to pick up the chips; they treasured the horseshit, as long as some other fellow had to roll in it.

Smoke's picture gallery jumped from wall to wall. With time on his hands as casting along Poverty Row slacked off, he passed hours at a stretch, even whole afternoons, teetering atop a step stool, sorting through sheaves of cowboy poses. He made his selections by impulse in the beginning, but soon gave over to puzzling out the riddles of best choice and alignment. He considered Mr. Griffith's words and let his mind range for the meaning. A generation in Hollywood, he realized, lasted about five years; the swinging door to the studios opened warm and wide to a few, but it slapped plenty more fannies on the fast way out.

Smoke invested in a better ladder and added a plumb bob to his store of tacks and tape. Often he would test a picture in a dozen different locations before he was satisfied with the fit. He moved around a close-up of Charley King for three years. The shot showed King as a "dog heavy" brandishing a lynch rope, but the true revelation of the photograph rested in the warped angles and gullies of King's whiskey-ravaged face. In a leap of thought that was new to him, Smoke perceived the fine paradox that Charley King was the gentlest of sots while several million American children had grown up mistaking the agony of a drunkard for villainy of the heart.

Well, listen to the shithouse philosopher, Smoke twitted himself, but he was secretly proud of his ability to reason about matters so shadowy. His mind sometimes ran away with him while he pored over the stills and posters. Like a cub explorer looking for footholds, he discovered a capacity for mental absorption that was strange and a little unnerving until he got the hang of it. Then his thoughts carried him along a zigzag path from free-floating concentration — another paradox — to satisfaction in focus and the pure wonder of invention. An urge to shape and arrange the pictures into an overall picture became a daily drive. His notion of order wasn't as clear and simple as birds on a wire. It wasn't one perfect line. . . . The proper mix, he decided, was something invisible finding a form.

He stole to piece out the single connected picture he envisioned, not often and nothing grand. He pinched a roll-up military map of the U.S. frontier from the set of a Randolph Scott cavalry opus at Columbia and hung it up in the alcove between his bedroom and the kitchen. He might as well have installed a magic lantern, he marveled, adjusting the drape. The change astonished him; the dim space took on a glow and a dimension of airy depth he imagined for an instant he could reach his hand into.

Rolled to full length, the map stretched from ceiling to just above his knee. Smoke mounted the ladder with a stack of posse shots and the faint stirring of an idea. Hours later, Harry Joe Hatton came down the hall for their usual evening bellyache and found him patching up a file of grainy horsemen across the Staked Plains. Harry Joe was barefoot and craving a drink after a day's location work out at Stoney Point; he left a trail of dusty footprints from the liquor rack across to the map. The hotel's hot water was the latest casualty to management thrift.

Harry Joe lifted a corner of the linen scroll and blinked at the Columbia property brand stamped on the back: *DO NOT REMOVE FROM GOWER LOT.* He gave out a low whistle: "Old man Cohn would wet his knickers if he ever saw this."

"Old man Cohn don't drop around much to drink up my booze like some others I could name. I spotted an Old Glory in the prop dock over there I'm going after, too. Dressy parade outfit with gold tassels all around the edge."

"Who's that white hat there?"

"Crash Corrigan. The guy on the end, swaddled up in the duster, that's Mitchum."

"The young Bob Mitchum," Harry Joe sniffed. "I had him for fifteen minutes in 1943, and bingo, he got hotter than a pistol. Too big for us now. How was I to know he could act?"

"Well, he's still making Westerns. Like Jake Del Rio and the Duke. I got a kick out of him in *Blood on the Moon*—"

Harry Joe downed his drink. "I'm hunting around for somebody brand-new who can handle a gimmick. Robert Tansey's minting a fortune with that bullwhip character of his, Lash LaRue. If I can't top a medicine-show gag like that, I might as well—" Harry Joe broke off and surveyed the map again. "Fits in right cozy with the other stuff, I'll say that. What's your main idea?"

"Just fiddling around."

"Looks like what they call a mon-tage, I guess. The Russians do it a lot."

"Hell you say."

Smoke couldn't sum up exactly what he was doing, didn't want to put a name to it. When visitors commented about the patchwork heroics spreading across his walls, he listened agreeably and steered the conversation on a neutral tack. He made up the rules as he went along, but he worked to cultivate an open mind. No cowboy singers allowed, he vowed in the beginning, scratching the breed; the same went for the swivel-wrist punies imported from Broadway to impersonate he-men against canvas badlands. He laughed to himself the day he taped up shots of Tex Ritter and Montgomery Clift side by side. The two belonged to the mix, and hairsplitting wouldn't alter the fact. So did Blackjack Ward, whose mean-eyed sepia mug he positioned opposite the gold-tasseled Stars and Stripes that he liberated from the Columbia prop deck under a mackinaw. Anybody who had made an honorable Western belonged to the mix, he resolved. It was the only rule that lasted or mattered.

A sense of fairness carried only so far, and Smoke winnowed out the faces he considered worthy to hang in a kind of honor circle. The ring of pictures saluted the famous and obscure, bygone giants and one-shot tyros bent on putting a fork to the Hollywood oyster. The legendary faces were almost inevitably Southern or bedrock rural; out in the dry sticks, the sons of the pioneers were weaned on visions of themselves as coming attractions. From old Hoot Gibson down to Audie Murphy, all the great Western showmen were razor-back country boys with nothing to live on except a dream of fortune, cut out for servitude but slipping the collar, practicing fast draws and working up their style to head west and try stardom. They were born grail chasers, Smoke reflected, not too different in life from the scrappy saddle aces they portrayed on the screen. The Kid had that look from the very beginning . . .

Dewey Street was literally a kid slapping leather when Harry Joe Hatton spotted him handling a long-barreled revolver in a courtyard on Western Avenue. "He favored the young Bill Holden in a glancing sort of way so I stopped to watch his workout," Harry Joe recalled in his memoir. "I saw at a flash his weapon was no plaything, but an old seven-shot top-breaking .44 Colt with a heavy fluted frame and whittled sights. I believe the cylinder of the pistol may have been a trifle loose, but it was a real gun, and the young man looked real to me, too. We struck up a conversation and when I determined that he was free of vice and 'game,' I used my standing at Grand Slam Pictures to enlist him for a screen test. This was around Independence Day, 1950. The rest, of course, is History."

Harry Joe holed up alone to fashion a role for his discovery, a Western true-heart with a fresh heroic twist. He blunted several gross of pencils in a week's close-mouthed effort, pacing and muttering to himself at all ungodly hours. Smoke, overhearing the agony of invention through the wall, felt a trifle put out by his friend's secretiveness. When Harry Joe tapped at his door one midnight to inquire about the spelling of "aborigine," Smoke replied tartly that he didn't know and didn't want to know.

The night before the test, Harry Joe brought Dewey around to the Sam Clemens to stand inspection. Smoke was listening to the war news on the radio — the next one had broken out in Korea — and he took his sweet time answering the knock. By then, he was seriously peeved. From broad hints, he had guessed the gist of Harry Joe's scheme and he considered the idea of a cowboy with a boomerang dumb as a wooden watch. Worse still was rating no say in the deal, having his good opinion taken for granted. Hell, that wasn't fitting; partners were supposed to be closer than white on rice. He screwed on a scowl getting to the door, meaning to even up the slight.

Harry Joe bustled in, primped up in his best suit and declaiming the introductions like a shyster salesman: "Lyle, this here's Dewey Street. Born to the movies, or I'm missing my bet. If the camera favors this lad like I think she will, we're about to be stepping in high cotton—" Harry Joe had brought a bottle for a rare change and he made for the kitchen to stir up drinks, chattering away in a hail-fellow filibuster that set Smoke's teeth on edge.

Dewey Street took a short step inside and offered his hand in a stiff shake. He was a strapping young fellow, handsome enough to stand out from the stew, and Smoke could see where he might promote the sale of a few show tickets, given some proper clothes and barbering. Young and hairy, paper-shack poor . . . probably unwhippable. No mistaking the shinnery stamp; the bones of his face marked him as a Dixie bitter-ender. Die-dog or eat the hatchet—old Matthew Brady had clicked the shutter on quite a few of the type . . .

"Toddy time, gentlemen," Harry Joe called out, "toddy for the body." Dewey stood rooted a bare step from the door, wringing the brim of his hat until he caught himself at it. He sensed the tension in the air, if Harry Joe didn't.

At the sink, Harry Joe hiked up his trousers with his wrists and popped his hands together, jabbering away merrily. Already half-lit, he cracked a couple of gossipy jokes about producers and kept winking to show he was above it all. Swabbing out tumblers at the faucet, the damn fool spattered his suit coat to the elbows and hooted it off as another joke.

Smoke was about to let fly with a spiteful remark but the urge stuck in his throat when the thought dawned on him that Harry Joe was showing off for a purpose, maybe even trying to buck up his own confidence. Whoa now—who was playing the fool here? Smoke turned toward Dewey. "Come on in the house," he offered. "Let me hang up that hat for you."

Dewey bobbed his head in gratitude and edged away shyly, drawn to the pictures and bric-a-brac on the walls from the first. He followed the line of display around the room with a little hitch in his gait, absorbed, nodding to himself. When he came to the honor circle, he paused and stood smiling at the roundup of faces until Harry Joe stuck a glass in his hand and draped an arm across his shoulder.

"Ready to break a leg?"

"Beg pardon, sir?"

"Drink at the spring, son—relax among friends." Harry Joe gathered Smoke in with his other arm: "Here's my surprise, Lyle. I'm going to put a boomerang in this lad's hand and feature him as the first Australian cowboy. You follow me? He plays a straight-shooter, see, same as always, but this one's been raised in the Aussie outback and he does everything Australian-style—"

"The fellow in the story," Dewey put in, "he's an American, in real life. He comes back home from overseas to revenge his daddy—"

"That's right," Harry Joe nodded, "he's sort of a young prince reared on foreign soil over there, but without an accent or anything like that. His dad's a big Arizona rancher with holdings all over the world, see. So when the old man gets snatched by a kidnap gang on a trip back to the home spread, the son drops everything in Australia and sails to the rescue. Oh, it shapes up as a dilly: I mean, that boomerang will be flying like a bat out of hell when he corners the badmen—"

"This fellow in the story carries an iron, too," Dewey explained, "in case of a tight where that other outfit might not work out."

Harry Joe broke out of the huddle and struck a dueling crouch: "Picture this for a teaser, boys. *The Buckaroo from Down Under*—'A gun in one hand, a deadly boomerang in the other.' We'll set the scene with a title card, see— 'The Australian Continent 1890'—and then cut to kangaroos, fuzzy-wuzzy natives, whatever travelogue stuff we can whistle up. Two minutes of 'Waltzing Matilda' and zippo, our hero's waltzing into Drygulch, Arizona, to save dear old Dad."

Smoke took a swallow of whiskey and grinned: "Corriganville, you mean. Or Stoney Point—"

"Hell, yes," Harry Joe said happily. "I see this thing as a fighting romance done on the quick, but souped up a little for the novelty trade. Fans nowadays want something new every time the marquee changes. I'd like to make about a dozen of these boomerangers fast and loose, build up a following, and then maybe try for a shot at a big two-a-day special. Shoot it in Trucolor, the works, see what I'm driving at?"

"Sounds like a pretty good send-off for this young gobbler," Smoke said. "I hope I don't have to play his aborigeney sidekick—"

"Oh, no, you're the cook at the home ranch, the old boss's right-hand man. I've got the plot pretty well thought out, but I'm still studying how to work in the boom displays—"

"What kind of displays?"

"Boom displays. They call boomerangs 'booms' in the down-under lingo."

Smoke turned to look at Dewey. "I was wondering about that. Can you throw a boomerang?"

Dewey stood up straight: "Well . . . if I can lift it, I'll throw it."

Harry Joe waved away the question. "Shoot, it's all settled. I got a trainer lined up to coach him. Fellow who works over at the Hollywood Athletic Club. He's a close pal of Errol Flynn's, they say—"

Smoke lit one of Dewey's Camels. "A sporty egg like that don't work for the fun of it. Who's going to bankroll all of this?"

Harry Joe drained his glass and chuckled: "Junior Gold. He don't know the half of it yet. I rented a suite over at the Roosevelt for a place to pitch the deal, sweet-talk him a little. I got to run over there right now." Harry Joe patted his damp sleeves and took a parting shot out of the bottle.

"Oh lordy, not another sport." Smoke laughed and clapped a hand over his heart. "Well, I'll work another lick for Junior Gold, but you tell him I want a cash advance. I need to get some slacks out of the cleaners—"

Harry Joe guffawed: "How about if I land us a bonus instead? Hardship pay for dealing with the prick. When we wrap this son of a bitch, Junior owes us all a three-week toot with the Dolly Sisters." Harry Joe crossed to the door, weaving a little. Before going out, he cocked a finger at Dewey: "We saddle up at eight o'clock; slick—Stage 1. Come out bucking just like we been talking about—"

"Yessir—" Dewey flushed, not sure just what was going on. Most of the talk had passed over his head, and he looked thunderstruck to find himself left to contend with a stranger. He hesitated an instant, then started for his hat, ready to bolt. Smoke motioned him toward a seat at the table.

"What's your rush? Pull up a pew."

"Well, I wouldn't want to put you out—"

"Pass me that bowl of ice there. Right behind you. Got any smokes left?" Dewey had barely touched his drink, but Smoke poured him a freshener and wedged a chair between the two of them for a common foot rest.

Dewey raised his glass and took a stiff swallow. His eyes smarted from the sting and he shook his head in disbelief: "Be John Brown, I've seen you in three hundred shows, and here we are drinking Old Crow together."

"Might as well get acquainted. Born to the movies, are you?"

Dewey blushed again: "I don't rightly know. Is this Junior Gold . . . is he an okay guy to work for?"

"He's the prick of the world, but don't let that bother you."

"I heard he was a Jew—"

"So?"

Dewey shrugged: "Never been around any Jews before. Are they all like that?"

"Bound to be rascals in any bunch and it's always been that way. In Junior's case, he's rotten on purpose and everything else is accidental—"

"Be John Brown—"

"Don't quote me on any of this."

"How does he get by with it? Dealing with big stars and all—"

"He owns the casino. Shaves the dice to suit himself—"

"Has he ever beat you on a trade? If that's not too personal—"

"I never counted up." Smoke leaned back in his chair and laughed. "You'll get used to it. Do whatever Harry Joe tells you to do and forget the rest."

"I will, yessir."

Dewey took a turn pouring the drinks. He was green as cowflop but natively quick and eager to please without seeming kiss-ass about it. His manners were scrupulous, right out of Matthew Brady's time. Instead of using the dinner plate set out for an ashtray, he pinched the coals off his cigarettes and tucked the butts in his pants cuff.

"Full moon," Dewey noticed. He had parted the curtain to look out into the summer dark. The smell of gardenias and traffic fumes floated up from the street. "This California," he said after a minute, "I never struck such a peculiar place. The weather stays the same and the air changes colors . . ."

"Been around town long?"

"About six months."

"Feeling homesick, I expect."

"Oh, I've been on the road for quite a spell." Dewey started to prop up his feet, then glanced around uneasily. "You don't have a missus?"

"No. Never found one to suit my pistol. Might yet, though. You?"

"I'm not married, nawsir, but I been thinking along those lines. The trouble is, there's two different ones I like, and . . . both real little sweethearts too . . . It's kind of complicated—"

"Women are always complicated. Two at once would tax old Einstein's brain."

"Yessir, for a fact—"

"Better wish on that moon for luck before the scene monkeys come and haul it off." Smoke pointed across the table. "Hand me my bulldog there—I'm tired of these pissy cigarettes."

Dewey passed over the pipe and pouch: "You're not much sold on this boomerang deal, are you?"

"Oh, it might work. It's anybody's guess what'll go over right now. The whole business is bottoming out—"

"Why's that?"

"Lots of reasons. I don't know bull about the high finance part, but TV's skimming off the audience. TV's got the whole country hopped up and it's free to boot—"

"Let me ask you something. I been studying about this in my mind. Did you ever dream about TV?"

Smoke snorted. "Never bother to watch it."

"I hate it myself. But did you ever hear tell of anybody who dreamed about TV?"

"Can't say as I have."

Dewey bounded up from the table. "That's because nobody ever does. Dogs can't even see it, I've noticed. But shows are different. People get caught up in the thrills, feel like they're part of it all. Me, I dream in Westerns half the time—" He paced across to the honor circle, moving with that odd stitch in his walk. He gazed up at the faces, excited and a little tipsy: "These old warhorses near about raised me. I want to be as good as they are. Joel McCrea, Jake Del Rio, old Gary Cooper—"

Smoke suppressed a grin: "That might be pretty hard to swing on a Junior Gold budget."

"Spirit's got to count for something. I'm willing to bust a gut—"

"It's a start; same as baby steps. Just hump along an inch at a time and don't confuse your pecker with your pocketbook. Who knows? Maybe you'll end up rich and famous—"

"That ain't it—" Dewey groped for words. "I mean I'd love to make a ridiculous fortune—shootfire, who wouldn't? But I'm out to see what I can do—" He turned in a circle, surveying the premises. "How come this place is called after Sam Clemens?"

"Damned if I know. Just the name of the place."

"I think it's an omen. You put any stock in omens?"

"Not much."

"I'm going to remember what you said about Jews. What's your thinking about niggers?"

"Why?"

"Because I got one dependent on me."

Dewey turned back to the pictures, looking as if he'd said more than he meant to say. When he took his chair again, Smoke topped off the drinks without comment, figuring the story would come out sooner or later. Meanwhile, they tested and prodded at each other in amiable ways to divine the possibilities for trust. It was a game of pursuit played by instinct, and Smoke excelled at the chase. Men became enemies or comrades for life on the basis of a gesture, an inflection, a half smile at the right or wrong instant. Dewey held his own in the give-and-take, only occasionally losing ground in a flash of boyish bravado. He seemed to be looking for a calling, not a job, but Smoke admired his spunk. The difference in their ages was no hindrance to the exchange because they believed in the same things. They believed in the Code of the West. They believed in the old manly rules the same way church people believed in the Holy Ghost and collection plates.

The whiskey helped. When the conversation stalled, Smoke poured a fresh round and Dewey naturally tried to keep apace. For a snack, Smoke broke out a supply of lunch cuts, and they wolfed down the lot. They turned on the radio and picked up the "Moonglow with Martin" program from New Orleans, then switched to a hillbilly station in Arizona when the static rose. Dewey knew the names of all the musicians, white and colored alike, discussed them the way he might talk about old friends. It put Smoke in mind of a long-ago conversation about Jimmie Rodgers and Vernon Dalhart. . . .

Dewey had read a scattering of books, too — drugstore paperbacks and the like — and he carried a notebook listing everything he had read. Smoke put on his bifocals to have a look. A sample page contained titles by Ernest Haycox, Jack London, and Raymond Chandler, with *The Foxes of Harrow* crossed out. Dewey used different colored pencils in a tricky kind of grading system. A note in red about *The Treasure of the Sierra Madre* said: "Clasic book & a clasic Western." The entry prompted a discussion with some real meat to it. Smoke had always considered *The Treasure of the Sierra Madre* a foreign-adventure picture, not a pure Western by any stretch. They debated the point like gentlemen seminarians, except they were both tight as ticks by then.

The talk spun on, ranging all over the map.

There was no further mention of Dewey's "dependent" or much else about his personal history. Smoke figured Dewey might have spent time traveling with a circus or carnival, but he held back from asking. It was part of the code, after all, to avoid beaking around the other fellow's business.

Dewey was clearly a novice at dissipation, although he kept his dignity, even half-pied. Somewhere along the line — the details were forever hazy — it was agreed that he would sleep over on the davenport since he was afoot and the Red Cars stopped running across town at midnight. Flushed and swaying, Dewey kept asking questions about Smoke's picture career and about the photos on the walls. To his amazement, Smoke found himself explaining his notion about the invisible rising to find a form. He had never discussed it before, even with Harry Joe.

"That's deep," Dewey said admiringly, sliding down on his spine. "I'll bet that's some kind of natural law you've got ahold of. Rivers do the same thing, jumping to a new bank. The wind, too—"

Smoke yawned, tamped out his pipe: "Call it Bailey's Law of the Wind, I guess. . . . Guaranteed hot."

Dewey smiled dreamily, fading fast. He laid his head down on his arms. "Just resting my eyes," he muttered.

Smoke stood up and took a stretch, half tottery himself: "What say we turn in?"

Dewey misheard, reared up in alarm: "Turn ourselves in? *Nawsir.* Don't ever say that. It's bad luck—" When he dropped his head again, he was gone for the night.

With a heave, Smoke maneuvered the younger man over onto the couch and discovered the cause for his eccentric walk. Dewey was packing an old plow-handle revolver in his boot. It was loaded, of course, and that made three of them. Smoke got tickled, hefting the antique cannon from hand to hand. Men were meant to go armed in a discourteous world, else He wouldn't have given them trigger fingers. In the early days, most of the Sam Clemens bunch had worn pocket pieces as a routine matter; Smoke himself often toted a pepperbox derringer back when he was more liable to stray into a jackpot in the helldives along Hollywood Boulevard. A "snake gun" used in the proper way kept discourse at a reasonable level. Only a dullard like Blackjack Ward ever overstepped the line to mayhem.

Smoke propped Dewey's comical-looking old pistol on the mantle, still laughing. Sugar mountains, he was thinking. The phrase floated into his mind from nowhere and conjured up an image of Art Acord adventuring in Mexico. . . . Dewey had some of the same qualities as Art had in his heyday, the good looks, the same good heart. . . . In bed, Smoke dreamed about a soaring, fantastical Mexico he had never seen in life. He saw himself jumping up and down on a glittery mountainside, playing the part of "Old Howard," the Sierra Madre prospector. Later on he was somehow transformed into a cross between himself and a handsome devil of a hero defending a pair of pretty señoritas while a barrage of boomerangs sizzled past his ears. . . .

Smoke put his feet on the floor at dawn as usual. He dressed and carried a pot of coffee into the living room. Dewey sprang to a sitting position, peering around in feverish confusion. His beard was the wiry kind, and he had sprouted a dark furze while he slept. He looked grubby in his tangled clothes and badly bent up all around. Hands jittering, he spilled coffee down his front plus a good deal else after he had sprinted into the donicker.

Smoke called through the door for him to use the razor in the cabinet, anything else he found handy. "Put on your Grand Slam smile," he joked in encouragement, stirring a hair of the dog in his coffee. It was a hollow joke, but Dewey wouldn't know it, and why spoil his rosy hopes for him? "Grand Slum" was the boneyard of Hollywood, run by a chinless degenerate who was hell to please and dangerous to cross. "The Baron of the 'B's'" . . . Junior Gold signed ads that way in the trades and then made the trashiest pictures on Poverty Row. He was a trashy little man who hoodooed everything he touched. He tormented the has-been stars who made the last-mile walk to his desk, corrupted the gullible young, and in general did whatever he damned well pleased to do. The cowboys despised him but lined up by necessity at his pay windows. . . . Smoke had debated whether to lay out the full score to Dewey the night before, but decided not. The hard rule, in the picture business or anywhere else, was to live and learn. It was an old saw, but old saws got to be that way because they were true.

Smoke drank a second cup of spike and called through the bathroom door again with no response. He entered after a round of knocking and found Dewey pitched weakly at the basin, inspecting his bloodshot eyes in the mirror. Dewey had soaped his face with shaving cream, but he said he was too "quaky" to trust himself with a razor.

"It's getting on toward eight o'clock—"

"Be John Brown," Dewey stammered, "I've come down with the stomach flu or something. Don't know what the devil's wrong with me—"

Smoke belly-laughed: "I'd say you've got a prime case of the whips and jingles. Drinking too much will do that, you know."

"Yessir, I've seen it happen, but I didn't figure on it happening to me—"

"Oh, it's democratic. Didn't you ever drink any whiskey before?"

"I was kind of saving up for the right time—"

"Look here, how old are you?"

"Be seventeen. In November."

Smoke's thoughts wove back and forth between total responsibility and none at all. He set Dewey down on the johnny lid and shaved him, scissoring off a rick of that hobo-length hair while he was at it. He located a vial of Murine in Harry Joe's rooms for the eye damage and stood by with a pan until the kid managed to keep down a dose of spike. Dewey was mortified to require doctoring, but he didn't piss and moan. He had pluck, a proper sense of pride. Before they set out for the Grand Slam lot, he found his gun on the mantle, slipped it in his boot without a word.

"Take your marks," Harry Joe snapped at them by way of greeting. He looked haggard and anxious—"It's shit or bust time," he kept muttering under his breath—but after the third or fourth take, he started smiling steadily. Harry Joe's strategy for the test was to forget about the test angle and film the guts of a sixty-minute feature in fast highlights. He reasoned that Junior Gold couldn't resist a picture already a third completed.

Dewey was half sick and the other half drunk the whole day, but the camera failed to notice. The camera recorded him in wonderful health, a fierce young avenger hunting down and punishing his father's tormentors. He was costumed in odds and ends from the company rag bin—Smith Ballew's faded vest, a pair of Eddie Dean's britches. To top off the outfit, he wore an Australian bush hat left over from a Tom Tyler serial. He kept punching up the crown, worried that it didn't look "American enough." The crew appreciated an attitude like that. Between takes, the old-timers began to offer him casual hints about stage business and pulls out of their flasks.

Harry Joe's story line was stock but elemental the way Dewey attacked it; in his earnest identification with the hero, he left a couple of stunt men counting their teeth after a pitched battle on the barroom set. They were all pretty much winging it by mid-morning, and Dewey was a whiz at improvising his own lines. "I'll see you around the next corner," he promised the "brain" heavy, making it a warning full of menace. In the next setup, a dialogue with Smoke, Dewey repeated the line as a token of respect and affection. Smoke grasped the pathos of the kid's invention and gave the scene more of an effort than usual. After that take, the crew whistled approval like youngsters at a Saturday-afternoon matinee.

Cowboy Movie in Black and White

From *I'll Be There in the Morning, If I Live*, 1973

I sighted the horses
    two miles away.
The burro groaned — he'd
    been on half-feed
Since Ruidosa, but, shitfire,
    so'd I — and we
Strained forward to catch
    the mare and her get
At Old Man Leonard Kafka's spring.

She had a fine, high sheen
    from the spring grass . . .
And when her hoof tore my temple,
I felt nothing:
Only free and sunfishing —
    through the air
Toward the water. My hand-gun,
    a right-smart bone-grip Colt
I'd saved up for and bought
    in Sweetwater,
Cleared my holster,
    hit the water,
And sank before I did.

Grover Lewis (left) made his second appearance in a major motion picture in a small role in Michael Ritchie's classic political film, The Candidate, *starring Robert Redford.*

Old Movies in My Mind

Unpublished essay commissioned by *New West*, 1990

"What is the scene? Where am I?"

—NORMA DESMOND in *Sunset Boulevard*

I had been out walking since dawn, playing old movies in my mind. By nine A.M., the gray coolness of first light had browned off into a smog alert sure to be unhealthful to everybody in the Los Angeles basin, and I slowed down to catch my breath every block or two. The early-morning heat hung over Hollywood Boulevard in grimy, undulant streaks, and the air was sticky and thick as syrup. I had a destination in mind, but I was in no hurry to get there.

Heading east, I passed the once-grand Hollywood Roosevelt Hotel and cut across the street to look for a patch of shade in the forecourt of Mann's Chinese Theater. Panting a little, I sponged moisture off my face with a damp handkerchief and leaned against one of the massive stone "Heaven Dogs" guarding the entrance to the lobby.

The courtyard was thronged with tourists snapping photos of the cement slabs bearing the handprints and footprints and squiggly autographs of the great stars of Hollywood's salad days—Humphrey Bogart and Clark Gable, Roy Rogers and Trigger, Tyrone Power, Susan Hayward, Alan Ladd, Judy Garland. . . . A heavyset woman in leather sandals and a pantsuit the color of eggplant darted from one slab to another, crooning the names aloud to herself. "My gunness," she murmured, "it's like . . . auld lang syne."

She had a sweet and open country face, and when she noticed me smiling at her, she smiled back. "I've been movie crazy all my life," she confided with a roll of her eyes. "Mama and Opal claim that I'm touched on the subject." I grinned and said I guessed I was a little touched on the subject myself.

I walked on, beginning to relax into the heat, letting it enfold me. A few hundred years ago, before this was a boulevard, it was a dusty footpath connecting a string of Indian brush camps. The Gabrielino Tribe had no specific word in their language to express love, but on the other hand they had no bad spirit connected with their creed. The first paleface interlopers took care of that. They left love a cipher, but they brought the Devil with them onto the set, and there'd been hell to pay in paradise ever since. . . .

The old footpath was a low crawl nowadays, in sore need of intensive care. I passed the smeary windows of burrito bars and tattoo parlors, junk jewelry stores, three-minute photo booths, electronic game arcades, discount wig outlets, and disco-flash boutiques sacrificing everything for half price.

Apparitions and phantoms glided along the litter-strewn "Walk of Fame" — mean tricks, hard dopers, low riders, and rubbernecking pilgrims. Scam artists planning world conquest loitered in front of novelty shops protected from them by wire-mesh gates. For seventy-five-odd years, America's oddest-bent birds had flocked in crazed squadrons to Hollywood in the hopes of getting what they thought they deserved. A few rose in the pecking order to become rich and celebrated. Most of the others ended up sacrificing everything for half price or the next best offer . . .

I walked further east and watched picture show epiphanies unreel against my eyelids:

"There's no sign of violence except these two tiny marks near the base of her neck."

"Do you think I *like* sending kids up in those old crates?"

"Cynthia, there is nothing medically wrong with your legs."

"Hold everything! I've got a story that'll set this town on its ear."

Growing up in the popcorn-smelling dark of movie theaters in the Forties and Fifties had left brassy arias like those forever turning green in the sepia-tone of memory. I didn't know or care anything about the "art of cinema" until I was almost grown, but I knew all about picture shows before I could read the credits. Even as a child, I intuitively grasped that America was "about" performance — showing off in high style and getting rewarded for it. As an operating model of the American Dream, Hollywood held out the gaudiest stakes and touted the grandest of all illusions. *Get into your dancing clothes,* the movies invited the world, *and forget about dying.*

In those days, Hollywood was a nation and a language unto itself, and ninety million Americans went to the movies every week. Neighborhood programs changed every two or three days, with a newsreel, cartoon, short subject, trailers, and a double feature. The very best pictures made you want to go and live in them. Lousy pictures were tolerated as petty swindles — apples starring worms. Going to the movies in the heyday of their great popularity was the equivalent of taking a long, cool splash. By contrast, living with television as a constant presence seemed like living in a brine.

The Pussycat Theater hadn't yet opened for the day's grind, and I slowed down to peer into the empty box office. In 1947, when I'd first visited Hollywood, the theater was called the Hitching Post, and it showed only "B"-grade shoot-'em-ups. Back then, the ticket girl wore a Western costume and sat next to a pegboard where the kiddie cowboys had to check their cap pistols before entering the auditorium. I attended a Saturday matinee just to say that I'd been to the place, and afterwards stood in line for an hour to shake hands with the serial star who played the Territory Kid. My ambition at the time was to work for Harry Cohn as a screenwriter at Columbia Pictures; Cohn had a reputation as a sadistic bully, but I figured I could last a few rounds with him, just as I figured that someday I'd come up with a story that would set this town on its ear. I was thirteen years old.

As it happened, I never chanced to square off with Harry Cohn, but twenty years later, on a magazine assignment at the other edge of the continent, I spent two hair-raising days barhopping around the Everglades with the mortal remains of the Territory Kid. By then, he had lost his stardom and most of his sanity, and he was permanently weirded out on booze and drugs. He grieved endlessly over the magic he'd let slip from his grasp: "The money counted out real fine, see, and there was more strange stuff around than a guy could shake his dick at. Then fate slipped up on me and slapped skates on my ass. You know who they based that *Sunset Boulevard* on?" he cried. "Me. *Me.*"

That Saturday afternoon in his prime at the Hitching Post, the Territory Kid handed out autographed 8 × 10 glossies of himself, and I took mine home to Dallas and put it in a dime-store frame and gave it to old LaZell, my grandmother's mildly cuckoo cousin. LaZell was past eighty, and as movie-struck in his second childhood as I was in my first. Whenever it fell my turn to see after the old man, I always took him to the Rainbo Theater.

We feasted on Butterfingers and saw scores of double bills together, as many crackly, old-time pictures as semifresh ones. We shrieked in terror at *The Mummy's Tomb* and wept like babes over *Of Mice and Men* and sang along with the bouncing ball. We talked about the heart-numbing suspense of *Foreign Correspondent* for days, and debated whether Jimmy Cagney had turned yellow on his way to the chair in *Angels with Dirty Faces*. During *The Petrified Forest*, LaZell dozed off amid the general talkiness, and I fell swooningly in love with the young Bette Davis. The old man and I sat through *Red River* three times running, and LaZell clapped his hands raw at the start of the cattle drive: *"Take 'em to Missouri, Matt!"* he would whoop in my ear at odd moments ever afterward . . .

To cool off again, I stepped inside the Larry Edmunds Cinema and Theatre Bookshop and leafed through Bob Thomas's biography of Harry Cohn [*King Cohn, the Life and Times of Harry Cohn,* 1967] until I located my favorite parable about the misanthropic "king" of the Columbia lot:

> *During a studio meeting Jack Cohn suggested that Columbia make a biblical film. . . .*
>
> *"What the hell do you know about the Bible?" Harry asked. . . . "I'll bet you fifty bucks you can't recite the Lord's Prayer."*
>
> *Both brothers laid down $50.*
>
> *"Okay, say it," Harry said.*
>
> *"Now I lay me down to sleep —" Jack began.*
>
> *Harry interrupted him and handed over the $50. "That's enough," Harry said. "I didn't think you knew it."*

I wandered through the maze of library shelves, searching for spines of books that had left their everlasting mark on me: James M. Cain's *Double Indemnity* and *The Postman Always Rings Twice; The Day of the Locust* by Nathanael West and Richard Hallas's *You Play the Red and the Black Comes Up; Fully Dressed* and *In His Right Mind* by Michael Fessier Sr. and *Build My Gallows High* by Geoffrey Homes; Horace McCoy's *They Shoot Horses, Don't They?* and *I Should Have Stayed Home; What Makes Sammy Run?* by Budd Schulberg; and anything and everything by Dashiell Hammett and Raymond Chandler. Edmund Wilson labeled the hard-boiled crowd "the poets of the tabloid murder" in a pecksniffish and poorly informed essay on Hollywood writers titled "The Boys in the Back Room." Well, to hell with paleface literary critics. They were a bare cut above film critics, and James Agee aside, I couldn't stomach the lot of them. Once, in New York, a leading lady cineaste astounded me by dismissing *The Wild Bunch* as "two hours of handsome killing." I managed to spill a martini in her ample lap on my way to the door, to the airport, "to the Coast." Hollywood had always been my spiritual hometown. . . .

Once more, I followed the sidewalk tides to the east, remembering the girls

I used to squire to the picture show, conjuring up faces without names and fumbling caresses in the brilliantined shadows and romances that sometimes didn't last two reels. To please the sturdy-calfed maidens I courted as a boy, I aped the winning ways of the stars. I was witty as Cary Grant, gentle as Jimmy Stewart, honest as Henry Fonda, tough as John Garfield, savvy as William Holden, cool as Robert Mitchum, whimsical as Gene Kelly, shrewd as Spencer Tracy, earnest as Joel McCrea, mysterious as Orson Welles, sensitive as Montgomery Clift, constant as Lassie, and manful as Gary Cooper. Or so I liked to imagine. Adolescent lust was the inspiration of my bravura performances, and it mostly went unrequited.

At issue, of course, was how to act, not merely in pursuit of the flesh, but in the conduct of life itself. For my generation, the combined physical and moral and spiritual impact of going to the movies was incalculable. Hollywood's penny entertainments defined the shapes of reality for the age, and shaped the nation into a community of shared experience. All of us learned the proprieties of love and war at the picture show. The movies were a garden of dazzling light, and the verities were familiar and comforting—basic decency and unsullied justice and the promise of happy endings for all. Wasn't that the universal goal? A common vision of goodness and virtue? Weren't those the bonds that held civilization intact and kept the bad spirits at bay?

The movies turned us one and all every way but loose. Still aping the stars when I reached young manhood, I went out in the world with the fixed idea that I wouldn't let anybody run over me. I used that, at my worst, to run over others. But ten thousand and one flickering myths later, I rated myself a better character for having been to the picture show. Or so I liked to imagine. . . .

I crossed Cahuenga Boulevard. At the news kiosk opposite Bela Lugosi's sidewalk star, I saw a headline that wrenched the breath out of me. I bought a paper, but didn't look at it until I found a seat on a bus-stop bench at the corner of Hollywood and Vine. The bench was unshaded in the smothering heat. I sat crowded in next to three or four women of retirement age and a vacant-eyed old man who was talking out loud to himself about trains.

The story was above the fold on page one. It was an account of the movie star Gig Young shooting his wife to death and then turning the gun on himself and taking his own life. Young was sixty years old, an alcoholic of record. His wife was thirty-one. They had been married for three weeks. The actor had appeared in fifty-five pictures and received an Academy Award in 1969 for his supporting performance in *They Shoot Horses, Don't They?*

A bus pulled into the curb and departed, and then another, and the retired ladies kept their seats. Their conversation made it clear that they served time on the bench every day, drowsing in the leaden air and listening to the old man chatter to himself about trains. Something that felt like a hairball churned in my stomach. I wadded up the newspaper and stuffed it in a litter bin and headed south on Vine Street. I walked fast for two blocks and turned left on Sunset Boulevard and stood at the literal heart of old Hollywood.

The ground there had once been planted in lemon and orange groves, and according to legend, Cecil B. DeMille shot the first feature-length Hollywood picture in a rented barn near the corner. The site was now occupied by a savings and loan association. A splashy mural above the building's entrance depicted the likes of Douglas Fairbanks and Greta Garbo and Charlie Chaplin. The likenesses were not very true to life, but that somehow seemed appropriate.

Movie stars, by and large, didn't end up in sharp focus or in happy endings. Gig Young's final scene was the grisliest flame-out imaginable, but Hollywood's sometime darlings often went up in apocalyptic smoke. They burned out their talent, if they had any, and the movie industry routinely dumped their ashes. The feds took most of their riches, and time and bodily hungers ate up the rest. The gorgeous young one-of-a-kinds grew old and unlovely, woke up to paunches and wattles and mortality. To shore up their perishing dreams, they shot themselves full of junk and sautéed themselves in liquor and strained against heaven to be born again. Used up and thrown away, they fell into permanent rage and despair like the Territory Kid, and descended finally into ruin and madness and tabloid murder like the Oscar winner on page one. Fate slipped up on the beautiful, pitiful creatures and slapped skates on their asses . . .

I turned off Sunset onto Gower Street and approached the studio that Harry Cohn had built. The weathered complex of four- and five-story buildings was still marginally functional as a moviemaking facility, but Columbia Pictures didn't live there anymore. Outside the reception lobby, I stepped off into the gutter to get a view of the third-floor window where Cohn used to spy on the comings-and-goings of his employees. He was a man who enjoyed cursing out his vassals, or firing them on the spot, or otherwise dealing them misery. He doubtless would have relished the sight of a writer standing in the gutter peering up and wondering about him.

Since the days of my juvenile call to work for Harry Cohn, I'd followed his history and talked with maybe a dozen people who knew him and/or had suffered some unpleasant association with him. The one almost invariably led to the other.

Harry Cohn had class with a capital K. He modeled his personal style after Mussolini. He was mean, venal, crude, abusive, vain, vicious, a monster of intimidation, a conscienceless greed head, the compleat vulgarian. He had a talent for alienating talent. He was a ravening egoist, an opportunistic seducer, a foul-mouthed, cold-blooded tyrant.

Cohn was sixty-seven when he died of a heart attack in 1958. I remembered Jimmy Fidler reporting the news on the radio. Two thousand people attended Cohn's last rites, and Red Skelton joked about the crowd at the funeral on his TV show: "Well, it only proves what they always say—give the public something they want to see, and they'll turn out for it." Skelton died with his tongue lolling out, and the audience whooped with laughter . . .

Harry Cohn's old demesne ended at Fountain Avenue, and the neighborhood south of there was full of prowling cats and hostile children. Puffing for breath in the thick yellow air, I hurried past the rundown bungalows and graffiti-smeared courtyards, and felt relieved to cross Santa Monica Boulevard and pass through the high iron gates into the sudden hush and immensity of the Hollywood Memorial Park Cemetery.

The burying ground was an old place by Southern California standards. Thousands of those interred there had been born in the first three or four decades of the Republic, and had migrated to the western edge along the overland wagon routes. The park's greenery was lush and well tended, and sentinel palms soared to great heights along the steep stucco walls that kept out the noise of traffic.

I rested for a time under an olive tree, then followed a familiar route through the rows of stone markers. I walked past the Confederate soldiers' plot and D. W. Griffith's thirty-foot plinth, and descended to the shore of the artificial lake. On the swell of ground above Marion Davies' tomb, a workman tinkered with the engine of an earth-moving machine. A satin ribbon curled on Tyrone Power's carved bench marker; the white cloth was attached to a Styrofoam cross and inscribed, "Daddy, I pray for you. Love, Romina."

In the Cathedral Mausoleum, a vase at Rudolph Valentino's crypt held a plume of roses, and I found fresh flowers at the biers of Peter Lorre, June Mathis, and Barbara LaMarr.

I circled the lake and came to stand at the imposing marble pile that marked the grave of Harry Cohn. There was no sign of any recent visitation there, and it occurred to me that in all the times I'd visited the cemetery, I'd never seen a tribute of mourning for the profane old king. The notion that nobody in life gave a faint damn about Harry Cohn struck me as obscene.

By all accounts, Cohn was fifty-seven varieties of a lowlife scoundrel, but he was also a crapshooter in the American grain and the greatest showman of his age. He had created luminous stars—Barbara Stanwyck and Jean Arthur and Rita Hayworth—and given the century the last romantic look at itself. He had put his stamp on some of the noblest picture shows ever made: *It Happened One Night, Mr. Deeds Goes to Town, Lost Horizon, You Can't Take It with You, Mr. Smith Goes to Washington, Only Angels Have Wings, His Girl Friday, The More the Merrier.* The roster was legion, and constituted a king's ransom.

It was wrong for the old bastard to lie unnoticed in his grave. Somewhere on the cusp between laughing at myself and crying, I went in the cemetery's flower shop. I grabbed up the first bouquet I saw and flapped it at the clerk. "For Mr. Harry Cohn," I blurted.

"The asters are nice today. Are you related to the family?"

"Yes," I said. "Yes, I guess I am."

I laid the flowers at Harry Cohn's resting place with a card signed, *See you, Harry.* Then I reeled out of the graveyard and tramped all the way to Melrose and Western before I found a cab. I was scorched and weary and lightheaded. I had been out walking since dawn, playing old movies in my mind.

part two music

Dirge for a Bird

Avesta, 1955

Maybe he wasn't for real at all. Maybe he really was a bird. His eyes were deep and black and you never could dig what went on behind them; he picked at things, too, like a sparrow shaking suspiciously around a bread crumb that he wants but is afraid to grab. He couldn't help himself, he was gone with it, I guess. No chick could quite soothe him, no food ever completely satisfied his hunger, not even his own music ever fully pleased him. If he was a bird, he was no ordinary one, though. You couldn't put salt on his tail, man.

His name was Charles Christopher Parker Jr. He left a few things behind, a trail of broads that he couldn't make happy and vice versa, a couple of friends scattered around, and some phonograph records, some good, no, great they were, and some so bad they made you sick at your stomach.

He was born colored into an ofay world and he never did learn to cope with that — born into this world in the first month of 1920 in Kansas City. It was cold that day — cold enough to make any bird crawl back in its shell. I guess that's just what he did. I guess Charles Christopher Parker Jr. slid back into his shell when he felt that first icy blast, and never came out again. And he never got warm either — this old world and all its rules and the people that made them became distant and untouchable and cold.

He was a bright kid, and that was trouble in itself. If he had been square, it all might have worked out right — he could have pumped a little gas or glossed shoes or ended on some chain gang and it would have all been the same, to him, to everybody. But no, he had to be a musician, man, be sharp — like with crazy threads, be a sugar daddy to all those lonely chicks — put something down. And he did. When he was fifteen, he was blowing a horn in the dingy clubs in K.C., just a boy, but he was doing a man's job and living a man's life. He was just a punk — a punk with wild music clawing its way out of him, music that picked him up and slammed him down, challenging him to tickle those keys on his horn in a little different way just to see what would come out.

Grover Lewis (right) poses with friends Larry McMurtry (center) and John Lewis at the University of North Texas in the late 1950s.

In those days during the Depression, Charlie could grab more gold in a month gigging with his tenor than his old man could make in a year.

It was a spinning-rainbow world. Guys like Harlan Leonard and Lawrence Keyes liked the way he played, gave him a job. He learned a lot, hard and fast. All the whiskey, all the women, all the wailing solos, and no time to hit the sack and knock a nod —

("Jesus, I'm beat, man."

"Here, don't lose your cool." A hand extended in the dark. "This'll pick you up, put you where it's Technicolor, man.")

And he conked his first weed. It was easy to go on from there, all the stuff, heroin, cocaine. He had a big habit almost before he knew it. Like the man said, it was Technicolor. Nothing could put him down.

He started working for Jay McShann and he was in; famous when he was just twenty-one. The jazz world screamed cheers for its new idol. There was money to be made, women to be laid, music to be played; what else was there? He had fresh ideas, different ideas like nothing before. He ran into others who were looking for a leader, who were trying to express something new, too: Dizzy Gillespie, Billy Eckstine, Sarah Vaughn. With Charlie blowing the lead, they created a new music. They called it bebop.

Bebop. (O vout orooney beep beep — are you hip? Do you read it? Do you dig the jive, Daddy-o?) It was nervous frantic music — neurotic and hard — fast dissonant rhythm and bubbling runs up and down the scale. It didn't last long, but it was a start, it paved the way for the Stan Getzes, the Chet Bakers, the Gerry Mulligans, the Dave Brubecks of today. It gave birth to progressive jazz and a whole new way of living, the hip way, be a cat, man. Play it cool.

There was a brief interlude with the army. When he came back, he had a new name: they called him "Yardbird," and eventually shortened it to just "Bird." Even the service couldn't tame him, put him down. But the rainbow was turning black around the edges. The hard living gave him ulcers, started eating away his liver. And the disappointments and frustrations — the hate for the squares who didn't dig the jive — began to eat away his heart.

Then it came. He cracked up at a recording session in L.A. in '46. Just like that. He stood up to blow "Lover Man" and he cracked up. One minute he was fine; the next he was standing with glassy eyes and sweaty fingers, playing a child's scale exercise. It all came down on him at once, the hate for a world he wasn't made for, the hurt that he couldn't bear anymore, the habit that got too big for him. They put him away in Camarillo to get squared away. Dial Records magnanimously released "Lover Boy" and it became a collector's item of perversion while Bird went through the hell of a watershock cure. When he came out, he played some more, made some more good records and a lot of bad ones. Even played in Paris at the International Jazz Festival and toured Scandinavia. They named the jazzman's mecca "Birdland" in his honor. But it was all over really; the Bird was getting ready to fly the coop, to split out.

You should have heard him walk out on "Laura," on "Relaxin' at Camarillo," on "She Rote." He was the greatest, the most, man; he wailed, he blew way far out. It was made dad, funky, hot and cold at the same time — like ice cubes on an atomic pile. He blew himself out of this world. He reached his millennium gate.

He cut out cool in March 1955. When he stopped by the Baroness' place on Fifth Avenue to jive over old times, he got sick, couldn't leave. Watching Tommy and Jimmy Dorsey on TV, he started laughing. He died right there in that plush pad, laughing out loud in hysterical peals at the commercial musicians he despised so, at the music he had put out of date.

He laid cold in Bellvue two days before one of his ex-wives claimed him. When the doctors cut him open, they found he had lobar pneumonia, ulcers, and a hardened liver. They listed his age at fifty-three. He was thirty-five.

The Bird's gone, this time for real, chilled, gone all the way and dead. But listen while I lay it on you — every time a guy blows a horn, Bird blows too. Every time a song hits the Top Ten, it'll have something in it that Bird invented. The things he did, his innovations, have been absorbed into the music, and the way he talked and thought and dressed has been copied by an entire generation.

Maybe he wasn't for real at all. . . .

R.I.P., Bird.

(Sit in with St. Peter. You'll gas 'em all.)

Later, man.

The Hard Traveling of Woody Guthrie

Essay Composed for a Reading to a Folk Music Club, Fort Worth, 1964

With training as an actor and a deep, compelling voice, Lewis occasionally wrote narratives for dramatic performance. When Woody Guthrie was near death, Lewis wrote this prose tribute that was accompanied by folksinger Ken Harrison. Lewis had become a friend of Jack Loftis when they were working on the copy desk of the Houston Chronicle. *Editor-in-chief of that newspaper for many years, Loftis recorded the program on reel-to-reel tape, producing a copy for Rae Lewis after Grover passed away. It is transcribed here without the song lyrics. Most of the Woody Guthrie quotes are from his autobiography,* Bound for Glory.

In the chill funereal silence of a mammoth New York State Hospital complex that looms up out of the soot-colored, antenna-bristling wastes of Brooklyn like a spectral black forest, alone and almost 2,000 miles from the wind-scoured mesquite prairies of his birthplace, one of the last great American folk heroes is dying. His name is Woody Guthrie.

Back in the 1930s, in that sad, brown zeitgeist stew, Guthrie was a kind of singing peatbog soldier and free-floating minstrel of the West Coast Okie camps. Always on the go, hustling and scuffling, sometimes playing his brave, angry music all night for only a meal, a bed, and a drink, Woody was permanently on the road when Jack Kerouac was still learning to punt a football at the Horace Mann School for Boys.

In praise of the one-thousand-odd songs Guthrie composed between 1932 and 1952, folklorist Ellie Siegmeister once described him as a "rusty-voiced Homer" and the Library of Congress called him "our best contemporary ballad composer." John Steinbeck's praise was no less lavish. "Woody is just Woody. Harsh-voiced and nasaled, his guitar banging like a tire iron on a rusty rim. There is nothing sweet about Woody and there is nothing sweet about the songs he sings. But there is something more important for those who will listen. There is the will of a people to endure and fight against oppression. I think we call this the American spirit."

Today, at the age of fifty-two, Guthrie is all but forgotten by an audience that at one peak period in the 1940s numbered in the hundreds of thousands. Stricken in 1952 with the incurable nervous disease Huntington's chorea, Guthrie is now confined as an indigent patient in a terminal wing in the Brooklyn State Hospital for the mentally ill. Spastic, suffering chronic attacks of mind-shattering agony, lingering out the bleak duration of his days in an era that seems both determinedly indifferent to his fierce artistic achievement and truculently hostile to his awesome, personal legend, to an uninformed observer, Guthrie might nowadays appear to be nothing more than an anachronism, a curious out-of-joint human reminder of a murky entrée act in recent American history that most people neither understand nor elect to dwell upon in memory.

To the handful who look closer, however, Guthrie stands solidly rooted as a towering monument to America's most tragic lost decade and an eloquent witness to the spiritual indomitability of the generation of Americans who grew to maturity in the blistering crucible of the Great Depression — a generation, many of us who are younger sometimes blush to recall, that was never chary about lifting its voice in thundering dissent or bawling its unequivocal "no" at the barbarous wrongs it saw around it.

Among my own generation of survivors, the young men and women born between the years 1930 and 1935, almost everyone retains a ghostly dream-textured recollection of the '30s. For the majority of us the period conjures up an inevitable blurred montage, a yellowing sequence out of a crude but poignant newsreel of the heart. As the reel unwinds, we see slow-shuffling ticket and bread lines, gray-faced men and women on the bum, a somber harvest of Soviet-influenced social consciousness films starring John Garfield or Humphrey Bogart, Paul Muney or James Cagney. The old Warner Brothers Stock Catalog now emasculated for showing on late night TV where the bleeding remains are sandwiched in between commercials for patent pile cures or H. L. Hunt's puréed products.

Deep from the heart of chicken land, the announcer chirps unctuously oblivious to the poetic truth of his copy. But the montage plunges dizzily on projecting the brooding face of Roosevelt and the gaunt austere symbol of the Blue Eagle, the ugly ranting bark of Hitler and Father Coughlin, the grisly national torment of the Spanish Civil War, wide ties for men and women's broad-shouldered fashions, the "Big Apple" and "Brother, can you spare a dime?" Endless volumes of heart-stoppingly bad proletarian poetry. Fibber McGee and Molly, Johnny stepping out of night-shrouded store windows all over America and the haunting, bittersweet strains of popular ballads like "These Foolish Things" or "September in the Rain," songs that you can never quite remember having heard for the first time, but only always forever in the poignant recall of former possession.

Yet, despite our perhaps overstylized pictorial anthology remembrance of the period, most of us are unable, or more precisely unwilling, to affect the preposterous pose of romantic nostalgia for the decade. In simple truth, the time was too damaging to our immediate elders and betters for us to redress so facilely or so soon their legacy to us of terror and bitterness; it still yaps and growls too close at our heels for comfort. And even for the few among us who have somehow contrived to salvage a fondness for the period, its shadowy image emerges in the furtive moments we allow ourselves to confront it in dead-on recall, much more like a collapsing gray collage of ghastly disaster than any kind of recognizable or bearable reality.

Such an admission seems particularly appropriate now in these bleak faceless years, these barren dog days of our era's spiritual menopause when we find that, catatonia-like, the latest version of "Bohemia" may have its sea coasts after all, when each of us in the private confessional of his mind attempts to come to terms with the wrenching realization that something has gone terribly, spirit-numbingly wrong in our collective life in the age of the cold warrior. For aren't we constantly reminded by the routine commonplace horror of our time that the world bequeathed us is neither a very wholesome nor a very safe place? And with moral confidence, or even elementary decency, can we assuredly posit any valid alternatives for today's young vanguard except the senseless, blind alley resorts of self-inflicted impotence, a middle course of clanking abroad in a world decked with abnegate bells wailing "unclean, unclean" or irredeemable madness?

Conceivably the most unwholesome condition of our age rests in the chilling fact that as a social and moral plenum we have our roaring fever chart of pathological symptoms and ills, an encyclopedic array of malignant virulence, but no healing knife skillful or ruthless enough to cut them cleanly away. For example, we have the shrieking fishwives of Little Rock and New Orleans befouling the hemisphere with their vile, scurrilous raillery, "Yeah, you little black SOBs, if you had any initiative, you'd turn white," and this filth to children, small children. And we have the chattering lack-wit whores of payola and the avaricious panderers to the corrupt spirit of the new cashism, none too immaculately conceived tin blackguards in search of white horses. We have the twittering Archaean bull dykes of fashion and the lisping female impersonators of the entertainment and subversive investigating industries, the squeaked-voice chinless wonders of the academic world and all the malevolent intellectually bankrupt yahoo hordes of blood-lusters and book-burners and people-burners, the gorilla bands of the warped, the diseased, and the merely evil. But precisely where, we wonder, in our Circus Maximus–like age of radioactive togetherness and exploding toilet seats, where amid the fey, tortured shriek of a million incessant jukeboxes vomiting forth the stricken mechanical yelps of Ricky Nelson and Elvis, Fabian and Frankie Avalon, those narcissist young troglodytes whose names resemble nothing so much as the brand names of detergents or ersatz dime store gadgets marked "Patent Pending"—precisely, where among us is the awful stentorian voice capable of drowning out the crazed and demoniac babble? The gigantic canned death rattle heaving up from the era's nerveless electronic bowels?

The simple aching truth is that we have no anathema-hurling moral leaders in our cliff-hanging tribes to scourge and blister us awake. No stern terrible Jeremiahs wailing corrosive prophecies at us from the wilderness, no Elijahs to task us with the fiery seers' ultimate either/or, God or Baal. As Claudia succinctly puts it in Antonioni's *L'Avventura*, "Everything has become so terribly simple."

The decade of the '30s nurtured a few such mythic endowed figures, the possessors of what Confucius perhaps meant when he praised the leaders of the Ying Dynasty for displaying Ling, but none of the American Depression breed was more stubbornly unswerving in visionary faith and stature than Woody Guthrie. Only a few dim time-pitted photographs of Guthrie survived from the Dust Bowl years. The best one shows him a lean-faced intense young countryman crouched in dreamy absorption over a well-traveled Gibson guitar. The guitar is inscribed with the terse hand-lettered motto "This machine kills fascists."

Most men of goodwill, of the Depression generation, were passionately antifascist in spirit but in the quaint, already archaic parlance of the period, Guthrie was known as a Labor Red. The term signifies that the singer lent moral, emotional, and artistic support to a number of progressive working man's causes, a kind of idealistic commitment which assorted Strangelove types today, armed with the spike-bristling bludgeon of omniscient hindsight and the impotent effrontery of the timid and the totally coerced, feel no twinge of conscience about denouncing as subversive or treasonous or—perhaps most damning of all epithets at a time whose collective consciousness could conceivably be represented by a paranoid sketch of a spider skittering along a dust-choked corridor leading nowhere—un-American.

Guthrie's various left-wing associations have long been a matter of public record, but contrary to the slanderous assertions of such cut-rate perjurers as Louie Budenz, Woody was never a violent, doctrinaire revolutionary. Instead, if he is correctly viewed in the turbulent political nexus of his day, he was a classic American hardhead, an instinctive troublemaker stung into angry recoil against the abuses of the Depression era by the tough warp and woof of his own searing experience of hardship. "Fights had a funny way of always ringing me in," he once remarked laconically.

In origin and orientation then, Guthrie was a lineal descendant of the squalling rock-fisted legions of loners and anarchists who filled up the Western frontier, and like his spiritual forebears, Guthrie was constitutionally incapable of adhering to anybody's dogmatic program or fluctuating with any group's mercurial party line. It is true, of course, as John Greenway relates, that Woody at one point reached the stage where he could wax eloquent and slightly vapid about the rigidity of class structure and capitalist society. In the ballad "Jesus Christ," for instance, he construed Christ as "a carpenter true and brave who was murdered by the rich for advocating grassroots socialism." A view of Christ as apocalyptic working stiff, which Guthrie shared with many artists of his time.

But like the best of our best must always be, Guthrie was never less than his own man seeking his own truth, whether it lay in the festering migrant jungles along Nevada's Truckee River or hung suspended sixty stories above Manhattan in the dizzying ethereal heights of the chic Rainbow Room, "where the shrimps are boiled in Standard Oil." And like the best of our best must always be, Woody Guthrie created his own morality, fashioning his precepts and convictions out of the raw stuff of his own vital existence; and these included love and grief, and blood and work, and want and the ravages of impossible necessity, courage and sweat and incessant trouble.

In describing Guthrie's experience, I mentioned trouble, and trouble came early for Guthrie and stayed late. He was christened Woodrow Wilson Guthrie in Okemah, Oklahoma, on Bastille Day in 1912, the second son of

Charles Edward Guthrie, a locally renowned bare-knuckled fistfighter-turned-land-speculator, and Nora Bell Tanner, an ear musician.

Charlie Guthrie maintained his family in baronial style during the hog-and-high-clover days of the first Oklahoma oil boom. But when the land bubble burst, shortly after the First World War, Woody's father "lost a farm a day for thirty days" and never fully recovered from the setback either emotionally or financially. In the aftermath of this first crippling reverse, tragedy stalked the Guthries with morbid regularity. The family's expensive new home burned to the ground in a flash fire. Soon afterwards, Nora Bell, Woody's sensitive, gifted mother, began to experience violent spells of insanity. "She commenced to sing sadder songs in a lost-er voice, to gaze out our window and follow her songs out, and up and over and away from it all, away over yonder in the minor keys," Woody recalled later.

But to climax all the previous disasters, Clara, Woody's older sister, died in an oil-stove explosion. Coming hard on the heels of the destruction of the Guthrie home, Clara's death was the second major loss by fire in a grim succession of incendiary calamities, which would blight Woody's entire life. And one day, as one commentator had noted, it would lend a peculiarly affecting note to his melancholy rendition of the old fundamentalist hymn "Sowing on the Mountain," one verse of which reads, "God gave Noah the rainbow sign, said, 'it won't be water but the fire next time.'"

Under the strain of ceaseless catastrophe, just as it would happen later with the uprooted Joads, among whose wretched and dispirited ranks Woody would one day count himself, the close-knit Guthrie family began to ravel and tear at the seams. Nora Bell, grown increasingly dangerous, was committed to the state asylum at Norman, where she soon succumbed to her dark malaise.

Charles, Woody's father, ill from burns received in yet one more fire, and hopelessly broken in spirit, abandoned his two sons, Woody and Roy, and drifted off to Texas to live in the care of relatives.

From the time of his early teens then, Guthrie was left to his own devices for survival. Passing from family to family as a kind of juvenile chattel deprived of the opportunity for a full formal education, he worked at a succession of odd jobs during the next few years: spittoon polisher, scrap collector, shoe-shine boy.

At the age of sixteen, leaving nothing more tangible behind him than the dread memory of his family's disintegration, he hit the road for the South, beating his way through the plague-blighted Gulf Coast states as an itinerant day laborer and strolling musician.

In his gutter-prowling street boy days, Guthrie had picked up the rudiments of the harmonica, the fiddle, and the guitar from Okemah's populist blues and religious players. Later he would recall the strident bawling milieu where he served his musical novitiate. "Preachers talked on hellfire and damnation and played music for their tips. Blind and crippled people rattled old tin cups, war veterans played mouth organs through shrapnel holes in their throats, Negroes blowed the railroad blues through their nose, Indians chanted up and down the curb, ballad singers of all kinds and colors hit the oil towns, and there was very little of their kind of singing that I didn't soak up. The color of the songs was the red man, the black man and the white folks."

Like most lone floaters of the period, Guthrie rode the blinds and boxcars of rattling gondolas on freight trains as he made his way South. Soon his adolescent muscles hardened to iron and his nascent bottom-dog sympathies began to crystallize. Traveling hard and fast, he had his first sharp taste of the liquory sweetness, rot, and terrible beauty of the land he would some day exalt and excoriate, as a line from one of his finer songs puts it, "From California to the New York Island."

Years later, Guthrie reflected, "I cannot help but learn the most from you who count yourself least." And learn he did from his first voyage out on the billowy American earth, among the nameless armies of nomads who drifted along the nation's railways. He learned from everyone he met: the grifters and panhandlers, the old bindle stiffs and billy-scarred ex-Wobblies, the harness bulls and the ancient bull jockers, the hopeful and the desperate and the lost and the violated and the luckless and the irrevocably damned.

He absorbed their rich talk and their withering understated humor, becoming at maturity a peerless master of American folk-say. "The only trouble was that I was lost in California," Guthrie once commented ruefully. "Since I lost the address of the railroad bridge my folks was stranded under." Or again, scratching his head and keeping a deadpan face, he might remark about the inherent uncertainty of final knowledge, "All I know is I add up all I know and I still don't know." Even the laboring man's sinew-grinding job of work, a generic motif in the raw joyous anthem of Guthrie's private and creative concerns, yielded laughter, aching as love and old as the earth.

The acquisition of this kind of terse, oblique comic viewpoint later stood

Guthrie in good stead with composition of several of his most stingingly effective protest songs, because he realized at an early stage that calculated acidity can be as implacable a weapon against injustice as any blow struck in white-hot anger. But Guthrie discovered more in his first stint on the road than the caustic potency of idiomatic folk humor. He also drank in the vital music of his restless fellow wanderers: the wild fellaheen plaints of Southern mountaineers; smoky, mournful Negro blues; aching, lonely cowboy ballads of the West; and the rollicking Christian hymns and gruff-voiced workman songs of protest from everywhere.

Woody liked the crude, primitive music he found in every hamlet and whistle-stop, often graceless, always "uncultivated." His virtues were more often reminiscent of human traits than aesthetic ones. A Negro blues maxim declared, "The blues ain't nothing but a good man feeling bad," and much like a natural man, the music favored by the people of the American earth was direct, unaffected, and as often as it could afford to be, pitilessly honest. "The human race will sing this way as long as there's a human to race," Guthrie once affirmed, "and the human race is a pretty old place."

But there was still more for the young Woody to absorb from his formative years on the bum. Long before he was himself legally a man, he came to know and reverence the motley, violent, impulsive ranks of working men among whom he daily rubbed shoulders in the corrosive struggle for existence. He shared their food and their thoughts. He competed for their women. He accepted their blunt, tough custom and usage as his own. The stifling netherworld of the American labor class in the 1920s was for the most part bleak, chill, and dispiritingly profitless.

Wandering wherever the promise of work led him, Woody, for one, discovered that bare subsistence was in most areas the general rule. In cities and in many chronically depressed rural areas bedrock privation wasn't unusual enough to invite comment. Toward the end of the decade of the 1920s, when scarcity became the most abundant national product, thousands of agrarian families had begun to desert the worn-out countryside for the semimythical security of town life. Author Edward Dahlberg cocked a cold savage eye on the massive flight from Camelot to city streets in that most tortured and phenomenal of all novels about the urban nomad, *Bottom Dogs*.

Woody also observed the restless exodus and he sympathized with its drawling spokesmen genuinely enough to endow him with a homely open face and a voice more accustomed to bawling across pastures than framing speeches.

But the majority of those who made the eager, hungry pilgrimage down the big, wide road, seeking the feast of urban pie in the sky, for the majority of those people, the trip to the city proved only a temporary stopover on the way to the rail yards and fetid hobo flats that had begun to spring up like wild, bitter weeds along the right-of-way of every spur line in the nation.

By 1929, the year of the great Depression crash, there were already tramping multitudes of the jobless and displaced, who had long ago earned the right to wrinkle up their faces in the wan counterfeit of grins and snort, ruefully, "The Depression? Oh, yeah, Mister. That's been here and gone."

As the grip of the national malady tightened, even counterfeit grins began to come at a premium. Woody sensed the numb paralytic despair gnawing at those around him, because he felt it himself, hurtling through the blackness of the national night in an overcrowded boxcar. "I set down with my back against the wall, looking all through the troubled, tangled, messed-up men, traveling the hard way, dressed the hard way, hitting the long old lonesome go, rougher than a cob, wilder than a woodchuck, hotter than a depot stove, madder than $900, arguing worse than a tree full of crows. Messed up, mixed up, screwed up people, a crazy boxcar on a wild track headed 60 miles an hour in a big cloud of poison dust due straight to nowhere."

Woody, of course, had never lived far from violence. He had been born and reared after all in Okemah, which by his own tally, was "one of the singing-est, squaredancing-est, yelling-est, preaching-est, walking-est, talking-est, laughing-est, crying-est, shooting-est, fist-fighting-est, bleeding-est, gun-carrying-est, gun club and razor-carrying-est of our ranch and farm towns because it blossomed into one of our first oil boom towns in the Southwest."

So from boyhood on, Guthrie had witnessed Okfuskee County's legendary shirt-staining fistfights and absorbed the endemic brawling spirit that prevailed in the blowing wild gusher camps, where as one roustabout sardonically told him, the only religion was "to get all you can and spend all you can as quick as you can and then get thrown in the can."

Still, inured as he was to the ingrained rowdiness of his native region, Woody encountered a new kind of violence during his trip on the road during these first years of the somber yellow leaf of the Depression and the experience jolted him into a precocious tough-minded social awareness that would govern his basic sympathies for the duration of his life.

Guthrie watched the appalling spectacle of the rootless poor, battling among themselves, not for the pure kinesthetic joy of combat (as had been essentially the case with the lusty roughhousers of Okemah), but striking at each other out of the fear and panicky helplessness that always accompanies chronic want. "Men fighting against men," he wrote later. "Color against color, kin against kin, race pushing against race and all of us battling against the wind and the rain and that bright crackling lightning that booms and zooms, that bathes his eyes in the white sky, wrestles the river to a standstill and spends the night drunk in a whorehouse." The itinerant life, of course, offered its compensations, its moments of somber silence, its interludes of soft drawling talk among men of rugged decency and sturdiness of character.

As he followed his vagrant instincts, Woody's convictions gradually hardened to the temper of tensile steel and his inherited prejudices disappeared, borne away by the profound sense of involvement and brotherhood he sensed in all the down-at-the-heels humanity he encountered. The raw, abrasive apprenticeship of his early wanderings at last came to an end and Woody discovered his true calling. With the thorough reckless abandon of a man who devotes himself unreservedly to the service of a high and holy and exalted faith, Guthrie accepted his incontrovertible involvement with humanity and pledged his ultimate commitment to love:

All the riders on the train, seeing how pretty the night was, walked, trotted, stretched their arms and legs around, moved their shoulders and took exercise to get their blood to running right again. Matches flare up as the boys light their smokes and I could get a quick look at their sunburnt, windburnt faces. Flop-hats, caps or just bareheaded, they looked like the pioneers that got to knowing the feel and the smell of the roots and leaves across the early days of the deserts.

Voices called out and said everything. "Hi, got a match on you?" "Yeah, shorts on that smoke when you're done." "Where are you heading?" "Frisco! Going to ship out if I can." "How's crops in South California?" "Crops or cops?" "Crops." "Celery, fruit, avocado." "Well, work's easy to get a hold of, but money's hard as hell." "Hell, Nelly. I was born to working and I ain't quit yet." "Working or looking for work?"

There was a big mixture of people there. I could hear the fast accents of men from the big Eastern joints. You heard the slow, easygoing voices of Southern swamp-dwellers and the people from the Southern hills and moun-

tains and then another man would talk up and it would be the dry, nosy twang of the folks from the flat wheat plains or the dialect of people that come from other countries whose parents talked another tongue. Then you could hear the slow outdoor voices of the men from Arizona riding to get a job, or see a girl, or to throw a little celebration. There was the deep, thick voice of two or three Negroes. It all sounded mighty good to my ears.

During a respite in his wanderings, Guthrie settled in Pampa, Texas, where in addition to being reunited with his father and briefly returning to school, he eked out an uneasy existence as a fortune-teller, a room clerk in a skid row flophouse, and a sporadically employed guitar-picker in his Uncle Jeff's hillbilly band.

In his early twenties by now, Woody courted and married a local girl named Mary Jennings, and, as he pungently recalled the period later, the pair of newlyweds "lived in the ricketiest of the oil town shacks long enough to have no clothes, no money, no groceries and two children."

Drifting from job to job, Woody soon found employment as a "root beer vendor," a none-too-subtle circumlocution during Prohibition days in West Texas for the more direct term, bootlegger. Instead of serving soft drinks, Woody peddled them a lime concoction called "Jamaica Ginger," or "Jake," as it was affectionately known to the hardy souls that it didn't either blind or permanently cripple.

Always an inquisitive man by nature, the young hawker once decided to give the whole thing a try himself and so he singled out a bottle of the woolly brew. He told the story later.

One day my curiosity licked me. I said that I was going to taste a bottle of that Jake for myself, a man ought to be interested. I drawed up about a half a mug of root beer and I popped the little stopper out of one of the Jake bottles and poured the Jake into the root beer. When that Jake hit the beer, it commenced to cook it and there were seven civil wars and two revolutions broke out inside of that mug. The beer was trying to tame the Jake down and the Jake was trying to eat the beer up. They sizzled and boiled and sounded about like bacon frying. The Jake was chasing the little bubbles and the little bubbles was chasing the Jake and the beer spun like a whirlpool in a big swift river. It went around and around so fast, it made a little funnel right in the middle.

I waited about twenty minutes or half an hour for it to settle down and finally when it was about the color of a new tan saddle and about as quiet as it would get, I bent over it and stuck my ear down over the mug. It was spewing and crackling like a machine gun but I thought I best drink it before it turned into a waterspout or a dust storm. I took it up and took it down and it was hot and dry and gingery and spicy and cloudy and smooth and windy and cold and threatening rain or snow. I took another big swallow and my shirt came unbuttoned and my insides burnt like I was pouring myself full of homemade soapy dishwater and I drank it all down and when I woke up, I was out of a job.

At the lowest ebb of the Depression in the drought-stricken panhandle, Woody was broke, threadbare, and desperate for any kind of work. "I got a few little jobs," he recalled later.

Helping a water well driller, hoeing figs, irrigating strawberries in the sandy land, laying roofs, hustling sign jobs with a painter. I followed the oil towns as far West as Hobbs, New Mexico. I slept in jails when my kitty didn't do so good and then cheap hotels whenever I had money. I made everything and nothing from one cent to $54 in one single night and then the dust storms began blowing blacker and meaner and the rain was getting less and the dust storms more and more.

I made up a little song that went, "'37 was a dusty year" and I says, "Woman, I'm leaving here." And on one dark and dusty day, I pulled out down the dark road that led to California, citizens' groups, deputy thugs, mean harness bulls and vigilantes.

"The further West you walked," Woody recalled, "the browner, hotter, stiller and emptier the country gets. I met the hard rock miners, old prospectors, desert rats and whole swarms and armies of hitchhikers, migratory workers squatted with their little piles of belongings in the shade of the big sign boards out across the flat, hard crust gravelly desert. Kids chasing around in the blistering sun, ladies cooking scrappy meals in sooty buckets, scouring the plates clean with sand, all waiting for some kind of a chance to get across the California line."

Woody's welcome to the "Golden State" hardly bore out the lush tourist enticements cranked out by the Chamber of Commerce. Because he was an

Okie, and in many striking respects a living counterpart of Steinbeck's troubled dog, Tom Joad, Guthrie's first encounter with the West Coast police was curt, business-like, and prophetically indicative of his future relations with California law enforcement authorities. "Cop said, 'Keep travelin'.' I said, 'I was born traveling, goodbye.'"

To his consuming fury and disgust, Guthrie soon discovered that the callously exploited Okies rarely traveled far or fast enough to suit the state's bellicose authorities. Police brutality was notorious during the migrant invasion of California, and Woody witnessed his full share of it as he followed the citrus harvest through the verdant Imperial and San Joaquin Valleys.

By now, Woody was a seasoned and compelling performer, if not a conventionally polished one, and his talent provided him an avenue of escape closed to most migrants. In the next several years, he divided his singing time between a succession of sustaining radio shows on KPVD in Los Angeles and XELO in Tijuana and a series of grueling stints in the Hoovervilles and strike-embattled fruit orchards of Southern California. The period was a taxing one, an exhausting one, but it was also the most fertile of Guthrie's career. In quick-fire succession, he composed the thematically related and intensely moving "Dustbowl Ballads." Songs of the power and stature of "Tom Joad," "Rambling," "Talking Dust Blues," "Pastures of Plenty," "Vigilante Man," and "This Land Is Your Land."

However zealous, Woody's championing of the dispossessed Okies was by no means all triumph. During the period, he acquired his damning reputation as a leftist agitator—an inaccurate and degrading stigma which would later earn him the humiliation of official surveillance during the McCarthy era.

On the eve of World War II, his activities in California at a standstill, Guthrie deposited his family in Texas, borrowed $35 from a relative, and bummed his way to New York. Alan Lomax ran into him there on the Bowery, and as a field researcher for the Library of Congress persuaded Woody to record all the songs he could remember, as Lomax says, "on a pint of pretty cheap whisky." On the strength of his fiery performances for Lomax, Guthrie was soon offered the opportunity to record for the Disc and RCA Victor labels, but two commercial sessions proved little more profitable to him than the first.

Guthrie lived for a time with Will Geer, a by-then-successful actor whom he had met while barnstorming in the California migrant camps, and he later moved in with "Leadbelly"—Huddie Ledbetter—and his wife Martha and through the intercession of these and other influential friends, Woody obtained a number of bookings on coast-to-coast radio shows during the World War II years. Shows such as *Pursuit of Happiness, Cavalcade of America, Back Where I Come From.* But despite a brief flurry of popularity, the singer was annoyed and felt constricted in the rigid system of network censorship, and he soon turned away permanently from the arena of commercial entertainment.

From the proceeds of his radio work, Guthrie managed to buy a car and he got in it and headed west. His next employer was the Bonneville Power Administration. Guthrie was commissioned to write a group of songs in support of the federal agency's construction of the Grand Coulee Dam. Working feverishly, he composed twenty-six songs in thirty days, including the memorable "Talking Columbia" and "The Grand Coulee Dam." The building of the dam itself took a little longer.

And Woody later wrote, "I saw the Columbia River and the big Coulee Dam and just about every cliff, mountain, tree, post and every other angle from which it can be seen. I made up 26 songs about the Columbia and about the dam and about the men." The records were played at all sorts and sizes of meetings, where the people bought bonds to bring the power lines over the fields and hills to their own little places.

For Guthrie, the year 1943 abounded with turning points, perhaps most important his extraordinary autobiography, *Bound for Glory,* which was published by E. P. Dutton. Further, his marriage to Mary Jennings ended and the ever-restless singer enlisted in the merchant marine. One of his shipmates was a longtime traveling companion, the late Cisco Houston. Woody recalled later, "I was in the Merchant Marine three invasions, torpedoed twice, carried my guitar every drop of the way. I fed 50 gun boys, washed their dirty dishes, scrubbed their greasy mess rooms and never graduated up or down in my whole 11 months."

From his oceangoing experiences came several of Guthrie's finest songs. One was the mournful elegy for merchantmen torpedoed in convoys crossing the North Atlantic, "Reuben James." Another was the dryly understated recitative blues, "Talking Merchant Marine."

Near the end of the war, Guthrie spent a brief hitch in the army. He also married again. His second wife was a former dancer with the Martha Graham Company, Marjorie Mazia. Their first child was a daughter, Cathy Ann, whom

Woody nicknamed Stack-a-Bones and for whom he created a cycle of children's songs as puckish and as tender as Pooh.

These years, these few months after the war, were perhaps the happiest, most productive phase of Guthrie's life, but another string of disasters, like those that had plagued his boyhood, lay in store. For a brief period, Woody rejoined the Almanac Singers, the group made up of Lee Hayes, Pete Seeger, and Millard Lampell, with whom he had toured after his arrival in New York in 1940. The group's postwar interests and political affiliations soon proved too doctrinaire for Guthrie's taste, however, and he severed the connection.

Then abruptly and disastrously, his beloved Stack-a-Bones was burned to death in an electrical fire. Simultaneously, the progressive political upswing which followed the war fizzled out in the tightening tensions of the Cold War. The new epoch of red-baiting and witch-hunting broke out chilled and ashen as a glacial dawn. Now no longer could Woody and all the rest who had nursed at the fecund breast of the radical reform Madonna of the '30s so clearly discern the enemy. The world had changed. It had become in some ways, more simple; in others, less simple. And also, it had become, as many had begun to feel, somehow less worthy of salvation than when Woody and Cisco could sing with husky-voiced fervor, "There's a better world a-comin', don't you see? Don't you see? There's a better world a-comin', don't you see?"

Although he still composed songs at a phenomenally prolific clip, Woody began once again to roam across the country—but aimlessly now, almost as though he was saying good-bye to it. Jack Elliot, then a twenty-year-old amateur busker from Flatbush, and currently one of the most electrically gifted young American folksingers, attached himself to Guthrie and became his ward, protégé, and inseparable traveling companion. On one occasion, the two of them, accompanied by the old jazz tenor man Brew Moore, hitched their way from New York to California playing in skid row bars and anywhere else a crowd could gather.

Then in 1952, the long, clean melody of Guthrie's life faltered, cracked, fell into silence. Classified as a public ward, he was admitted to Graystone State Hospital in New Jersey suffering from Huntington's chorea. Occasionally, according to John Cohen, of the New Lost City Ramblers, Woody is allowed to leave the New York hospital, where he's presently confined, to spend a weekend at home with Mary Jennings, with whom he's become reconciled, or visit any of his children who might be in the New York area. But the dimensions of Guthrie's personal tragedy continued to swell.

Two years ago, his firstborn son, Will Rogers Guthrie, was killed in an automobile accident in California. "Woody's still a kind of overgrown kid," Jack Elliot told me. He paused reflectively, rubbing his hand across his face in a characteristic Guthrie gesture. "Those weekends when they let Woody go home with Mary, you know what he does? He eats candy bars and listens to records by the Carter Family." And Elliott thought for a moment with his face averted and said, "He's the greatest man I've ever known."

The literary achievement of Woody Guthrie is utterly unique in the annals of American literature. It consists of an undetermined number of songs (probably around a thousand) and *Bound for Glory* (reportedly condensed by the publisher from a million words to its present length of 428 pages), an unpublished anthology of folksongs assembled in collaboration with Pete Seeger in 1941, several edited volumes of songs, such as *California to the New York Island*, and a few rare pamphlets, fugitive articles and letters, and now almost unobtainable magazines published during the late 1930s and the 1940s.

To characterize such a heterogeneous output is, of course, well near impossible. For one reason, it's not yet all readily available for examination, but with regard to Guthrie's available works, one might do well to begin with Grandma Joad's observation, in *The Grapes of Wrath*, in a different connection, "Maybe it ain't nice for pretty, but it's nice for nice."

Commenting about his own earthy style of singing and playing, Guthrie once explained,

I can't play any chord by looking at any book and never could. I learned how to play the guitar by ear, by touch, by feel, by bluff, by guessing, by faking, and by a great crave and drive to keep on playing. If I'm sort of lazing it around, I'll leave out a few of the extras. If I'm scattering wild oats for my goats, I lay in a few more just to keep my string finger oily and limber. If I play with one other instrument, I do this way. If it's two others, I play some other way. If it's at a 16-guitar hoot, I'm forced by the law of nature and averages to naturally find some seventeenth lost part that nobody else is using and tickle around with that.

I won't say that my guitar playing or singing is anything fancy on a stick. I know that my voice is not one of the smooth writing kind because I don't want it to sound smooth. None of the folks that I know have got smooth voices

like dew dripping off the morning violet. I'd rather sound like the ash cans of the early morning, like the cab drivers cursing at one another, like the longshoreman yelling, like the cowhands whooping and like the lone wolf barking.

If Guthrie's standards of performance were unorthodox, so was the manner in which he created his chronicles of the Depression. One of his close associates, Pete Seeger, offers this recollection. "His method of composition was to pound out verse after verse on the typewriter or in his precise country-style handwriting and try it out on his guitar as he went along. Later the song could be pruned down to usable size. He put his rhymes to tunes, which were more often than not slightly amended versions of old folk melodies. He was often not exactly conscious of where he got the tune until it was pointed out to him. The songs were rarely written to order. Anything worth discussing was a song, news off the front page, sight and sounds of the countryside he traveled through and thoughts brought to mind by reading anything from Rabelais to Will Rogers."

Songs were composed for himself and for his friends to sing and he had faith that a good song would get around in spite of the music industry. For the most part, of course, Guthrie's songs are meaningless without the catalyst of his singing and playing to jolt them to raw, vital life. One can, however, get a clear sense of that exultant and lyric joy, not only by hearing someone sing Guthrie songs, but from one of the composer's own comments. He wrote,

I hate a song that makes you think that you're not any good. I hate a song that makes you think you were just born to lose, no good to anybody, no good for nothing, because you're either too old, or too young, or too fat, or too slim, or too ugly or too this or too that. Songs that run you down or poke fun at you on account of your hard luck, your hard traveling.

I'm out to sing songs that will prove to you that this is your world and that if it hits you pretty hard and knocks you for a dozen loops, no matter how hard it's run you down and rolled over you, no matter what color you are, what size you are, how you're built, I'm out to sing songs that make you take pride in yourself and in your work.

Guthrie's main achievement in prose is his freewheeling, Wolfe-ian autobiography, *Bound for Glory*, which recounts the major events in the author's life up to the year 1943. Without overstatement, the book is a little sublime, one of the great single American literary landmarks. One might rhapsodize over a score of the episodes. Woody's gradually dawning awareness of his mother's madness, for instance, is brilliantly accomplished, a masterpiece of abbreviated indirection.

Equally artful is a lengthy, graphic description of an adolescent gang war in Okemah, a deadly combat fought by boys with names like Buckeye, Sawdust, Slug, Rabid, and Star Navy. The emotional center of the book flashes and arcs to life in Guthrie's repudiation of a lucrative but degrading singing job at the elegant Rainbow Room in the high-rent district of Manhattan's Rockefeller Center.

In conversation, Guthrie once recalled, "They offered me a job at $75 a week. That was about $70 more than I'd got for regular singing before, so I said to myself, 'Boy, you got you a job.' But when they tried to rig me up in whiskers and a hillbilly clown suit, I ducked into the elevator and rode the 60 stories back to the USA. Made up a song about it as I was going down, went, 'Never coming back to this man's town again. I'm never coming back to this man's town again, singing, "Hey, hey, hey."'"

As he re-created it in *Bound for Glory*, Woody's rejection of the Rainbow Room job is akin to Huck Finn's resolute decision to suffer hell for Nigger Jim, an expression of uncompromising moral principle. Afterwards, Guthrie wanders along the Hudson River and hops aboard a barge resolved to resist his temptation to return to the Rainbow Room and apologize for his impulsive exit.

I drug my thumb down across the strings of the guitar. In the river waters at my feet, I could see the reflection of fire and kids fighting gang wars. Clara didn't look burnt and mama didn't look crazy, not in that river water. They all looked kind of pretty. I'd seen the oil on the river and it might have come from somewhere down in my old country, West Texas maybe, Pampa or Okemah. I seen the Redding Jungle Camp reflected there too and the saloons along Skid Row. I saw a girl in an orchard and saw how she danced along the mud bank of a river. Sail on little barge, heave on little tug, pound your guts out. Work, dig in, plow this river all to hell, it'll heal over.

Like the greatest American writing, Guthrie's literary canon constitutes a single, long, glorious cry of survival without compromise. A stubborn anthem of determination and faith in the face of unceasing adversity. It is the poetry of bedrock survival, stripped of ostentatious adornment, stripped of all puerile aesthetic affectation: "My belly is hard from hard traveling and I want more than anything else for my belly to stay hard and stay wound up tight and stay alive."

This is the testimony of a man who can sum up his aims by writing, "Let me be known as just the man who told you something you already know." In his *Paris Review* interview, Hemingway said, "From things that have happened and from things as they exist and from all things that you know and all those that you cannot know, you make something through your invention that is not a representation but is a whole new thing truer than anything true and alive and you make it alive and if you make it well enough, you give it immortality."

In his finest writing, I believe that Woody Guthrie gave us something alive, something truer than true, something ultimately immortal. Particularly now in these arid days when even the best of us seem to have compacted mutually to feign being what we are not, and probably couldn't be at our collective worst, Guthrie more than gloriously fulfills the obligation of greatness by reminding us of the extremities of courage and faith and unquenchable personal integrity.

In the beginning, I remarked that Guthrie is almost forgotten today, and it's true that his songs and prose writings are for the most part sadly, perhaps even criminally, neglected. Like it or not, agree with it or not, Guthrie's views are socially and politically out of season. Nonetheless, Guthrie as an artist has his admirers and in some circles his name already conjures up the unmistakable aura of immortality. Jack Elliot, for example, feels the obligation to Woody to perpetuate not only the older singer's music but his personal mannerisms and idiosyncrasies of speech as well, and as you're already aware, another young folk performer, Bob Dylan, has composed a moving tribute song to Woody. But there are other and even surer indications of Guthrie's steadily mounting stature.

Several years ago, wandering though the deserted depot yards of a small town in the northeastern part of Texas, I stopped for a minute to watch a freight train hauling out for Oklahoma. Something was written on the side of one of the clattering, empty boxcars and a blur of tears stung my eyes as I made out the sloping, painstakingly scrawled legend, "Woody."

In better and braver times than ours, Guthrie will undoubtedly be accorded more permanent and expensive honors, but until that day arrives, the stark, eloquent tribute I saw that day suits me perfectly. I'm fairly certain that given a choice in the matter, Woody wouldn't care in the least for anything more grand or elaborate.

Looking for Lightnin'

Village Voice, 1968

I.

Turning off the racing cabal of the Gulf Freeway a couple of minutes south of downtown Houston, I had my first glimpse of Dowling Street, main artery of the Third Ward and—so I'd learned after a hard day's night of marathon phone inquiries—home base for the legendary country blues singer, Sam "Lightnin'" Hopkins.

The neighborhood, once an opulent residential enclave, was now, in the summer of 1960, a black ghetto, shabby at the elbows and knees. Towering Victorian houses, sandwiched in among bleak rows of shotgun shacks and paint-flaking juke joints, still reflected some of the old, baronial splendor, but the baroque cupolas atop the weathered mansions had bleached and cracked and begun to fall and the ornate gingerbread lacing on verandas and spires was saggy with rot.

Locating the intersection where I'd been directed, I parked beneath the marquee of a theater featuring a triple-threat combination of horror thrillers and walked past a dry-goods store's sidewalk display of outsize denim overalls— "If They Fit You, You Can Have 'Em," a hand-scrawled sign challenged— back to the tin-roofed café on the corner.

The first encounter set the tone for most of the others to follow.

I opened the screen door, plugged with cotton tufts to ward off flies, and stepped into an electric-charged silence. Conversation died away without a murmur; bottles suddenly stopped ringing against glasses. For a long instant, the eyes of the half dozen cab drivers sitting at checker-clothed tables in the rear—any of whom, I'd been assured, could help me find Lightnin'—all turned my way. Then, with no appreciable movement, everyone was looking somewhere else.

"What you need, man?" one of the two waitresses inquired cautiously.

I explained that I'd driven in from Dallas to try to locate Sam Hopkins, a guitar player—

"Ain't no gittar player here," the second waitress said quickly.

"What you want to see this man about? You a law or does he owe you money?" the other waitress asked.

I explained I wanted to hear him play.

"What's his name again?" After I told her, she shook her head with finality. "Naw, there ain't nobody around here like that. You know any Tom Hopkins, Lottrell? Any you boys know him?"

Lottrell shrugged and moved off behind the counter. None of the men answered for a long moment. "Naw, I don't know nothin' about him," someone finally drawled. "I never heard of him, my own self," a companion chimed in.

"You come back now," Lottrell called out brightly to my back.

Outside, waiting for the light to change, I heard the café's jukebox begin to throb—a nervous, high-pitched boogie played without accompaniment on an amplified guitar. The song was as harsh and dreary in its dogged reiteration of a mocking, sardonic central riff as the urban slum where I stood.

Now and then, the guitarist injected caustic asides on his own playing: "Now ain't that *good*," he sneered, a note of self-parody in his voice, after a brilliantly intricate succession of volatile, ringing runs.

There could be no doubt about the performer's identity: I'd first heard him in '48 or '49, when, browsing in a grimy, secondhand record shop in Dallas' "Deep Ellum" section, I'd stood stunned with recognition listening to the raw, mournful guitar and a smoky, galvanic voice chanting:

> *I come all the way from Texas*
> *Just to shake glad hands with you*

It was Lightnin' Hopkins, the man I'd driven three hundred miles to hear.

When the song ended, I started walking east, laughing and looking for a likely place to resume the hunt. Midway across the intersection a battered jalopy whipped around the corner in front of me. On the rear bumper, inscribed in red tape, was the motto: "SON OF ZORRO—LOOK OUT."

Still laughing, I did, and he missed me a good eight inches.

II.

At night, Houston's Dowling Street, pulsing with jukebox music and flickering neon signs tersely announcing "Beer and Tavern and Dancing," radiates an electric musk—the edgy, sinister reek of something akin to violence held in too long and spoiling to explode.

But strolling east in the steamy afternoon heat as I searched for the fabled Lightnin'—passing a grocery with banana stalks outside, a fortune-telling parlor, a used furniture store, a string of dingy bars held together by a surrealistic patchwork of metal signs, the echoing galleries of ancient boarding houses, a church called the First National Tabernacle of Matthew, Mark, Luke and John, African—I was reminded of the small, islandlike business corners of the late Thirties, before the component-parts shopping centers. In an eerie sense, walking down Dowling Street was like retreating twenty-five years into the past.

Buttonholing passersby and shop clerks to ask about Hopkins I was repeatedly rebuffed. Several people refused to talk to me at all; others were studiedly vague or evasive in their answers. The reaction of a saleslady in a record store was typical.

With narrowed eyes, she listened to my questions, and at first professed to know nothing about Hopkins. When I persisted, she blinked innocently, puckered her forehead in feigned concentration and free-associated: "Hopkins, Hopkins . . . hmm, Harry, maybe? No, he was in the New Deal."

Trying to keep a straight face, I pointed out one of Lightnin's LPs on the rack behind her.

"Oh, that," she grinned amiably. "That's $3.98."

I had better luck with a chance acquaintance named Junco Red at a bar in the next block.

"Well, I be John Brown," he boomed when he heard my question. A wizened gnome with bloodshot eyes, he tipped his truck driver's cap at a rakish angle and wheezed a phlegmy chuckle as he swung around to shake hands. He had only one leg; propped beside him at the bar was a pair of yellow pine crutches. "So you're lookin' for Lightnin', is you?"

Yes, I nodded. Had he seen him?

"Has I *seen* him?" he exploded with laughter. "Why, Sam and me's like brothers. Him and me used to travel all over the country together workin' on the ray road." He pointed at the door. "That scoun'el passed this place not five minutes ago. Well, maybe it were ten, but I know it were soon."

He mentioned a café across the street where Hopkins traded regularly and suggested I check over there. "I'd go with you," he offered, draining his glass and winking, "but I'm afraid I'd freeze my heat."

I asked Red if he could describe Hopkins.

"What he look like?" Red thought a minute and motioned vaguely. "Be John Brown, man, I can't say. He be just a cat put his pants on one leg at a time like everybody else." Red stared down into his lap, looking at the empty trouser leg. "Just a black man," he nodded reflectively, "like everybody else."

At the café, a waitress pointed through the window to a dusty row of shotgun houses on the adjoining street. "Mr. Hopkins lives in either the fourth or fifth house," she said, "I'm not sure which." When I looked surprised at her help, she smiled: "What's the matter—the people along the street giving you a hard time?"

I knocked at the fourth house and a gaunt, impassive Negress, bearing on her hip, in the immemorial posture of the country woman and her "chap," a plump, sleeping baby, answered the door and eyed me warily as I explained what I wanted.

After I finished, she studied my face a few seconds longer and then un-latched the screen door to point across the yard to the next house. "This here be my place," she explained. "Lightnin', he stays over yonder. He be gone around the corner to the barber shop, if you want to wait." She waved at a man sauntering toward us from Dowling. "There be Spider Kirkpatrick now—he Lightnin's drummer, and he can more than likely holp you."

Thanking her, I walked to meet the small, dapper drummer. Dressed in a skull-hugging corduroy cap and tightly pegged "drapes" dating back to the be-bop period of the Forties, Spider moved with the poised, head-in grace of a jockey.

"Are you the cat he been lookin' for Lightnin'?" he asked politely.

I nodded yes and asked where Lightnin' was.

"Aw, he be around here somewhere," Spider drawled, glancing back at the intersection where a battered '54 Dodge was rounding the corner. "Some of them heads at the poolroom, they told me you was huntin' him, so I figure I'd come out and meet you . . ."

I didn't notice a poolroom, I told him.

"Everybody on Dowlin' seen you, whether you been seen them or not," Spider snorted with a short laugh.

The Dodge had pulled into the curb now, motor idling, about a hundred yards up the street. Because of the sun glinting on the windshield, I couldn't see the driver's face.

"Yehr," Spider mused, accepting a cigarette. "I been knowin' and drum-min' for Lightnin' ten years, and he be well-liked, I can tell you that . . ."

"Is that him?" I asked, motioning to the car which had pulled up abreast of us.

"Yehr," Spider nodded without looking. "That the man."

Stepping off the curb, I leaned in the car window. The driver was a thin, sinewy, middle-aged man dressed in rumpled slacks and a heat-wilted sport shirt. Draped around his neck in the manner of an ascot, a spotlessly white barber's towel contrasted startlingly with the deep-chocolate hue of his skin. Tilted over his eyes, he wore a jaunty, Sinatra-like porkpie, and mirror-rimmed sunglasses further obscured the spare, angular features of his prominent-boned face.

"Are you Lightnin'?" I asked him.

Chuckling, the man pushed his hat back with a lazy gesture and squinted across the seat at me. "Lawd have mercy," he said in a warm, raw rush of whiskey fumes. "I got to cop a guilty plea to that one. Yea, I'm Lightnin' Hopkins. What's happenin', baby?"

III.

Looky yonder what I do see —
Whole lots of 'em comin' after me,
But I'm gone.
  — Sam "Lightnin'" Hopkins, 1960

"You ain't just signifyin', is you?" Lightnin' asked warily. "You mean you come all the way from Dallas to hear me play?"

When I nodded yes, he searched my face quizzically and then slapped his knee and rocked back and forth with laughter. "Climb in this ol' hoopy, white boy," he crowed, leaning across to flip open the passenger door. "There's a little hell-dive around the corner that sells the coldest beverage in Houston town. Less you and me go over theh and get our heads all tore up."

Which we did. The head-tearing-up process, which was enacted in a succession of piss-smelling little beer parlors, wore on for days, at the end of which I knew considerably more about sour mash whiskey than I had counted on. But in the end, I also knew considerably more about myself, and the South (and that knowledge ultimately freed me to leave it forever), and my own forebears, who, like Hopkins in his young manhood, had been sharecroppers. Somewhere along in there, too, in those feverish, rushing days and nights of sweet, raw whiskey fumes and mournful guitar cadenzas — even as we shyly began to feel each other out over the clattering racket of the Dodge's hoarse engine — I realized with a dawning sense of wonder that the quest I'd initiated in looking for Lightnin' had begun long before.

In the years after my first exposure to Lightnin's music, the legendary singer had become a human talisman in my breviary of values, an associative touchstone around which clustered most of my precariously balanced, double-edged feelings about the Southwest. This was 1960, recall, before the Kennedys, before McLuhan and the Beatles, before the Mississippi Summer and Lee Harvey Oswald and Jack Ruby and Sirhan Sirhan and Chicago and — oh, hell. A time so remote, in retrospect, that it virtually paralyzes memory.

Texas had changed greatly since my childhood days when, striding beside my grandfather, I roamed the heart-burstingly beautiful dogwood trails of the lower Red River Valley. The transformation, roughly coeval with my own lifetime, hadn't all been for the good.

Much of the wilderness had vanished in the decade after World War II. The vast metropolitan areas spawned by the dizzying changeover from an agrarian to an industrial economy extended suburban purlieus into the countryside, swallowing up pasture, forest, limestone hills, even rivers. The homeplaces in most outlying rural districts stood empty and desolate. The part of Texas from which I'd sprung was now a dying landscape full of sere, brown cemeteries and decaying ghost towns.

The fact that urban existence differed from country ways wasn't what disturbed me. Rather, it was the haunting feeling that something basic, vital, and valuable had been lost in the transition.

Somehow, all of us in Texas, I gradually began to understand, had left behind the old fierce, personal capacity for love and anger that engenders and sustains tribes. Collectively speaking, we were all running scared and alone. Later, traveling and living in other parts of the country, I would understand that the referent "we" encompassed not merely Texans, but Americans at large.

Growing up absurd in the Fifties, as Paul Goodman had it, I found myself increasingly attracted to the few dwindling areas in Dallas that hadn't changed beyond recognition in the span of my own memory: the hustling, feverish Farmers Market; "Deep Ellum," with its bawling street singers and gaudy pawnshops; a rundown "back o' town" section with massive stone staircases soaring crazily out of the debris-strewn foundations of demolished Victorian mansions.

Invariably, I'd encountered the two most fully articulated esthetic expressions of my rolling, lonesome native country: the wild, fellaheen plaint of the hillbilly ballad and the brooding, archaic blues sung by men like Lightnin' Hopkins.

As time passed, I'd accumulated a piecemeal fund of information about Hopkins. I learned, for instance, that he was born and raised at Centerville, a small, dusty cotton community halfway between Dallas and Houston on U.S. 75.

Hopkins' records — many of them unmistakably autobiographical — spilled over with the texture of his life. From such songs as "Tim Moore's Farm," "Sad News from Korea," "Racetrack Blues," "Penitentiary Blues," "Short-Haired Woman," and a score of others, the patterned progression of his past and present emerged — from his earliest days as a sharecropper in the black loam country of Central Texas to his abrupt appearance in 1946 as a prolific recording artist ensconced in the night club and sporting-life milieu of Houston.

All the pungent flavor of his experience, I discovered, was hidden somewhere in the canon of his music: the country dances and Baptist Association suppers in Leona and Groesbeck and Buffalo Springs, where he first heard the harsh, intense poetry of singers like Blind Lemon Jefferson and Hopkins' own cousin, Texas Alexander; the cutting scrapes that followed the dances and the prison stretches that followed the cutting scrapes; the faithless, evil women he knew in both the country and the city as a hobo, a policy gambler, and finally as the cherished pet and musical idol of Houston's black underworld.

Yet it wasn't merely the cold facts of Hopkins' day-to-day life nor his anguished, esoteric music that accounted for my unflagging interest in him. Instead, it was the burgeoning realization that, lying at the heart of both his existential experience and his intense, personal creative efforts, there existed a working fund of values of profound significance for a generation such as mine, born circa Munich.

From Hopkins' music, I learned long before I met Hopkins himself something of the essence of the bleak, barbaric microcosm of his fallen and perishing world — and in the end I understood that he had come to full terms with it. Unlike many in my generation, he'd passed far beyond the lachrymose, self-pitying posture that accompanies a frightened, solipsistic preoccupation with survival. Accepting the bedrock necessity of unceasing struggle for existence as a simple, inflexible condition of life, he had summoned up the strength, courage, and raw marrow to forge ahead and confront a vaster dilemma: the problem of fashioning something outside oneself worthy of continued life.

At his creative zenith, Hopkins had given form and life to the kind of triumphant, victorious music that, after Faulkner's last ding-dong of doom has pealed, surely will come bubbling and ringing from the lips of the first human to ascend into the light again from his tangled underground lair.

Lightnin' Hopkins, I understood at last, had accomplished in his fashion as much as any man can do. With only one good arm and a splintered toothpick for a bat, he had coolly stepped up to the plate and knocked the concrete ball aimed at his head clear out of the largest goddamn park there is.

IV.

Houston—the South's first feverish megalopolitan dream—resembles a cocky, overdressed, temporarily successful club fighter showing off for a gallery of poolroom bums and petty chiselers on the corner.

In scant minutes, you can drive from the lawless, squalling strip of malarial bayou east of the downtown district, where nine out of ten cons discharged from the prison farms at Huntsville and Richmond congregate after release, to high-on-the-hog Afton Oaks, where oilman Glenn McCarthy's town house scowls sullenly out of a sunless clot of trees like a sybaritic weedhead who thinks the world owes him a lid.

Strolling along heat-shimmering Dowling Street with Lightnin' toward a cluster of tin-and-tarpaper bars, I was in Houston's "third city"—the black ghetto of the Third Ward. Watching our approach, a gangling, stiff-haired shine boy shot out of his cubbyhole rhythmically snapping his cloth. "How you, gate? Lemme put a glaze on them skates for you."

Hopkins waved him away moodily, a distracted frown on his face. "Naw, I ain't got no gig at a club right now," he was saying. "Me and John Lomax Jr.— you're too young to recollect Ol' Man John Lomax, which he got Leadbelly out of the penitentiary in Loozyana—me and John Jr., we got a revival out at California University, one of them little towns out there . . ." Berkeley? "Yah, that's the one." Hopkins darted a quick, troubled look at my face. "You ever go up in the air in one of them flyin' ships?"

I nodded yes. "Man, I ain't woofin' you," he sniffed emphatically, "I'm *scared* of them molly-trotters. Why, one of them flimsy little ol' outfits could crash and burn up in a minute, and then where'd you be?" After an instant, he brightened. "Aw, well, I'll worry about that tomorrow or the next day," he grinned, recklessly. "It ain't no hurry."

Leading the way into a dim, grimy lounge called Zito's Jungle Hut, Hopkins stopped, recognizing a thin, wrinkle-eroded woman in a maid's uniform sitting at one of the scarred tables. After my eyes grew accustomed to the gloom, I could see she was young and very drunk.

When Hopkins touched her shoulder, she stared at him without replying. "Get wheelin', Mottie," he ordered sharply. "Split your ass on outta here before the man comes along and sets you to pickin' peas." Still wordlessly, the girl rose and lurched toward the door. Watching till she was gone, Hopkins shrugged self-consciously. "Ol' Mottie, she all right," he explained, "but sometimes she get too much beverage to drink."

Maybe Mottie had—but we didn't—not in Zito's, at least. When Hopkins approached the bar and ordered, the waiter answered tonelessly, "We all outta beer today, man."

"What?" Hopkins asked, uncomprehending.

Looking steadily at me, the barman mumbled, "I told you, we ain't got no beer today," and turned away to begin mopping the counter.

Stunned, Hopkins spun around and, motioning curtly for me to follow, plunged back out into the sunlight. Shifting from foot to foot, he tried to dismiss the incident as a joke, but the more he talked about it, the angrier he got. The episode seemed to trigger some hair-fine edginess in him, and in the moments that followed, he grew increasingly morose, only occasionally breaking into abrupt, unprovoked fits of hypertense laughter.

"One thing that man's still got to learn," he grumbled darkly, inspecting the ridged, hairless skin on the backs of his black hands. "This here stuff don't rub off one way or another, you know what I mean?"

Our reception was more affable next door. A gaudily lighted jukebox played a slow-drag blues, and the husky, bald bartender greeted Hopkins as we entered: "How things shakin', Sam?" "Everything copacetic," Lightnin' nodded. "Hit us with two more of the same, will you do that, Curly?"

One of the selections on the jukebox was a song by John Lee Hooker. Curious to find out Hopkins' reaction to what I supposed to be one of his rivals, I asked him about Hooker's style. "Aw, he'd be all right," Hopkins smiled crookedly, stripping the label off his bottle with a thumbnail, "if he'd just woodshed a spell and learn how to play the damn gittar."

Uneasily, trying to stave off the awkward silences that began to develop, I continued to ask Hopkins questions. Gradually, he grew more spontaneous and animated—at one point, he raised his trouser leg to display the scars left on his shin by a leg iron he wore during a stretch on a Central Texas work gang—but it was clear that he wasn't over the depression anger caused by the ugly incident at Zito's.

"Tell you what," he said finally, cutting his eyes nervously around the room and scraping a raspy palm across his stubbled cheeks, "I never did get that shave I set out for this mornin'. I think I'll roll on down to the barbershop and get cleaned up while you got this cool place to wait for me in. Okey-doke?"

I nodded, sure.

"Won't take but fifteen, twenty minutes," he estimated. "Then I'll meet you up we'll go by where I stays at and get my box, and I'll hit a lick or two for you."

The jukebox fell silent. Swiveling around to watch Hopkins' tall, stooped figure move through the shadows toward the door, I wondered if I'd see him again and thought about the long return drive to Dallas, and then stopped thinking about anything at all and simply sat, waiting, watching Mottie, slumped half-hidden at a table in the rear, lifting and lowering her pint of Tokay until it rang empty.

V.

Oh, if it wasn't for lovin',
I believe this big world would come to a end.
But I want you to remember—
This world's gonna stand forever.
　　　　　　　—Sam "Lightnin'" Hopkins, 1960

Looking frail and worn, swaying precariously on the edge of the rump-sprung divan on his front porch after picking me up at the Dowling Street bar more than an hour past the time he'd promised, Hopkins opened the pint of bourbon, drained off a deep, hungry swallow, weighed the cap in his hand a moment, and then flung it far out across the packed-dirt yard. Twilight was settling and a faint, tangy breeze had sprung up from the direction of the Gulf, but Lightnin's face glistened with a sickly rime of sweat.

"Well, I done made it up in my mind," he announced hoarsely, picking up his guitar and striking a jagged discord that seemed to linger, brooding and tangible, in the wan light. "I'm gonna call John Lomax Jr. tareckly and tell him I ain't goin' to California nor no place else in no airplane."

He tilted the bottle again and a tic leaped in his cheek. "Ol' John's been good as gold to me, and I hate to jump salty on him, but when it comes to any outfit that goes up higher off the ground than a fast rattler, that's all she wrote for this mother's son."

Ducking his head and muttering under his breath, he began to tone his strings. Next door, a sullen-faced teenager with the wispy beginnings of a mustache and boot-shaped sideburns was monotonously bouncing a tennis ball off the dust-grimed wall. After a minute, Hopkins grunted irritably, and called out: "Hey, hotshot, how you expect a man to get this box talkin' American with you makin' all that racket?"

Taking his time, the boy bounced and caught the ball twice more before sauntering across the yard and leaning indolently against the banister. "You really think you're somethin' else, don't you, doctor?"

Hopkins stiffened but didn't glance up. "Naw I didn't say that," he murmured.

"Well, you ain't me, doctor," the boy drawled, "'cause I think you're somethin' else, and that's a fact." He reached over and flicked one of the guitar strings and Hopkins' head snapped erect. "You know, doctor," the boy said, calculating his shot before turning away, "there just ain't nothin' sadder in the world than a old hipster."

Wincing as though he'd been struck, Hopkins watched the boy saunter away across a yard and resume bouncing and fielding the ball. Then, lurching to his feet with a mixed look of terror and unutterable weariness, fumbling with the guitar and the capless whiskey bottle, Hopkins reeled off the porch toward his car. "Come on if you're comin', white boy," he called in a vacant, stricken voice. "I ain't got all day."

Revving up the Dodge's engine to a throbbing, feverish wail, Hopkins jammed down the accelerator before I got the door closed, and staring dead ahead, roared through the stoplight at Dowling, heading south. After he'd whipped around a series of blind corners and careened past a vast, desolate graveyard for junked automobiles, the engine began to knock, making the car pitch and buck.

"Sounds like it's throwed a rod, don't it?" Lightnin' remarked distantly, mopping moisture from his face with the barber's towel draped around his neck. "But maybe it ain't."

The pavement ended and the road abruptly dwindled to a single span of dirt tracks. The last house fell behind. In the middle of an open field, facing a motte of sycamore trees, Hopkins braked the hissing, protesting car to a halt. The engine wheezed once and died.

Wordlessly Hopkins started toward the grove trailing the guitar through the high scorched Indian grass. As I got out and started after him, a swarm of birds soared up from the trees like a pall of dark, oily smoke. Somewhere close by, the sound of running water rustled.

Hopkins sat down on a stump near the verge of the grove and cradled the guitar under his arm, and I stood a half dozen yards away. He had just begun to play when he heard the sound.

Rising involuntarily, all the muscles in his face working in frantic chorus, his fingers unconsciously sweeping the guitar strings, Hopkins recoiled in blind, panicky anguish as the jet airliner, climbing for altitude, swept straight toward us, its metal belly gleaming only a few hundred feet above the earth in the last, thin wash of light.

Then Lightnin' pulled himself fully erect, his fingers still ripping the strings, and cried out in tormented protest — not words — but a roar of mingled horror and triumph old as the earth itself.

After the plane had passed, Sam Hopkins of Centerville, Texas, remained erect and his fingers began to remember how to play mere music again, and I sat across from him in the warm, enfolding summer grass, rapt and grateful and listening very hard.

Hitting the Note with the Allman Brothers Band

Rolling Stone, 1971

Shortly before Duane Allman's fatal motorcycle accident on October 29, 1971, Lewis spent a week on the road with the Allman Brothers while on assignment with Rolling Stone. *He turned in his story two days before Duane Allman's death. It was the most controversial piece of his career.*

There are sixteen seats in the first-class compartment of the Continental 747 flight from L.A. to El Paso, and the tushy blonde stewardess greeting the boarding passengers beams the usual corporate smile until she does a fast snap and realizes that a full baker's dozen of the places are being claimed by this scruffily dressed, long-haired horde of . . . Dixie greasers. Her smile congeals, then goes off like a burnt-out light bulb when one of the freaks asks her matter-of-factly for a seat-belt extension and starts packing guitar cases — seven of them — upright into seat 1-D.

"Well, now, wait, I don't know," she stammers, fidgeting from foot to foot. "Who are you, anyway?"

"We're the Allman Brothers Band from Macon, Gawgia," Willie Perkins, the band's road manager, announces in a buttery drawl. He searches patiently through his briefcase and produces a round-trip ticket for the seat in question. "It's OK," he assures her, "we paid cash money for it. It's the only safe way to transport our gittars. We do this sometimes six days a week. Now would you please get the extension; please, ma'am?"

Reluctantly, the stewardess fetches the cord, and Willie finishes lashing the vintage Gibsons into position. Then, just before takeoff, he does a quick head count of the entourage to be certain that no one's been left behind. The members of the band — Duane Allman, Greg Allman, Dicky Betts, Berry Oakley, Butch Trucks, Jai Johany Johnson — all are present and accounted for. The three roadies — Joe Dan, Kim, and Red Dog — and the sound technician, Michael Callahan — all aboard. The proud bird with the golden tail lifts skyward to Texas.

By the time the No Smoking sign flashes off, both of the Allmans are fast asleep, their mouths characteristically ajar. Duane, whose nickname is "Sky-dog" but who resembles a skinny orange walrus instead, looks bowlegged even when he's sitting down.

Dicky Betts, alternate lead guitar to Duane, whiles away the flight swapping comic books with the bassist, Berry Oakley. Butch Trucks, the group's white drummer, pores over a collection of sci-fi stories by Philip Jose Farmer. Jai Johany Johnson, the black drummer, who's also known as "Frown," stares somberly out the window the entire trip.

Willie Perkins, wearing a faded Allman T-shirt, offers a fellow traveler a filter-tip and concedes that yes, there're quite a few hassles involved with being on the road almost constantly. "Coordination is the key to the whole thang," he says as if it's just occurred to him. "Gettin' all the people and the equipment to the right place at the right time. Then, too, I've got to mess with gettin' us paid, all that shit. These days the band averages about $7,500 a gig, and we don't ordinarily have no trouble gettin' our money. When the band was younger, though, playin' smaller clubs, sometimes I had to . . . well, *lean* on some of the shadier promoters.

"Sure, there's a bunch of headaches. Me, myself, I wouldn't do my part of it if it was just a pure-dee ol' gig. I wouldn't do it at all unless I really dug the band. Business-wise and musically, see, the boys are all equals. Unofficially, Duane is the leader — everybody looks to him for makin' the major decisions. Family is an overused word, I reckon, but here it fits just fine."

While a second, less nervous stewardess serves lunch, Willie points out the three married members of the group — Greg Allman, Berry Oakley, and Butch Trucks — "Greg just got married two weeks ago, was you aware of that? Yeah, sweet little ol' girl, too. But the wives don't travel with the band 'cept on special occasions. Everybody has purty well adjusted to the situation, you might say." Willie signals to the stewardess that he needs some help with his tray. "Would you fix this doohickey for me, please ma'am?" he asks pleasantly.

"You bet," she says, bending to the job. "Did you fellows play someplace last night? Everybody looks pretty sleepy."

Willie grins. "Naw, we was up all night, but we wasn't workin'. Truth is, we up all night purty near *every* night."

From the seat behind, Red Dog reaches forward to tap Willie on the shoulder, jostling Greg awake in the process. "Hey, brother," Red Dog asks Willie excitedly, "is that snow down there on them hills?" Greg squirms angrily in his seat. "Kiss my dyin' ass, brother," he mumbles. Willie peers out the window for a second and shakes his head at Red Dog: "Naw, brother, that's the desert. That's a right smart of dust down there."

As the plane makes the descent to El Paso, Berry Oakley squints down at the brown, hilly town. He nudges Butch Trucks: "Hey, my man, this is where the Kid got it, you know that?" Butch dog-ears a page in his book and yawns, "Billy the Kid?" "Naw, brother, that cat in the Marty Robbins song. Marty Robbins is my hee-ro, man."

Inside the terminal, after Willie and the roadies have rounded up the group's thirty-odd pieces of luggage, Joe Dan rubs his palms together in a parody of lustful anticipation. "Man," he crows to Michael Callahan, "I can't wait to put skates on the ass of some of these nice Texas ladies." Callahan tells him that the night's gig is in Las Cruces, New Mexico, and that they won't be in Texas more than a few minutes in transit. "Well," Joe Dan says philosophically, "they got nice ladies in New Mexico, too, I reckon. We'll put skates on *their* asses."

Under a lowering sky, the entourage crowds into two Hertz station wagons for the sixty-mile drive to Las Cruces. During the ride, Jai Johany plays lacy Afro jazz on a cassette machine, frowning, saying nothing. At the wheel, Willie reminisces to the fellow traveler about the band's gig on the last paid-admission night at the Fillmore East: "Oh, my God, the boys was hittin' the note for sure, brother. They smoked up the place till seven in the mornin'. That was a *great* place to play. The World Series of rock and roll."

In the backseat, Duane leafs boredly through a copy of *Cycle* magazine and grumbles about the group's travel arrangements. "It's a drag not to have your own plane, man. That way you could go where you wanna go when you wanna go. Jesus, I'm wasted." He falls asleep almost instantly, as does Berry Oakley. The wasteland miles roll past, and the first quarter-sized spatters of what will turn into a furious rainstorm blur the windshield.

Las Cruces is the kind of vanishing Western town where you can leave your motel room safely unlocked, except almost no one ever does because most of the people in the motels are from places where you can't leave anything unlocked. At the Ramada Inn, where the Allman ménage disgorges for a rainy afternoon of sleep, TV-viewing, card-playing, comic-book reading, coke-snorting, and pure listless boredom before the evening's concert, there is a stenciled sign on the door to the hotel's cocktail lounge. It reads:

N. Mex. Law:

ALL CUSTOMERS MUST WEAR
SHOES & SHIRT

Wearing neither, Dicky Betts sits in his room just before the show, strumming his guitar and softly running through the lyrics of "Blue Sky," a muted country-style air he's just written in honor of his Canadian Indian lady friend, Sandy Blue Sky. Joe Dan, one of the roadies, sits hunkered on the carpet across the room, sipping a can of beer, and when Dicky has finished singing, Joe Dan nods and murmurs respectfully, "That's hittin' the note, brother." Betts acknowledges the tribute with a sober bob of his head; he has just cut his hair short, and he has the kind of bony, backcountry face that calls to mind the character Robert E. Lee Prewitt in James Jones' *From Here to Eternity*.

"Hittin' the note," Betts muses, cradling his guitar snug against his bony chest, "it's kinda hard to explain to anybody outside the band. It's like gettin' down past all the bullshit, all the put-on, all the actin' that goes along with just bein' human. Gettin' right down to the roots, the source, the truth of the music. Lettin' it happen, lettin' that feelin' come out . . .

"See, we got a lotta blues roots, the old-timey blues players—Robert Johnson, Willie McTell. Myself, I do a lot of the old white country players like Jimmie Rodgers, some of those fellows. . . . Hell, I'm a big fan of Merle Haggard. The truth be known, I bet ol' Hag set down with his manager and schemed out 'Okie from Muskogee.' . . .

"Ten years from now? Well, I'll still be playing music. That's just in me to do. Where I'll be at or what kinda music I'll be playin' . . . shit, I don't know. Naw, this band won't be together by then. I don't see what point there'd be in tryin' to keep it together that long. Everything's got to change. The times'll be completely different. But I'll still be playin', somewheres or other."

There's a knock at the door. It's Willie Perkins, rounding up the boys for the gig. It's time to go hit the note.

But it doesn't happen this night. At the Pan American Center of New Mexico State University, a cavernous, sweltering-hot gym where the concert is scheduled to begin at 9:45, there's a forty-five-minute delay while Greg Allman's rented organ is located and installed on stage. During the wait, Greg and Duane Allman and Dicky Betts sprinkle out little piles of coke on a table in the backstage locker room where the band is sequestered and sniff it through rolled-up hundred dollar bills. Duane calls it "Vitamin C," and after his second snort, he buttonholes the fellow traveler in expansive praise of Betts' guitar-playing: "Brother Dicky's as good as there is in the *world*, my man. And he's gonna be *smokin'* tonight. Listen to him on 'In Memory of Elizabeth Reed.' Fuck, he wrote that fuckin' song after he fucked this chick on a fuckin' tombstone in a fuckin' cemetery in Macon. On a fuckin' *tombstone*, my man!" The other members of the band sprawl listlessly about the room on wooden benches, drinking Red Ripple and reading comic books in a tableau that will be ritually repeated every evening for the next six days.

When the band finally files on stage and Duane kicks off "Statesboro Blues" to a scattering of cheers and applause, the principal revelation of the occasion is that Greg Allman is not, after all, a stone catatonic, as he appears to be everywhere except in front of a microphone. His voice rises and swoops, circles and jerks the old blues staple to a frenzied, hair-raising climax that's explicitly sexual enough to be rated "X." The usual contingent of snowbirds and total-loss farmers, massed ten-deep in front of the towering amps, howl their pleasure — "Boogie my *mind*, motherfuckers!" a pudgy cockatoo in head-shop plumage screeches as the band runs through its more or less standard repertoire: "Elizabeth Reed," "Please Call Home," "You Don't Love Me," "Stormy Monday," "It's Not My Cross to Bear," "Dreams," and "Hot 'Lanta."

But the crowd in the farther reaches of the hall seems considerably less enchanted. For one thing, the sound is soggy at the rear, and a long-haired kid who says he's majoring in Police Science (yes) estimates the crowd as "25 percent freaks, 25 percent cowboys, and 50 percent who don't give a fuck." The band manages one encore, "Whipping Post," but halfway through the number the audience is busily streaming toward the exits.

Afterwards, back in the locker room, Greg Allman morosely doles himself out another dollop of coke. "I couldn't hear *shit*," he snorts, and snorts. "Sounded like we'us playin' acoustic," Dicky Betts chimes in disgustedly. "Coulda been a dynamite gig, too, man," Berry Oakley laments. "Coulda been, but it wadn't," Duane snaps. He sinks down on one of the benches, frowning. "I thank mebbe it was the audience," he sighs, "but then again . . . it coulda just been too much fuckin' coke. You know what I mean?" He snuffles and reaches for the coke vial.

Off to one side, Red Dog is whispering in the ear of the lone groupie who's shown up, a big-nosed redhead with deep acne scars. The girl listens expressionlessly, then finally nods yes to whatever, sucking on a joint as if it were the last sad drooping cock in the world.

Under Willie Perkins' persistent proddings, the Allman retinue is out of the Ramada Inn and settled on a flight back to L.A. by noon the next day. Again, most of the boys spend the travel time dozing or poring over comic books. Before zonking out on the plane, Duane shows Berry Oakley a crumpled letter he's just received.

"Know who this is from, brother?" he crows. "Ol' Mary ——. You 'member Mary? Man, I hitchhiked 2,500 miles to see that chick one time, and then her daddy caught me fuckin' her in the garage and threw me out. Sheeit, I'm still in love with that chick, man . . . I . . . thank." Within seconds, Duane is snoring, and when a saucy-hipped stewardess stoops to pick up his letter from the aisle, Red Dog leans over and says to her conversationally, "Honey pie, you got the sweetest lookin' ass I've looked at all year. Lawd, I wish you could sang: We'd take your sweet-lookin' little ass right along with us."

"Oh, I can't even carry a note in church," the stewardess sings out, flustered and flattered.

Red Dog is the undisputed king of the Allman roadies. He's been with the Allman Brothers Band since its earliest permutations—first, with the Allman Joys in 1965; then with the short-lived Hourglass, a West Coast–based studio group in '67; still later, when the present band was formed, principally from the personnel of the earlier groups, from '69 on. Red Dog was there toting instrument cases when the Allmans cut their three LP's to date—*The Allman Brothers Band, Idlewild South,* and *The Allman Brothers Band at Fillmore East*—and he'll likely be around as long as there are any Allman instrument cases to tote.

Right now, he winks slyly, orders three cocktail-sized bottles of Jack Daniel's Black Label from the stewardess, serves himself one, and pockets the other two. "Gawddamn," he cackles to me, "I gotta whole suitcase full of these leetle fuckers. Why not? They free when you fly first-class."

Rubbing his back, he complains that he feels achy all over, "See, I tuck and fell off the fuckin' stage last night while I was settin' up Butch's traps. One or the other of us is always fallin' off the fuckin' stage. And I got a pimple on my ass, too, man. Hurts like hell. This just ain't my trip, brother."

Teasing his scruffy red beard with a swizzle stick, Red Dog remarks that the band's success has brought some changes. "Aw, it's still fun awright, but not anywheres the way it used to be. Time was, we'd blow our last five bucks on a case of beer in Flagstaff or someplace. Now it's big bid-ness." He makes a face, then laughs aloud: "I still get off behind the chicks, though. Man, we get chicks ever'where we go. What really knocks me clean smooth out is to get head. Did I tell you? This weird chick was eatin' me on stage at the last Fillmore East blast. Naw, the audience couldn't see it, but all the boys could.

"Another time, in Rochester, I was standin' against the stage wall while the band was hittin' their note and some chick come up and unzipped me and started gobblin' me *alive*, man. The cat in the booth saw what was happenin', and he flashed a spotlight on us. Shit, man, I didn't know what to do. Three thousand people out there, see, but goddamn, it felt so *good*. I thought, well, fuck it, and I grabbed her ears and said, '*Let it eat!*'"

A black-suited, middle-aged limo chauffeur named Artie, self-styled "driver for the stars," meets the band at L.A. International Airport, helps Willie round up the mountain of luggage, and drives the boys to the Continental Hyatt House high atop Sunset Boulevard. During the ride, he prattles on cheerily about what groups are playing in Vegas and Tahoe, and he looks away discreetly as Duane snorts coke through a short-stemmed surgical straw.

At the hotel, Bunky Odum greets the group with bear hugs for all. A bluff, hairy grinner with a build like a crocodile wrestler, Odum books the band in the East and South and serves as second-in-command to Phil Walden, the Allmans' sharp young manager. In a poshy suite on the fifth floor, he seizes the fellow traveler's hand and pumps it like a hydraulic jack. "Gawddamn, boy," he booms, "you gonna have to come down to Macon and get laid back with us when this bid-ness is over. We'll take you ridin' on our motors and get you laid and feed you some *down-home collard greens.*"

In another suite on the same floor, Berry Oakley orders a meal from room service, then kicks off his boots and plops heavily on the bed. "Tourin'," he grimaces, "I'm gettin' just a little tired of it, but that's what I been doin' ever since I could do anything on my own. Started playin' gigs eight, nine years ago when I was about fifteen, and I been more or less livin' on the road ever since.

"I can't say what's gonna happen with the band. It could be somethin' great, and then again it might just go away like all the rest of 'em. We could do ten times more than we do, actually. There's so much that's in us that we haven't played. We're gonna have to start rationin' ourselves out, like goin' on the road and then goin' home and workin'. Lately it's been just goin' on the road.

"All of us like to play to an audience and get response back. That's what we call hittin' the note. How should I say it . . . Hittin' the note is hittin' your peak, let's say. Hittin' the place where we all like to be at, you know? When you're really feelin' at your best, that's what you describe as your note. When you're really able to put all of you into it and get that much out of it. We just found it out along as we did it. We learned some from the audience, and they learned some from us, and things came together that way. It happens, I'd say, 75 percent of the time. There's some special places we play where we've done it before, and everytime we go back, the vibes are there and it ends up happening again. We'll end up playin' three or four hours, and when we finish, I'll be so high I can hardly talk. When you start hittin' like that, the communication between the members of the band gets wide open. Stuff just starts comin' out everywhere."

Stuff starts coming out everywhere that evening at the Santa Monica Civic Auditorium, beginning with the little white piles of coke backstage. This time around, though, the acoustics of the hall are crisper, the audience is more responsive, and the band's music flows more smoothly, although there's little if any variation from the previous evening's program. The crowd bawls its approval, but begins to disperse after one encore.

Afterwards, there's a party like an open running sore in Phil Walden's tenth floor suite at the hotel. The booze flows, the smoke blows, the coke goes up, up, and away. Around midnight, a trio of female freaks, including a Grand Guignol–painted dwarf, crashes the festivities, chanting gibberish, doing stylized little dance numbers, groping cocks. Somebody says they're part of Zappa's grass menagerie. When the hotel manager finally flushes them out of the room, Dicky Betts nudges the fellow traveler and guffaws: "Haw! You better get out yo' pen and pencil and write down their names, my man!"

The next morning, while Artie and Willie Perkins are loading the black limo with luggage and instruments, Greg Allman sidles up to the fellow traveler in front of the hotel and palms off a plastic vial containing a quarter ounce of white powder. "Hey, brother," Greg mutters, "hold these goods for me till we get to Frisco, will you do that? I'm scared of them fuckers at the airport, man. They got them gun detectors and all, and they down on people that look like hippies."

On the way to the airport, more comic books and boredom. As the car passes the Super All Drugs, Butch Trucks cranes around to stare at a flamboyant leather dyke. "Well, theh's ya big city," he philosophizes. Willie is fascinated by the dizzying onrush of traffic. "These California people all got to be good drivers," he drawls, "or they'd all be dead by now."

Grover Lewis (right) arrives on the set of The Candidate.

At the airport, Duane draws Dicky Betts off to one side. "Did you hear them tapes of last night, brother?" he asks, shuffling excitedly from foot to foot. "Man, I was *inspahred.* Listen, we got to get at least six more killer tunes right away. My composin' chops are gettin' rusty. What say when this tour is over we woodshed and write for a coupla weeks?"

"I dunno," Dicky says, looking dubious. "I was thankin' about goin' to Canada to see Sandy."

"Aw, come *on,* man," Duane groans.

An hour and a half later, in a rented station wagon headed for what turns out to be a fleabag tourist warren near San Francisco's Fisherman's Wharf, Dicky is reading aloud the marquee billings along Broadway in North Beach: "Cal Tjader, hmn . . . the Modern Jazz Quartet . . . hey, Mongo Santamaria. Shit, I thank I'll bop in there and ast ol' Mongo when he's gonna record 'Elizabeth Reed.'" He double-takes at a sign above a topless joint that reads NAKED SEDUCTION. "Crap on that stuff," he wheezes. "I druther do it than look at it."

Pausing at the hotel only long enough to drop their gear, Duane and Greg and Berry Oakley race back to North Beach on a shopping binge. In a super-expensive leather shop, Duane freaks over a hand-tooled shirt with a colored panel on the front that resembles a drive-in theater façade in, say, Ponca City, Oklahoma; he eagerly pays $200 for it. Within minutes, he and Greg have dropped over $500 for a few shirts and trousers, and then Butch Trucks, accompanied by his slender, shy wife, Linda, briefly joins the group and buys a cowboy-style coat. Then Dicky shows up, looking for a maxi-length white leather dress for his Indian lady friend. After Butch and his wife have paid for the coat and drift on to rubberneck the bizarre upper–Grant Street mise-en-scène, Greg curls his lip derisively: "Shit, you see that ratty-lookin' coat ol' Butch bought? Fucker didn't even fit him."

Duane shrugs contemptuously: "His ol' lady probly put him up to it. She don't know shit. She made him buy that Dee-troit car, too, man, and he coulda bought a fuckin' Porsche for the same bread. Shit, man."

"Yeah, shit, man," Greg agrees.

The band plays for a near-capacity audience at Winterland that evening. Before the music starts, while Bill Graham's rent-a-goons are nastily hassling reporters on what seems to be sheer lunatic principle, Greg draws on a joint backstage and mumble-explains his concept of hitting the note: "Uh, achievin' . . . the right . . . frame of mind, man. You smoke enough grass, you'll get there. Uh . . . three joints, maybe."

Ten minutes later, Greg is squalling out the opening lines of "Statesboro Blues," and a joy-transfixed chickie in the balcony shoots to her feet in a writhing dance. "*Oh, baby,*" she screams, "*joy up and jump on me!*"

Early the next afternoon, enter the photographer, looking cheery. An easygoing zoftig lady, she's been promised a two o'clock shooting session with the band, but whatever else they're doing, the boys are *not* hitting the note today. Half of them, in fact, are still asleep at the appointed time, and to a man they resist being roused. "Aw, Duane and Greg'll do that, you know," Willie Perkins explains sheepishly. "They'll stay up for three, four days, and then crash like they'us dead."

Bunky Odum promises solemnly that he'll deliver both Allmans to the photographer's studio before the evening's concert at Winterland. "Gawd-damn, honey," Odum booms, "you gonna have to come down to Macon and git laid back with us when this bid-ness is over. We'll take you ridin' on our motors and . . . uh . . . feed you some *down-home collard greens.*"

But Odum fails to deliver on his promise that evening when both the Allman brothers balk at the notion of being photographed apart from the rest of the group. They seem, in fact, outraged by the notion. They seem, in fact, like cranky, petulant children, coked to the gills. "Fuck, man, we ain't on no fuckin' *star trip*," Duane snarls. "Naw, man, we ain't on no fuckin' *star trip*," Greg echoes. Trying to smooth things over, Odum arranges for the photographer to join the group's swing back to Southern California the next day.

Exit the photographer, looking addled.

Exit the fellow traveler, looking for a movie far from the madding goons at Winterland.

Sleepy and hanging over, the group assembles in the hotel parking lot the next morning for the drive to the airport and an early flight to Santa Barbara. Only Dicky Betts seems in high spirits; after last night's gig, he'd gotten a new tattoo at Lyle Tuttle's south-of-Market studio—a dove entwining the name "Sandy" on his right bicep. "Ever'body in the band got one a these, too," Dicky says proudly, pulling up his pant leg to show a tattoo of a mushroom on his calf. Willie Perkins nods shortly, "It's the band's emblem. We all got one, and we use the same design on all our litachoor, too."

Dicky catches sight of Duane and guffaws: "Hey, brother, you got coke all over in your muss-tache." Peeved, Duane rakes the white grains out of the hair on his lip and glares steadily at the photographer, who's snapping individual candids of the band members. When she moves in toward him, he turns his back with a growl.

On the drive to the airport, Berry Oakley is literally holding his head with both hands. "I run into this ol' girl last night who had a whole purseful of tequila," he groans. "Then when that run out, we got into some Red Ripple. *Jesus.*"

On the flight south, Butch Trucks reads the opening chapter of D. T. Suzuki's *Zen Buddhism.* "You read this un?" he asks Dicky Betts. Betts' eyes flick over the title. "Yeah, good, ain't it," he grunts. An hour later, one of the stewardesses remonstrates repeatedly with Duane to return his seat to the upright position for landing. Irritably, he complies, but when the stewardess moves on, he reclines the chair again, muttering balefully under his breath. "The boys are gettin' pretty tahrd," Willie Perkins sighs.

The band puts up for the night at the Santa Barbara Inn, a poshy beach resort for the middle-aged rich, where, once again, Duane refuses to show up for a picture session with the photographer. Looking positively shell-shocked by now, she pleads her case to Bunky Odum. "Goddamn, honey," he booms, "you gonna have to come down to Macon and git laid back with us when this bid-ness is over. We'll take you ridin' on our motors and feed you some *down-home collard greens.*"

That night's concert is held in Robertson's Gym at the University of California–Santa Barbara. The band plays a tight, subdued set that sets a gaggle of braless nymphets near the stage to jiggling like fertilized eggs frying in the ninth circle of hell, but the general ambience in the hall—high humidity, surly security guards, a surfeit of bum acid—gives the evening a jagged, unpleasant edge, and streams of people begin leaving before the set is done.

Duane and Dicky lope backstage afterwards to "do some sniff," as Dicky terms it. Duane grabs a towel and mops his streaming face while Dicky spoons out the coke. "Goddamn, I'm *sopped,* brother," Duane complains.

Dicky snorts the powder and bobs his head in pleasure, "Sheeit, my man, I druther sniff this ol' stuff than a girl's bicycle seat."

Jo Baker, a black singer with the Elvin Bishop Group, hovers nearby, eyeing the coke. Duane fixes her with a cold stare. "Looka-here, sister," he says loudly. "I'm sorry, but I got just a little bit of this shit left, so I can't give you none."

"Oh, that's all right," Jo says, looking embarrassed. "Sure, as a musician, I understand."

Early the next morning, "Frown," Jai Johany Johnson, is living up to his nickname in the hotel restaurant. Slurping a triple Gold Cadillac, which is a positively depraved concoction of liquor and liqueurs, he growls, "Bullshit, my man. I'm into playin' music, not this sittin'-around bullshit. Seems like when we was unknown, all we did was play. Now all we do is get publicity. . . . Ten years from now, if I be livin', I expect to be playin' music. . . . Naw, not with this same band. . . . I got my nickname, the full thing of which is 'Jaymo King Norton Frown,' from drinkin' Robitussin H-C, that cough syrup. It makes you nod and frown. All the cats in the band used to drink that shit, so they finally got me to drink it, too. . . . Shit, I don't know what my attitude is towards dope. I don't guess they ever gonna stop it comin' in the country and all that shit. Sure has caused a lotta hang-ups, if you can dig what I mean. . . . Hittin' the note is—well, that don't be nothin' but a phrase. What the cats in the band mean by it is . . . gettin' out of it whatever you're lookin' for . . ."

Bunky Odum has again promised the photographer that he'll line up the boys for some shots when the group checks out of the hotel, so she stations herself near the parking garage and nervously waits for them to show up. Soon, Butch Trucks and his wife join her, and Butch apologizes to her for the runaround she's been getting. "Aw, ol' Greg and Duane don't mean no harm, I reckon, but they still ortn't to act that a way," he mutters, looking pained. "We been on the road too long, I guess. It's been five weeks now, and you get awful tahrd and wore out bein' out that long, playin' the same tunes every night and all. It gets to where sometimes it ain't any fun. And this definitely ain't the kind of business to be in if you ain't havin' no fun."

One by one, the boys straggle out to the cars, again looking sleepy and hung-over. When they've assembled in a loose semicircle, the photographer explains that she'd like to get a group shot showing the tattooed mushrooms on the calves of their legs. There's some grumbling, but they begin to fall in line and raise their pant legs. Then Duane shakes his head angrily and stomps out of camera range. "This is jive bullshit, man," he rasps, "it's silly." "Yeah, silly," Greg echoes, and follows suit. "Jive bullshit," Dicky Betts agrees, stuffing his pant leg back into his boot. At my teasing suggestion that it's no sillier to shoot a picture of everyone's tattoos than it is to have them put on in the first place, Duane coldly offers to punch me out on the spot. Well, what the fuck, hare krishna; Duane is, after all, the walrus.

The entourage crowds into two rented cars for a tensely silent ride down the coastal highway to L.A. Along the way, Duane gruffly agrees to stop for a last try at the photos on a beach road. When the photographer tries to position the group around the cars so all their faces will be visible, Duane goes out to lunch entirely. "Fuck it," he bellows at her, "either take the fuckin' picture or don't take the fuckin' picture. I'm not gonna do any of that phony posin' shit for you or nobody else."

He's still grumbling and snuffling when the cars swing back onto the highway. "I don't like any of that contrived shit, man. We're just plain ol' fuckin', Southern cats, man. Not ashamed of it or proud of it, neither one. Ain't no superstars here, man." When he finally shuts up and falls asleep, the fellow traveler gladly crouches down toward the floorboard so the photographer can shoot both the Allmans with their mouths agape in the rear seat. It's uncomfortable for a few miles, but it beats the hell out of getting punched.

Quartered once again at the Continental Hyatt House on the Karmic Strip in L.A., the Allman group whiles away the afternoon snorting coke, reading comics, mounting a seek-out-and-buy raid on Tower Records, and watching

The Thief of Baghdad on color TV. When it's time for the evening's gig, Willie Perkins rounds them up and herds them toward Artie's black Cadillac limo for the half-mile ride down Sunset Boulevard to the Whiskey-a-Go-Go. "C'mon, brothers," Michael Callahan, the soundman, calls out as the band mills about the driveway, "they gonna eat you *alive* at the Whuskey-a-Dildo."

In the upstairs dressing room at the Whiskey, amid the usual groupie babble and turmoil, the photographer determinedly tries to shoot some final pictures. Politely, she asks a busboy to replace some burnt-out light bulbs in the ceiling. When the busboy fetches a ladder and the bulbs, Greg Allman saunters up and mumbles, "Don't screw that bulb in, my man. I like it in here the way it is."

"Please screw the bulb in," the photographer entreats.

"Don't screw the bulb in, man," Greg says to the busboy stonily. This happens a few times.

"Oh, screw it," the photographer says finally in exasperation and leaves.

When the band's set gets under way downstairs, the usually comatose Strip crowd yells its lusty approval from the first chorus of "Statesboro Blues." By the time Dicky Betts thunderballs into his solo jam on "Elizabeth Reed," people are standing on their chairs, yodeling cheers. As the band jam-drives to a sexy and demonic close, sounding not unlike tight early Coltrane, a flaxen-haired waitress is passing up draughts of beer to the screaming patrons in the second-story gallery. The beer is streaming amber and glistening down her bare arms, and the Allman Brothers Band from Macon, Gawgia, is—what else—hitting the note.

Stones Concert

Village Voice, 1968

Altamont Speedway, Alameda County, California — All across the scalded brown hills looming above this seedy, out-at-the-elbows drag strip located fifty miles northeast of San Francisco in the monotonous, sepia-tone wastes of the Livermore Valley, there hung in the already-polluted air the mingled odors of burning grass and patchouli oil, that heady, almost suffocating body scent so favored among the now-nameless nomads who used to be called the hippies.

In the course of the day — last Saturday — four babies were born in the midst of the multitudes assembled here, and an undetermined number of expectant mothers suffered miscarriages.

That evening, four people from the throng died violently, three of them by violent accident. The fourth, a still-nameless black man, was kicked and stabbed to death in full or partial view of a crowd that various professional head-counters put between 300,000 and 500,000 people — quite possibly the largest throng ever assembled for a rock music event anywhere in the nation, including Woodstock.

The immense crowd had come together, on less than a full day's notice, for the long-promised and often-canceled free Rolling Stones concert, first planned for Golden Gate Park, then scheduled at another equally remote racing strip in Sonoma County on the coast. On-again, off-again, it seesawed for a time, and here comes your nineteenth nervous breakdown.

As soon as the Altamont site was selected on Friday, the hordes began to arrive by the tens of thousands, virtually in tandem with the fleet of rented trucks ferrying in electronic equipment for the sound system and raw lumber for the stage. Early arrivals staked out choice vantage points in the parched grass near where the stage was being frantically erected in the natural amphitheater adjacent to the race track stands. The overnight campers found (1) no public water supply, (2) no stable food concession, and (3) scanty sanitation facilities.

On Saturday, I saw men and boys by the score urinating against a fence near the long queues leading to the line of portable johns.

With some friends, I arrived at the mingle, mangle, and jam of the amphitheater, well before noon. We'd had to walk four miles after a grinning California Highway Patrolman directed us into a parking space on a feeder road off U.S. 580 with the good-natured crack, "Rock festival to your right. It's outasite." Along the march route to the performance area, dope of all shapes, sizes, and colors was being openly dropped, smoked, bartered, and sold. The only police in sight were the far-too-few highway patrolmen, who were concentrating exclusively on directing the nightmarishly snarled traffic. Over a squad car radio came the report that a nude man had leapt into the line of traffic from an overpass on the highway, and required ambulance assistance. "I'm Mick Jagger's brother—ball me," a stoned kid bawled, groping at a passing girl's breasts. With a panicky look, she shoved him away and hurried on.

In the crush of the amphitheater, my friends and I found a place to sit perhaps a quarter of a mile away from the bandstand. I scanned the crowd with zoom-lens binoculars. The sheer magnitude of the gathering was awesome, and, as the day progressed, not a little disquieting. In the main, the audience struck me as benign, passive, and unutterably stoned. But more than once, I had the troubling feeling that if the mammoth crowd was itself capable of feeling anything on a mass gut level, the mass gut immediately devoured its own feeling, swallowed up its own capacity for spontaneity by its very enormity. It wasn't a good feeling to feel.

Sam Cutler, the Stones' Cockney road manager, took the mike a few minutes before noon to plead access for a truck attempting to deliver music equipment: "If all the cowboys will get off the Hertz van please . . ." A cluster of kids clung to the sides of the truck in order to get into the already perilously packed area near the stage; only a scattering of the easy riders dropped off as requested. Cutler shrugged and said, "All right, then, let's all have a party."

The speed-oriented rock band Santana opened the program. During the group's second number, which sounded depressingly like its first, someone hurled an empty wine bottle at the stage. Slivers of glass rained across the platform. The band's guitarist broke off playing and savagely cursed the heckler. An unidentified stage functionary took the mike to request that the Hell's Angels come on stage to serve as a security force. The Angels didn't hesitate; strutting and preening in their colors, lugging cases of beer with them, they swarmed onto the platform in a cadre forty-odd strong. At that precise instant, nobody — Sam Cutler included — could have had any way of knowing it, but the "party" was already well on the way to being over.

After a characteristically lengthy delay, the Jefferson Airplane followed Santana. Nothing, but nothing, went right for them. To begin with, it was one of their unhappy days to start off sounding maddeningly off-key. Then, just as they were beginning to pick up a little altitude, a nude black man, obviously freaked-out, somehow managed to clamber up on the apron of the stage. An Angel braced him, and the black man clumsily threw a punch that didn't connect. Four Angels kicked and beat the man to his knees and, still flailing at him, dragged him offstage. There was ominous surging and shoving in the tight-packed throng near the platform. Grace Slick crooned over and over, "Please sit down, people, please sit down." The band continued to play a mechanical semblance of "The Other Side of This Life," with Grace lividly improvising: "Find yourself someone to love, but don't fuck him around."

At the song's conclusion — it just sort of went away after a while — Jack Casady, trembling with emotion, snapped caustically, "Will the Angels please note that when somebody's freaking-out, you don't help him by kicking the shit out of him. I'd also like to announce that Marty Balin was punched unconscious in that little comic number you just saw staged and I'd like to say —"

At the rebuke, the Angels charged bullishly into the band. It was a sick, scary moment as fists flew and bodies blurred in a confused tangle. When the pandemonium ended, only Grace was left untouched. Sam Cutler grabbed an open mike and requested that all "unauthorized people" — meaning the Angels — leave the stage immediately. The Angels defiantly stood their ground. Somehow, the Airplane managed to get through "Volunteers of America" — dedicated "to all those people who wouldn't let us play in Golden Gate Park" — before abandoning the stage.

In the audience, a rusty-haired kid from Fresno shrugged fatalistically: "The Angels are just red freaks, that's all. Those dudes used to be heavy, man, but nowadays they're stone geeks. That's what reds'll do to you."

While the Flying Burrito Brothers rousingly jammed the kicks out of "Six Days on the Road," the nude black man reappeared at the border of the stage. The Angels made a halfhearted grab at him, but this time some friendly longhairs led him off in the direction of the medical tent.

Since I'd promised to call in a report on the day's doings to Howard Smith at WABC-FM, I went searching for a phone. I found one — exactly one telephone for perhaps a half million people — in the firm grip of a local radio newsman who explained that he couldn't relinquish it for a minute because, in addition to his own news chores, he was coordinating the helicopter flights landing and evacuating the performing rock groups. "Sorry, pal," he smiled wanly, and for a lingering moment I almost felt sorry for him.

In the medical tent, I talked to the physician in charge of the volunteer first-aid operation, Dr. Richard Baldwin. A pleasant, round-faced man who looked close to exhaustion, he estimated that his staff had treated three hundred bad-trip patients by the middle of the afternoon. "But the concert's not over, you know," he added in a soft, rueful tone. At the flap of the tent, a volunteer medic shook his head in incredulous wonder: "There's enough bad dope changing hands in this field to paint-and-paper the whole Haight-Ashbury. Even bummer brownies. Who the hell ever heard of bummer brownies before?"

On stage, Crosby, Stills, Nash, and Young began their set unannounced. By now, the platform was aswarm with more Angels then ever, despite Sam Cutler's earlier warning that the bandstand might collapse under their weight. At times, the swaggering bikers and their old ladies obscured the performers from view. Inching my way back to where I'd been sitting in the crowd, I took a quick personal inventory of myself: I was wind-chapped and sunburned and shaken by the fracas on stage and more than a little pissed-off that I'd have to drive all the way to Tracey, a ranching town fifteen miles away, just to make a simple goddamn phone call.

The concert's organizers had promised to conclude the program before dark, but the sun went down about 4:30 and there was no sign of the Stones. The crowd began to thin out, but not in large numbers. The Angels stood in a solid phalanx across the front of the stage, arms akimbo, glowering at the audience. Cutler announced, "The Stones positively won't come out to perform while the stage is in its present state." "Get off the stage, get off the stage!" a sizeable portion of the crowd began to howl. None of the Angels budged, and the cry soon faded away.

After another tense delay, Cutler reappeared and surveyed the audience for a long, grave moment before saying simply, "I'd like to introduce your friends, the Rolling Stones."

It was full dark now, scores of bonfires were flickering on the trash-strewn slopes, everybody present was standing and craning, and suddenly the Stones were before us in a dazzling burst of noise and lights, Mick Jagger bumping and grinding in exquisite nastiness and rasping out "Jumping Jack Flash." For

Grover Lewis (left) and Jesse Ritter in Lewis's Rolling Stone *office in San Francisco in the early 1970s. Ritter, a faculty member at San Francisco State University, and Lewis edited* Focus: Media *together.*

the first time of the day, the day seemed to have some significance. A frail young girl in wire-rimmed glasses standing near me in the crowd sang and danced in near-delirium: "Oh, Mick, I love you—you make me so excited! Everybody in the whole world is watching us—even God!"

After the song, an Angel attempted to block Jagger's path to the edge of the stage. Jagger stepped around him. "There's so many of you," he said admiringly to the audience. "Stay cool now, and try not to move around too much."

The prelude to the final trouble came a third of the way through "Sympathy for the Devil." Apparently angered by hecklers in the first few rows, a half-dozen Angels swan-dived off the stage into the audience and began whipping heads. The music stopped abruptly. In a pleading voice, Jagger, who was wearing a long, red robe, cried: "Everybody, brothers and sisters, cool out, listen to me, please cool out. . . . Is anybody hurt? Who's fighting, and what for? We've got to stop this trouble right now." After a few confused moments, the music resumed.

At that point, my friends and I gladly left the amphitheater so I could make my phone call in Tracey, which I did, which in turn threw us back into the heart of the postconcert bumper-to-bumper turtle derby headed toward Livermore and the city two hours later. It took us three hours to travel twenty-five miles. On the radio, we heard that the freaked-out black man the Angels had stomped had made his third and final appearance at the concert stage. The poor bastard had gone off somewhere and gotten himself a piece, and then he'd gone back and gotten himself kicked and cut to death for his trouble.

When we reached the Alameda County line, about a mile north of the amphitheater, I spotted a teenaged girl wrapped in a poncho sitting alone on the shoulder of the highway. Something about her posture made me get out of the barely moving car to see if she needed a ride. She didn't raise her head at the question. "Mister, I don't need a ride," she said in a thick, stoned slur. "I need to go to a hospital." Involuntarily, her hand twitched out from under the poncho. Apparently she'd lit a cigarette sometime back, and then forgotten about it. Her fingers were on fire.

The Wreckage Children

From *I'll Be There in the Morning, If I Live*, 1973

Must I go,
Or must I shake 'em on down?
Gettin' so tired of haulin'
I believe I'll shake 'em on down.

—FURRY LEWIS

Take this cup from me:
I am able only to say the Wrong Thing.

—DONALD COTTON

Consider the distances we've run,
All the fevers and hungers we've endured.

(THIS IS TIME PASSING/HISTORY'S
    GRASSHOPPER LAUGHTER.)

What feasts we've been
    to each other,
And how barren a harvest;
How touching and terrible
That we've loved each other
    so hotly
And wasted ourselves so coldly.

Victims/lovers/travelers,
Ravaged pistils/junk children,
Dope monsters/American Moorsoldaten:

I think we must be
    The end of a world.

To dole out my pulpit's passion,
Feed my blood's bread
    to the rushing travelers
Has been my vanity/my lust,
    my aching lovelessness . . .
Now I leave all that cold time behind;
I shut my windows and steal away.

—Oh yes/kind friends/I have to leave you
And I bid you all goodbye.
Oh yes/I know you all are hungry
But/my darling friends/don't cry.

Sweet bruised stalks,
Lovely stricken blossoms,
The nature of the pandemonium flower
Is to bloom and flake
In drowning silence,
Exploding finally in a thin wisp
Of equivocal dust:
    —Ah-ah-ah-ahhhhh-uh-uh.
Antonioni could scald the eye
    with the black process,
But his jet vapor-trails are horror enough —
. . . Sticks lifted over a dying dog.

—I am now traveling on the geography
    of my temper.

What an indictment a man's face
    can come to be —
A ruined contour map of remorse,
    a white blur of fatality.

Reiser says I look like an American,
    but I've wept

Seeing myself suddenly in mirrors.

Sorry truth/I'm tired and broken
  and without hope.
My milky engine no longer stirs and arcs
  in the dark drip of trees:
I hear no more horn music from windows
  and overcoats;
My mind is bitter and rank as a mushroom's
  muscled heart—

Only my eyes continue to rave.

The scene changes/but nothing actual changes.
Memory is a succession of perishing Happenings.

SHOOTING SCRIPT FOR A POST-EXISTENTIAL NEWSREEL:

Some drenching time in fugitive doorways
  (those gaudy tightwire orgasms the Swede
  and I stole from the snatch
  of the old tragic whore);
Mirrors and muscatel
  (—Religion lasted three months,
  Balzac jeers):
Cruising the gangster mudtracks of Backotown
  (pissing in the blind eye of a
  Plymouth under a come-stained
  poster of James Dean):
Whirling in dumbshows on the dark edges of towns
  (someone's upraised thighs
  in a cottonfield . . .):
Trembling in profane cathedrals
  (wailing beyond anguish in the
  lynched Wobbly Hall in Houston):

—And always/all of us stabbing each other
  with sex and pills and music
  like knives,

And always the wild orange trucks
 of my Southland,
And always our wild young faces pitted
 with old volcanic burning.

O FATHER / MY GAUNT FATHER,
 THE GROIN STIRRINGS OF 19-
 42 ARE NOT YET RENDERED.

Three hours wandering alone
In the maple-hazed streets
Of Backotown / smoking and
Praying; then a raw mug of
Coffee at desolate Rafael's
Near the market / weeping.
Afterwards / high / reeling
In panic through the feral
White dusk / the dog quiet,
The black glass of eyes:

 Prowling south on the Main
 To score for dex / I run the
 Gauntlet of grifters and
 Losers / all the enamel-eyed
 Zombies of the lush fringe.
 They snake out scabby claws,
 Hustling me for change;
 If my father had survived
 Himself / he'd be there among
 Them now / lustrous as shattered
 Bone in the dead arcade light:

Outside Texas Ted's Cafe,
The old Negress plays the
 Soprano saxophone / a slow,
 Foamy rocking sound / pat-
 ting her foot in its raggy

Man's shoe. Her husband blows
A scored electric guitar,
Using a half-closed jack-
Knife instead of picks.
His pink eyes bleed
Out of the barbecue ruts
In his face. As I stand
And watch/the two of
Them collect $2.71 and
Three immortal souls.

I voyaged across the prairies
To my grandfather's grave,
Solitary in the pregnant
Bursts of country trees,
The ghost of smoke/the
Floating music of long-distance
Trucks and diesel whistles.
WILLIAM MEDFORD LEWIS . . .
1872–1959 . . . a good man
Passed up. Wretched and awash
In my thin bones/I lay in
The Indian grass and sobbed at
What he'd make of the strange,
Rootless wanderer I've become.

Always loneliness
 and
Lean traveling —

And once/in winter/hurting
 very fast
I tasted my face turn blue.

(This is time passing,
 I tell you,
History's grasshopper laughter;

Survival can become
        merely an addiction,
A numb wringing of hands.
History's grasshopper thirst . . .
Now I yearn for well water,
        Ache to halve peaches
Into spring water
In my grandfather's bucket
Under our vast/hundred-year elm,
        where Indians once
Dreamed/dreamed . . .
But I pity none of us,
        can you understand?
None of us —
No more than I pity
        that ritual hill
Where we sometimes stumble
To watch the world come back,
To hear the dawn improvised
        by birds
And dim/neighing horses.)

— Dr. Bigelow's formula was,
that fevers are self-limiting;
afterwards that all disease
is so; therefore no use in
treatment. Dr. Holmes said,
No use in drugs. Dr. Samuel
Jackson said/Rest/absolute
Rest/is the panacea.

Wrecked at midnight,
I lurch through the still rooms,
Blindly touching the stigmata
Of old dream friendships:
A collage of Doolittle's
        another of Nolan's;

Jo's blue self-portrait,
And the brutal mugshot of Prez
    brooding in the house of mirrors . . .
The dumb and dusty spines of books:
    Trocchi/Mailer/Marx,
    Wieners/Sigal/Freud,
    Brammer/Rechy/B. Traven,
    McMurtry/Reich/Meltzer—

—So the heritage passed on
to me/poor hope/and the
little object as well/and
I went out into the world.

Claudia is right:

—Everything has become so terribly simple.
In our years in the wet,
History absolves no one/nothing:
History reduces to neon graffiti,
    paying dues/night watches,
    double-bill horror movies,
    exiles/departures/terror
    sweats/the ruined snapshots
    and poison pen letters of time:
History is the suicide of philosophy;
It ends like Seneca,
Or the anabatae in the Circus Maximus,
And reappears in duello scrawls
    on pisser walls
In fetid highway taverns:

—VIVA LA REPUBLICA!
ABAJO EL PUTO FRANCO!

—HAVE YOU SENT YOUR CONTRIBUTION
FOR THE STAN MUSIAL MONUMENT?

—RED CAMPS
WAGE WAR
OVER PEACE
—LONNIE F. X. VON SPIDER LIKES TO
STROKE RABBITS AND SMELL FISH

—WHAT ARE WE GOING TO DO
ABOUT THIS MAN CALLED JESUS?
—BLOW HIM

— OH LORD/REVIVE THY CHURCH
BEGINNING WITH ME

In Backotown/where I once twisted
     and burned and exorcised ghosts,
There are eerie stone stairways
     winding up to nothing.
Gazing down from the rubble-strewn landings,
You see the scalded traces
     of gingerbread mansions,
Long since moved or destroyed,
Smell the raw reek of ironing
     and harried women,
Listening to noonday radios . . .
Hanging there once on the heights,
Chilled with recognition,
I heard the enraged squall of the child
     who'll one day kill me,
Or wish he had.

For the benefit of those
Who first prize my pelt,
Then shred it to loose hair
     in wanton vengeance:
I am a lover/a hater,
A mystic/an existentialiste,
A blackhaired wandering American,

An illuminated manuscript,
A frothy scum of names/shrouded glances,
   faces;
I've been heard to mutter
   Fuck you/darling,
And mean it;
I bleed most copiously for cannibals,
Unknown to themselves
   and their mothers;
I am a chattering emptiness of love,
A frozen sonofabitch in my heart,
A boiling sea of compassion:

   I forgive nothing.

Tatting together the rotting skeletons
   of hillbilly songs,
I invented humanity at the age of eight;
I've built cities in my sleep.
In my young manhood,
I lay in ambush for myself
   but never appeared;
Became a catalyst instead of a novelist,
A teacher of Engel-ish to mixed groups
   of all sexes.

Like all revolutions,
I was betrayed from within.
. . . What remains is the shape
And the ash
   of my old gone dreams,
The distances,
The iron stub of my tongue,
A haunt of guitars,
The shards and naked bones of poems.

American in the marrow,
I was an un-American boy;

Looked for my father in the smoky streets
    of Melville/the lilac-yards
    of Whitman;
Found my mother in fugitive expression;
Learned my green iconography
    on the wet wood of porches,
    under the yelling cottonwoods
    of Backotown;
Spent my passion wantonly;
Fought the bears and tigers of dreams;
Kissed hell on the mouth;
Fucked girls in the cock/mouth/teats;
Smoked shit in underground attics,
    thinking: — Roualt once painted
    these same stricken clowns in
    another moment of failing light.

I expected too much
And hoped for nothing.
Now/to keep from shaking to pieces
Is the only problem.
Still . . . I'm somehow a survivor
    of all this —
Like one of those swelling staircases
    in Backotown.

What complex/pointless machines
We make of ourselves.
Do you recall that ugly sign of distress,
    when/burning to the ground,
We entreat each other in gray terror:
— Are you all right?
ARE YOU ALL RIGHT?
Yes. No.
There is no word to suggest the imprecision.

The scene changes/but nothing actual changes.
Nothing good enough can happen.

    Bruised fruit/trampled chaff
    Of my gnarled generation's bloom:
    Victims you fell.
    Victims/lovers/travelers,
    Ravaged pistils/junk children.
    Dope monsters/American Moorsoldaten:

All our fathers are psychopaths,
    the lees and scum of what
    could have been a country
    of men;
All our mothers the pale memories
    of blowing taffeta dresses . . .

I tell you/there is no use talking
    about it any more:
Tribes fall and die.
Victims you fell,
The climacteric of a mad fever,
And when in new-orphaned grief
You made my arms a womb
And rushed breasts agate with loss
    to my straw bones,
I was vacant and mute as an old man
    feeling crumb pockets
For the times of trains that came
    and left a life ago.

Does it matter that fish and history
Murdered in all our bowels
    since infinite fathers?
Or that dream and reality,
    those caul-spring siblings,

Only meet to do cold love
  in colder places?

Categories—what degrading pigshit!

Only this/then:
Be mad/be insane!
If a level man prowled in these shadows,
He'd hemorrhage in his deep throat,
  flame his lungs red
  with insatiate laughter.
So go hobbling crazed on salt-and-pepper legs,
And if it's in you/do your things.
It isn't weakness/but absolution,
To know that nothing is fixed
  and that nothing changes.

  O bitter boys,
  Withstand this day.
  O bitter boys,
  Going away,
  Let me sweeten
  Your wounds.
  O summer/let me
  Endure your clawings,
  Drive these bones.

If it's in you/do your things:
There are no reasons,
There are no motives,
There are no rewards,
There is only blood pulsing
  and no explanations.

  O LORD/REVIVE THY CHURCH
  BEGINNING WITH ME

  Sing the song/children.

Goodbye If You Call That Gone

From an uncompleted memoir, 1994

Everything in nature is lyrical in its ideal essence, tragic in its fate,
and comic in its existence.

—GEORGE SANTAYANA

History and legend bind us to the past, along with unquenchable memory.

In the spring of 1943, my parents — Grover Lewis, a truck driver, and Opal Bailey Lewis, a hotel waitress — shot each other to death with a pawnshop pistol. For most of a year, Big Grover had stalked my mother, my four-year-old sister, and me across backwater Texas, resisting Opal's decision to divorce him. When she finally did, and when he finally cornered her and pulled the trigger as he'd promised to do, she seized the gun and killed him, too.

A next-door neighbor of Opal's — called "Dad" North because of his advanced age — witnessed the mayhem shortly after dawn on a rainy Monday morning in May. Big Grover was twenty-seven years old, Opal twenty-six, and they'd been married for almost eleven years. My father survived for half a day without regaining consciousness, and died in the same charity hospital where I was born. Opal died where she fell, under a shadeless light bulb in the drafty old rooming house where she'd been living alone and struggling to keep Titter and me in a nearby nursery school. No charges were filed, and a formal inquest was considered unnecessary since the police and the coroner's office declared the case solved by mid-morning. My uncle Dubya Cee, Opal's older brother, talked to one of the detectives involved and found out some additional information, which he shared only with the Bailey elders. Such, anyway, were the bare bones of the story as passed along in family history that soon blurred off into murky family legend. It was the sum of what I was allowed to know, although there remained to be answered, of course, questions I had not yet learned to ask.

Grover and Opal were strong, attractive, hardworking people with no history of wrongdoing. They'd started out as Depression kids who'd eloped from the working-class district of Oak Cliff in Dallas, where they'd both been youthful friends of the notorious Southwestern desperadoes Bonnie Parker and Clyde Barrow, who'd died in a police fusillade six months before I was born. Like Clyde, my father was an unschooled country jake who fell — or jumped — into low ways in the big city. Big Grover and his two older, rakehell brothers, Lester and Cecil — "Leck" and "Cece" — had been coughed up by the dust storms of the 1930s and were among the first generation of Texas boys to grow up without the idea of the American West beckoning them to fortunes untold. By their time, America was "all took up." Opal, like Bonnie, was a bright student who'd left school early to help support her family before meeting and running away with her first true sweetheart — a moral girl, everybody agreed, with high ideals. Like Bonnie's, Opal's main crime seems to have been picking the wrong man to love. In the end, she managed to save my father from everybody but himself.

The fatal events took place in my hometown of San Antonio when I was eight. By then, I had experienced at first hand such a numbing amount and so many varieties of violence that I was left with the choice between an invitation to death and the will to live. My sister, still only a toddler, was almost oblivious to the calamity and would forget our parents completely within a year or so, but complex guilt and mourning and survivor's self-loathing gnawed at me without letup. In my foreshortened child's perspective, I worried about my own culpability in the bloody strife that had descended on us, overcome with remorse that I might have been more watchful, that I ought to have tried even harder to protect Opal and stave off our fate. In the secret, nonverbal chamber of the heart where unquenchable memory takes root in childhood, I knew many things on a dim level — but I knew them well enough. In our year on the run and its desperate aftermath, I had stored up memories I couldn't get rid of and memories I wouldn't let go, including the awful knowledge that Opal had been betrayed by one of our own family circle — that news of our whereabouts had repeatedly been passed along in secret to Big Grover in his darkening rage by a man who had often sat at our table in happier times and pretended to love us all. In an icy flash, I understood the horrifying extent to which life is shaped by chance and happenstance, and how abruptly the unexpected can strike and obliterate everything you most cherish. Chaos, I sensed, lay hidden beneath the superficial order of the normal, where the solid rules of right and wrong were displaced by treachery, corrosive passion, and sudden death. I was, you must understand, just at the threshold of the age of reason, trying to sort out for the first time without Opal's help the possibly true from the wildly improbable.

With Big Grover commonly understood to be the wrongdoer and the case closed, the bereaved families assembled to pay their respects, some missing a day or two's work and driving in from such distant points as Dallas, the Red River Valley, and rural Oklahoma. The mourners made over Titter and me with tears and smothering hugs, but their faces, normally stoic and set, were seized with grief, astonishment, and anger that soon turned to muted discord, at least on the part of my mother's people. Some wounds of the heart never heal, but leave a shadow and a scar and a family stain that even crushing sorrow can't ease.

Matthew Bailey, Opal's hot-tempered father, caravaned into San Antonio at the head of a posse of Baileys, all armed and bristling. When Matthew was notified by the police about Opal's death, no mention was made of Grover's condition, so the old man rounded up his clan with the idea of hunting down Grover and evening the score in the old-fashioned frontier way. At joint services held for Opal and Grover at a neighborhood funeral parlor—caskets were open for viewing—Matthew and his band stalked outside when the Baptist minister began intoning the obsequies for my father. The few Lewises present shifted uncomfortably and looked abashed—crushed, in fact—but they were, I am certain, just as aggrieved by Opal's loss as by Grover's, and despite the tenuous connections between the two families, they must have realized that Matthew was hopping crazy even on his best behavior. Later—I felt like I remembered it, but maybe I was just told—it struck me that Matthew and some of his brothers and sisters were actually glad that Opal had dropped her killer, proud of her grit and nerve and sure aim. Big Grover had been shot just once, squarely in the eye.

Because of my age, I wasn't supposed to know or even find out such things, but the details, usually meant to pass over my head, seeped into my consciousness and became part of the tangle of facts and fancy and immutable mystery that marked my parents' deaths. From our year of "running the roads" in fear of Big Grover's wrath, I'd been exposed to an atmosphere heavy with whispered accounts as Opal and her younger sisters talked strategies of escape. By then, my mind was like a racing engine, and there was a part of me that was already a spy with an instinct for grown-ups' hidden purposes, for shadings and

nuance and that knowing adult tone that promises to reveal forbidden knowledge. It set me considerably apart from other children, along with my thick,
gold-rimmed eyeglasses and some other eccentricities, and gave me a prissy,
"know-it-all" manner that rubbed some of my elders the wrong way, not least
Big Grover at our final meetings, when even I could see that he was hell-bent
for destruction — ours or his, whichever came first.

In those last days, he was a man dusted with a certain odd mixture of innocence and menace, the hint that at any instant he could swing wildly right
or wrong. What drove him beyond all normal bounds and left him nothing to
break the fall was the thought that somehow he'd let Opal best him — belittle
him, really — and because of her selfish, twisted-up thinking, he was about to
lose everything he'd ever held dear, including his self-respect. No man worth
the powder to blow him away could let that happen without a fight to the finish. Hell, he'd *raised* Opal, put food in her mouth and clothes on her back for
ten years. The way he'd been taught, the family was sacred with the daddy su-
preme, and he'd sired not only a smart-mouth, half-blind son who was bound
to be a burden forever, but a curly-headed little baby girl, normal and sweet as
pie. He loved us all was the only thing that mattered. Oh, he'd messed up a
few times like most men do, but overall he'd toted fair. Then, right out of the
blue, just over a couple of silly arguments, Opal took it in her crazy Bailey
head to leave him for good, taking his kids away with a court paper. *What kind
of happy horseshit was that? No woman was fixing to divorce him, take away his
own flesh-and-blood.*

Big Grover's plans for getting us back never took failure into account. On
our last outing together, a street photographer snapped a candid shot of the
four of us walking along Travis Street, and in the picture you can see the fury
in my father's stride, the hard set of his jaw, the storm of rising blood. If love
means to close all distance, death can accomplish the same end. That afternoon in downtown San Antonio was approximately two weeks before the
killings.

The touchiness and mistrust between the Baileys and Lewises at the mortuary underscored their essential likeness. Opal's relatives were Appalachian
hillbillies who'd cotton-picked their way in stages to Texas to get out of the Al-
abama minefields, while the Lewises had settled in Texas before the Republic
when the place was still called *Tejas*. On both sides, they were simple, unas-
suming people of limited skills and ambitions — white, poor, Protestant, "salt
of the earth," streaked with sentimentality and dark superstition. But the two

clans were perhaps most truly kindred in having a deep sense of themselves as being "common folks," not created by a vast and conscienceless society, but by a small, homely one in which human character bloomed in stages and by precept. In an almost tribal way, we knew where we belonged and to whom we belonged, and that our allotted territory was very small, ranging from forty acres of played-out shinnery to three or four city blocks on the poor side of town. Work and endurance, fortitude and self-reliance had seen both families through the hardships of the Depression and would get everybody through anything else that came at them. The Baileys and Lewises alike were insular people who lived in a world defined more by the past than the present, more toward the country than the city, more Southern than Southwestern. Drama, in the form of extraordinary events, had never touched either line with the exception of occasional disgraces best ignored or blessedly forgotten. Vide Matthew, the outrageous wild man of the Bailey side, and the outlaw Lewis boys, Cece and Leck—bank robbers, it was whispered, or anyway failed bank robbers—and the special case of my lost and fallen father, who had been a good provider and family man like all decent Lewises until he turned strange and departed the firmament of sanity.

We believed we belonged to that old marginal world because we belonged nowhere else. *Old-timey*—that's what everybody boasted about being, still clinging stubbornly to country principles. No one I knew, with the sole exception of Opal, looked at living as a matter of weighing alternatives and then picking the best choice. You simply took the pattern that awaited—marrying one of your own kind and multiplying until death did you part, serving in the armed services if called, working the land or some menial town job into premature age if the bosses left you alone. A dab of reading and ciphering was fine if you had the time and the knack, but talking or singing or even fancy whistling served just as well when work was endless and recreation rare, and the real things you had to know how to read were the heavens and the waters and the forests. Our old unsung grandsires—hillbillies and Texians, all hide and bone like the longhorns—had opened up the country, and even when I was small, there lingered among us a poignant and powerful longing for that unspoiled America the elders had seen before urbanization, when the world beyond the horizon was nothing but dust and rumor. But those times were gone, fenced in or padlocked or clear-cut or blacktopped over. The power of caste rarely being generous, history was something created by Them that happened to you.

One of the most basic ties linking the Baileys and the Lewises lay in the fact that both families had been ensnared in a web of peonage since the Civil War and Reconstruction days. The Lewises, originally colonists from England, had pledged their prosperous Texas holdings to the Lost Cause — and lost everything. The Baileys, always landless and also on the losing side, were forced off their mountain hunting grounds to work as hirelings wherever necessity drove them. Inflexible as slavery, the caste system of the South in defeat decreed the sizing down of the person, the whittling away of the individual to fit the prescribed social and fiscal molds. Born poor and despised, three or four generations of my Southern ancestors experienced the imprisoning realities of subsistence drudgery through the institution of cotton sharecropping — endless stooping and picking along wormy turn-rows, dragging twelve-foot-long cotton sacks by a harness over the shoulder. Women and children were expected to drag and fill those sacks, too. Big Grover had just missed that kind of labor by a hair, but Leck and Cece had both pulled bolls on the shares until, as young, almost destitute men in the late 1920s, they'd thrown off their harnesses and gone "on the scout" — "running them ol' hard roads," as the Barrow Gang put it, in search of adventure and easier money.

If times were bad, ran the old-timey wisdom about such things, then a man's real worth might not always square with what he was reduced to doing in a "tight." Besides, as Oak Cliff's own Bonnie Parker and that Oklahoma fellow Pretty Boy Floyd had proved, some thieves from decent working families weren't half as sorry as "the laws" sent out to chase them. As boys, Leck and Cece had unaccountably "gone to the bad," chasing down raw country girls and drinking liquor on the sly by the time they were twelve or thirteen. To their credit, they always excluded their beloved "baby bud" from their openly criminal pursuits. During that attempted bank holdup — whenever, wherever it took place — Leck had escaped, and Cece had been caught in a cotton field and sentenced to a cotton field. So went the family legend as whispered by the Baileys, and I assumed that's why Leck was present in the Lewis pew at the viewing of the bodies, trying to comfort his mother, and Cece's absence was never even mentioned. It was part of the immutable mystery that I wouldn't be able to puzzle out for some time to come.

The Baptist preacher, hired by the undertaker, paced between Opal's and Grover's biers, talking about "estranged souls" and how some were called to the light and others to darkness. Grandma Annie and Daddy Will Lewis, my father's parents, wept in shame and grief, all the more humiliated, I knew, to be showing their feelings in front of a roomful of strangers who seemed to despise them. They'd ridden a Greyhound bus south from the little Hill Country town of Lampasas, packing a sack lunch and bringing along a cake for us children. Next to Opal and Grover, they were the people closest to me in the world, and I kept wanting to run to their sides, but I was firmly wedged between Bill and Millie Cox on the Bailey side of the aisle, and Millie wouldn't let go of me. She was my mother's next-youngest sister, a woman I'd known only a short time but had already begun to fear.

The Legacy of Huckleberry Finn

St. Petersburg Times, 1985

> *"Dad fetch it, how is I gwyne to dream all dat in ten minutes?"*
>
> *"Well, hang it all, you did dream it, because there didn't any of it happen . . ."*
>
> *Jim didn't say nothing for about five minutes, but set there a studying over it. Then he says . . .*
>
> *"When I got all wore out wid work, en wid de callin' for you, en went to sleep, my heart wuz mos' broke bekase you was los', en I didn't k'yer no mo' what become er me en de raf'. En when I wake up en fine you back again, all safe en soun', de tears come en I could a got down on my knees en kiss yo' foot I's so thankful. En all you wuz thinkin' 'bout wuz how you could make a fool uv ole Jim wid a lie. Dat truck dah is trash; en trash is what people is dat puts dirt on de head er dey fren's en makes 'em ashamed."*
>
> —MARK TWAIN, *The Adventures of Huckleberry Finn,*
> Chapter xv

Dr. Martin Shockley, who could recite most of Huck Finn from memory, was the first man I ever knew who actually twirled his mustache. He was well into middle age when Larry McMurtry and I began to take his American literature classes at North Texas State in the mid-1950s, but still robust and vigorous—"well set up"—with a boxer's watchful eyes and wide shoulders, and the broad, smiling face of someone who likes to laugh and often finds sufficient reason to. And his voice was of a wonderfully sonorous and sarcastic bass that seemed to come up from the depth of his belly, so that everything he said was in a way a gut statement, and you tended to believe him even if you had some evidence that he was exaggerating.

He twirled his mustache in canny glee at the impression he was creating by twirling it, and given the somnolent backwater ambience of Denton, Texas, back in those years—North Texas State was not yet the "multiversity" it would become nor as yet far removed from the teachers' normal it had recently been—Dr. Shockley was conspicuously donnish in his dress, most often wearing a tweed coat and matching billed cap, old school tie (University of Virginia), handmade English brogans, and a cane to spritz about with and lean on. The cane was imaginary . . . or at least you thought so until you felt the invisible tip of it grazing close to your liver and lights.

Dr. Shockley fiercely opposed the McCarthy-type incursions against intellectual freedom common to the period and was considered an irritant or worse by the campus powers-that-be. A noted Twain scholar and nineteenth-century generalist, he published regularly in the leading academic journals and was always immersed in some new line of research.

Legend had it that he had declined a partnership in his family's Virginia banking business to pursue scholarship, only to be hounded from distinguished job to lesser job, to his present position by the racist yahoos who largely controlled Southern education back then, just on the verge of mass desegregation.

Perhaps that explained the air of exile about him at odd moments. He seemed a man of brooding scruple, alternately cordial and aloof, flinty and compassionate, "public" and reclusive.

If Dr. Shockley was a maverick to the watchdogs of the administration, he was an unholy terror in the classroom. His overall attitude toward students was to fire them up or drum them out. In a plummy Tidewater accent, he would make it clear from the outset that he abhorred humbug and all things "picayune and stew-pid."

He lectured with the fluency of an angel—and then devised term examinations like a demon. You couldn't fool him. You were either smart or dumb, and he was for the one and against the other. His passion—it is not too strong a word—was for the kind of books, in Lawrence Clark Powell's phrase, "which distill truth from the bulk of human error."

One of Dr. Shockley's pet peeves was the horde of semiliterate biddy schoolteachers who flocked to his advanced classes interested only in the course credit. In those circumstances, he always demanded a plentiful supply of fresh air—even when it was snowing.

One winter's night before a roomful of terrified ladies, it was rumored, he had whacked out a windowpane with his invisible cane to illustrate the point.

No "sentimentering" for him. The good doctor was a gentleman of the old stripe, but he dearly loved to disturb those blue bouffants.

The school was a kind of gulag operation in the boondocks, a mélange of ugly buildings surrounded by greasy eating joints. I lived on the main drag in a rickety rooming house with a pool table on the second floor, taking my suppers at a farmers' café downtown because I could get a week's meal ticket there for $3.

Nobody in my family—what was left of it—had possessed $30 all at once since the Civil War. I had been married early, worked a couple of years, and then entered college as a kind of private dare to myself.

Webster defines character as "strength of mind, individuality, independence, moral quality." I wrote stories and poems in the evenings, and looked up quite a few such definitions. I harbored the dread that Dr. Shockley would find me "stew-pid."

Larry McMurtry, my closest student friend, felt the same insecurity, and we tried to keep each other's spirits bucked up.

Dr. Shockley kept his eye on McMurtry and me. We were the aspiring young writers on campus, the two who had begun dividing up the literary prizes awarded each semester by the school magazine, *Avesta*. We had done it three or four times running, splitting the prize money between us for best short story, poetry, and essay.

We had found a sponsor in the form of the brilliant creative writing instructor, Dr. Jim Brown, but as the awards mounted up, various formerly snobby teachers in the English department began angling to counsel us and "shape" our talents.

Dr. Shockley didn't care about any of that flapdoodle, but he meant to keep tabs on any self-styled young turks running around loose in his bailiwick.

"Mistah LOO-WIS! Mistah MUG-MURTRY!" He was waving his stick like a baton. "Step over here closah, if you please, gentlemen."

Dr. Shockley usually took a brisk constitutional after lunch, slowing on the return trip to his office for a smoke or a chat or a chance merely to appraise the passing students at the campus fishpond. The pool and its canopy of trees was a small, wilting patch of sylvan green the administration had not yet figured out how to pave or put to loftier use.

McMurtry and I approached warily. "I hope he doesn't have a magic bulldog or anything," Larry said in a worried tone.

"Umn-hmnnn . . . yas, yas . . . I thought so." Dr. Shockley twirled his mustache while looking us over crisply. He tucked his cane under his arm like a riding crop.

"I've seen you two boys togethah like this for several yeahs now . . ." Dr. Shockley said with a mock-dolorous shake of the head, "and I still can't make up my mind which one of you is in low company."

"Young turks" in a backward school freighted toward business and education degrees—well, of course—but "four-eyed bookworms" was another term we heard. Thirty years ago you could be judged violently nonconformist just by liking jazz.

In the lone-star land of raw machismo, McMurtry and I stuck close for reinforcement, each being the only writer the other one knew. We were matched as competitors, but with the saving grace of mutual friendship and encouragement. People remarked that we were vastly different and "just alike." We truly wanted to shine as writers and were more than willing to apply the seat of our pants to solving the problem. In all other things, we shared a clean brand of idealism and ignorance.

McMurtry and I were both "country" measured by frat-rat standards—but far too sophisticated from our reading to be considered hayseed. Between us, we had devoured hundreds, perhaps thousands, of books before entering college—and we were perpetually on the lookout for more.

Larry's father, a prominent West Texas rancher, took a rather dim view of his oldest son's education in general and frequently summoned him home for a weekend of forced-march cowboying. Once in a while, I tagged along to help with the chores—always too intimidated by the stern old man to step a horse in his presence.

At other times—on duty-free weekends—Larry and I took off in his barely factory-equipped Ford for more private destinations.

Larry knew a trick that would have outshone Dean Moriarity in Kerouac's *On the Road*: He could drive and read at the same time on the barren stretches of highway out in the middle of nowhere. We identified to an extent with the Beats if only because we loved to clock off the miles rolling past.

I had moved from the rooming house to an apartment just being vacated by Pat Boone, who was quite the milksop even then. McMurtry would honk beneath the window.

Paul Newman and Grover Lewis (right) chat on the set of The Sting. © *Universal Pictures.*

"Got your toothbrush?"

"Sure."

"Any money?"

"Not much."

"Let's go to Juárez." Or Austin, or Houston, or — just riding, following the white line.

Anywhere would do. We would drive 100 miles for a milkshake. Dallas and Fort Worth were nearby, and gas cost only 20 cents a gallon.

One night in a sports arena at SMU, we witnessed the poet T. S. Eliot, visiting from England just before his death, being solemnly invested as an honorary deputy sheriff of Dallas County, complete with badge and ten-gallon Stetson. On another evening, we saw Elvis Presley — not yet famous outside the South — get the living tar whaled out of him by an irate fan in the parking lot of a rural dance hall.

McMurtry and I justified our excursions as "bookscouting," but we were nosing around, really, poking into obscure nooks and crannies. We checked out distant truck stops, county fairs, and junk auctions, the fading towns bypassed by the new interstates. We went to old fiddlers' contests, rodeo dances, favorite shoot-'em-up movies playing half the state away. We nursed beers in the strident honky-tonks on the infamous Jacksboro highway outside Fort Worth, trying experimental conversations with the B-girls and earnestly hoping not to get caught in the Wild West gunfire that periodically erupted there.

And the bookstores—we found and ransacked them all, often skipping meals for the privilege. We searched the dusty corners in old furniture shops where used books might lurk, anywhere books might lurk.

One of our prized haunts was a three-story warehouse of books in the black "Deep Ellum" section of Dallas. The place was so crowded and jumbled that the proprietor offered us a standing reward for his pocket watch, which he had mislaid in the stacks years before. The watch never turned up, but I unearthed a brittle copy of *The Dial*, an avant-garde magazine of the 1920s, which contained a portion of T. S. Eliot's *The Wasteland* in the original publication. Thrilled, I bought it for a quarter.

"You blame boys float through here just like ghosts, carry away all my best stuff," the book dealer grumbled, not really meaning anything by it. He liked the two of us, thought we were "college gentlemen," all high seriousness.

There was, of course, a serious side to our wanderings. The Southwest was literally perishing in front of our eyes, its old landmarks and heroes being nudged aside by tract homes and SAC bases—and the likes of Elvis Presley. McMurtry had already pegged the theme of changing values in the region as his own literary territory. For my part, I had begun the slow but liberating realization that Texas wasn't going to be my exclusive subject.

Still, we were both mesmerized by the collision of cultures, and burning twenty-cent gas was our way of paying homage to the dark and bloody specters of our ancestry. It was idyllic, now that I think of it, running over those hard country roads past the winking Christmas-tree oil rigs, humming along with "T for Texas" or "Fraulein" on the late-night car radio.

Larry and I had long, searching conversations on those midnight rides about our work and ambitions, the young men's dreams we were bound to chase. At the beginning of our senior year as honor students, we were gaining a fair amount of recognition for our craft, both on and off campus.

McMurtry had made promising publishing contacts with *The Texas Quarterly* and *Southwest Review*, both prestigious publications; meanwhile, he was working on the stories and sketches that would in a couple of years comprise his first novel, *Horseman, Pass By*. In addition to publishing in *The Nation* and several other magazines, I had just won the annual *Carolina Quarterly* short-story prize and the Samuel French Playwriting Award.

Larry and I were headed in different directions after school was over, and both of us wanted to find some special way to express our gratitude to our mentors, Dr. Brown and Dr. Shockley. My copy of *The Dial* finally gave us an idea. We decided to put out a literary magazine of our own.

To maximize the fun, we would keep it a surprise. We wouldn't tell our professors about it until we took them the first copies. Our own "grand bulge" we thought. If there was a subtext of mischief in the undertaking, it was to let everybody know they had been to the picture show with us.

> *Just keep punchin', boys.*
> —JAMES DEAN as Jett Rink in *Giant*

A few weeks ago, I sat down to read *Huckleberry Finn* in the handsome edition designed by Barry Moser for the University of California Press to commemorate the hundredth anniversary of the novel's first American publication in 1885.

As always, I let myself drift on the raft down the Mississippi with the two fugitives from "sivilization." Around Chapter XV, it occurred to me that I was rereading the book for perhaps the fifteenth time since the close of my undergraduate days. And for a very good reason . . .

McMurtry and I took on a partner to put out the two issues of *The Coexistence Review*—a devout young preseminarian named John Lewis, no relation to me, who happened to possess a key to the mail room at the Episcopal student center near the school. The three of us shared the grunt work of production—typing cardboard plates, turning the crank on an ancient duplicating machine, collating and bradding the piles of pages.

We agreed on using the topical buzzword "coexistence" in the title because it signified to us that we were all embarked on separate paths but getting along amiably just the same. A friend drew us a stylized "lone star" for the cover. The available ink colors for the illustration were red and black, and we naturally chose red.

The finished magazine was no beauty, but it proclaimed our allegiance to the hip literary muse and gave us a heady sense of achievement. We were well aware that it was the first campus-related publication to circulate free of the petty censorship imposed on *Avesta* by official fiat. In that sense of breaking ground, it was a challenge to the establishment — or, to our way of thinking, another application of the principle of "coexistence."

Interest was brisk, and copies of the two-hundred-plus press run began to be grabbed up at once. We sold them for 50 cents each and gave away quite a number to friends. Overnight, the issue was a sellout — and our world began to collapse.

The administration sent out growls of disapproval via channels. The biddy claque of students, followed by quite a number of our teachers, began to high-hat us — giving us the silent treatment or walking away at our approach. Was this the result of the mild profanity we had printed?

Somebody had to explain the "political error" of the red lone-star cover to us. Soon it began to be whispered around that there was going to be a loyalty investigation of some sort . . . whether conducted by the school or the state legislature, nobody could say. Everything was back-channel. You couldn't pin anyone down.

Much of the bad blood seemed to be emanating from the office of the college vice president, who was said to act out his superior's edicts. On impulse, McMurtry dropped by the office to offer a cowboy handshake and a copy of the magazine with the compliments of the editors.

The vice president launched into a furious tirade. This learned man — an ex–English teacher, a vanity poet — said he didn't care to read such trash. He said we were nobodies who would never be genuine writers. Terminating the interview, he dropped the broad hint that we might not be smart enough to graduate with the rest of our class.

Shortly after this bizarre display of mental penury, it was announced from on high that McMurtry's and my work was ineligible to appear in the upcoming *Avesta*. This was unfortunate since we had already been named winners of the semester's literary awards. The campus magazine shut down and did not publish again for five years.

We were staggered by the severity of these reprisals, and as reckless romantics often will, we counterpunched to let off steam. Naïveté, not sedition, was our crime, and we hastily put out *Coexistence Review No. 2*—this time around with an unadorned cover featuring the standard text of a loyalty oath jointly signed by the editors.

Our stab at irony hardly countered the vicious smear campaign being waged against us—sometimes in the classrooms where we sat. Our former allies—the same folks who had hailed us as local literary lions—were now heaping dirt on our heads. The injustice of being painted as subversives and moral degenerates made us feel soiled and heartsick—ornery enough to take a swing at somebody. The campus newspaper, which had found us pretty reliable copy in the past, wasn't interested in airing the situation.

Bewildered—well in over our heads—we turned to Dr. Brown and Dr. Shockley for advice, and as always they gave us wise and proper counsel, urging us to moderation in our behavior. Dr. Shockley is today professor emeritus at North Texas State University. Dr. Brown made a number of highly placed enemies during his vocal defense of us in the magazine scandal but taught on for another year, then left the profession for a time. The two of them were brave and inspired teachers—better men than the institution they served. They taught us honor in the midst of its opposite on a campus with a very small pond.

An investigation never materialized, but the threat of expulsion was a daily worry. Still, there were bright moments at the close of our sentimental education.

McMurtry and I had to laugh out loud at our inclusion in *Who's Who among American University and College Students*. And a burly sophomore from the Piney Woods returned both issues of *The Coexistence Review*, demanding his money back.

"You against us on politics?" John Lewis asked.

"Not enough s-e-x in the doggone thing," the kid said, spelling it out.

The hostilities never ceased, and as a calculated parting shot, Larry, John, and I were left in the dark as to whether we would graduate until we had the diplomas in our hands. McMurtry wore blue jeans under his baccalaureate robes at the ceremonies, as I recall.

Afterward, at a private function, a group of faculty stalwarts and scrubbed new B.A.'s stood around someone's living room, holding glasses with something brown in them.

"To your health, Mistah Loo-wis," Dr. Shockley proposed.

I returned the sentiment, and after a couple of sips, I fell to confessing my uncertainties about the future.

"Ah, the fantods of youth . . . umn-hmnnn . . . yas, yas." Dr. Shockley lifted his glass and clinked it solidly against mine.

"Reread *Huck Finn* every two yeahs, young man," he said, ". . . and you may develop some charactah yet."

Cracker Eden

Texas Monthly, 1992

> *. . . home, in the twentieth century, is less where your heart is, than where you understand the sons-of-bitches. Especially in Texas, where it is the vitality of the sons-of-bitches which makes everything possible . . .*
>
> —DAVE HICKEY, *Art in America,* 1972

I.

History and legend bind us to the past, along with unquenchable memory. Growing up in Dallas's working-class suburb of Oak Cliff in the 1940s and '50s was the second experience in my life that I never got over. I hadn't been back to those boyhood haunts in thirty years, and I wasn't as calm as I thought I'd be about returning. Under a patchy October overcast, the houses along Marsalis Avenue looked beat, maybe even whipped. I had to slow down to read the sign for my old street because all the landmarks were gone.

When I first saw East Ninth in 1948, the street was a leafy tunnel running past tidy bungalows and well-kept Victorian mansions dating back to the original settlement of the City of Oak Cliff before the turn of the century. Now, it was food-stamp country—a jungly midden with a Third World flavor. I knew in advance that the house where Spook and I lived had been demolished during the Latino incursions of the 1970s, so I eased past its replacement, not ready to look at it yet. Turning south on Patton, the area changed from merely seedy to wasteland.

At Tenth and Patton, I pulled over in shock. The devastation was total— an entire neighborhood sunk in rot. The surviving houses were vine-choked, boarded up, literally atomizing in a ghastly mockery of the thriving community I recalled. The burnt-out hulk of an apartment warren stood on the site where Lee Harvey Oswald allegedly killed Officer Tippit after the Kennedy assassination.

Leaving the car, I paced up and down the broken sidewalks searching in vain for the duplex where my best school pal had lived. The blasted terrain looked as though war and pestilence had swept through, leaving behind only feral silence.

Turning away, still on foot, I started back toward Ninth. Oak Cliff's soul had changed or maybe died, I couldn't tell which. And what exactly had been lost? Well, a civilization . . . Growing up on these streets, I'd started learning about all the things I was still trying to comprehend — love, sex, money, art, death. But then I knew a thing or two about death when I first came to Oak Cliff . . .

In 1943, my parents — Grover Lewis and Opal Bailey Lewis — shot each other to death with a pawnshop pistol. Big Grover had stalked us for a year, fighting divorce tooth and nail, and when he finally cornered Opal alone and pulled the trigger, she seized the gun and killed him, too. They'd started out as Depression kids who'd eloped from the Trinity Heights area of Oak Cliff, where they'd both been friends with Bonnie Parker and Clyde Barrow. Like Clyde, my father was an unschooled country Jake who fell — or jumped — into low ways in the big city. Opal, like Bonnie, was a bright student who'd left school early to help support her family — a moral girl with high ideals. Like Bonnie's, Opal's main crime seems to have been picking the wrong guy. In the end, she managed to save my father from everybody but himself.

The fatal events took place in my hometown of San Antonio when I was eight, and I became the ward of a brutish Fort Worth in-law who amused himself by trying to break my body and spirit. By today's standards, he'd be deemed abusive enough to serve jail time. After five years, when I realized that my options were either suicide or homicide, I ran away and refused to return if I died in the process. Many of my mother's kin considered me unsalvageable because I was "a pure Lewis." They'd give me that look: *Just like his daddy* . . .

Spook — my great-uncle, C. E. Bailey — saved my life. When he took me in, I was badly damaged — withdrawn, lacking confidence, blind as a bat, smart as fire, dumb as hell. Still, with a friendly home base only a block's walk from my high-school classes and the local library also close at hand, I began to mend. My case was extreme, but hardly singular in a workingman's district where a lot of families got blown to smithereens.

A sagging condo pile with a no-drugs sign out front occupied the lot where our old family boarding house had stood. Spook and I had lived upstairs in a bare room with a bare bulb above the iron bedstead. When I started working after school, I bought us reading lamps, feeling grown-up about pitching in.

Spook's insight—his special grace—was to treat me as a younger brother instead of a ward. In his fifties by then, a union machinist and lifelong bachelor, he kept his mind sharp by studying the Bible and parsing out "the lies in the papers." Half a Wobbly in his secret heart, he taught me a multitude of useful things, one of the germinal ideas being that decency and common sense were most likely to be found in common people. He offered general advice—specific if asked—and never raised his voice nor hand to me. In the long haul, I think I was less trouble to him than his loony sisters, both of whom constantly schemed to lure him into their religious cults.

If Spook was our family Samaritan, Matthew Bailey—my mother's father—was our scourge. A Snopesy little jackleg-of-all-trades—he'd been Bonnie and Clyde's favorite bootlegger—he worked for thirty-odd years as a maintenance engineer at the Wholesale Merchants Building in downtown Dallas, where he routinely slept with all the maids as a condition of their employment. With a flame of rage perpetually flickering in his head, he once put a black man off a city bus at knife point for sitting in front of him. I loved the old devil regardless and helped him out sometimes on weekend plumbing jobs, mostly just handing him his bottle. Matthew approached everything with the maximum violence required for the job, but he never swatted me around because, as a rule, he only beat on the people who lived under his own roof.

I lived on the outskirts of the family, craving acceptance but shrinking from ties that didn't bind so much as strangle. The pervasive racism of the time was part of the rub with me, but then the Bailey clan encompassed a whole panoply of bonehead prejudices. None of them had a dime's worth of schooling, and few showed much regret about it, rejecting out of hand any view that didn't strike them as "comp'terble." The women tended to be pop-eyed with faith in one nostrum or another, the men long-winded dullards. The backwardness I figured they couldn't help, but I resented their willingness to lick the hands of their oppressors. By Spook's dictum, they were just plain people muddling through as best they could. Over time, I came to regard them—tribally, anyway—as patsies on a treadmill. Trying to reason with them was like slamming into a wall of soft cheese.

My people, holy and profane, were "pure-dee Oak Cliff," of course. In mindset, our community on the hard-luck side of the Trinity was a paradise of the deepest redneck dye. The fear of race mixing was a constant topic because the district's communal identity hinged on being white, conservative, "saved," and married with children.

The gabble of bigotry thus became a daily canticle, a sacred text. The ethos of the place—what it promoted—was absolute white supremacy, reinforced by old-time religion and male chauvinist prickism. In our primary-color culture—97 percent white in 1950—the No. 1 rule was: Don't mess up. If you swerved from the True Path, you messed up. Above all, you had to "cut it." Cut the yard, keep your hair cut, cut the mustard . . . *cut the crap, boy* when you spoke out of line. Docility was preferred over intelligence, guaranteeing the whittling-down of the individual to fit unvarying social molds. This bred the kind of multiedged boredom that comes from poverty locked into place by spiritual poverty. As a jumpy adolescent, I was starved for ideas in much the same way that I yearned to sleep with somebody besides Spook—some like-minded, bookish girl, I hoped. But if racism was obligatory, sex without benefit of clergy was out of the question.

Following a zigzag route, I walked to the intersection of Marsalis and Jefferson Boulevard, where the Carnegie branch library had once stood. The building, erected in 1914, had been bulldozed in 1966 when, as someone later told me, "Dallas was tearing down everything old and throwing up junk." It had been an elegant little sanctuary set in a wooded park—one of the community's few true gems. The structure located there now—a Dallas Department of Transportation cubicle—resembled a postmodern pillbox.

The old library had saved my life as much as Spook had. I'd found my own sacred texts in there, groping for direction in that period when the self doesn't really know what it is yet. A precocious reader by the age of twelve, I read an average of four or five books a week all through high school, including trash, the classics, and everything in between. Above all, I learned how to read and think critically, with no clear sense of vocation yet, but at least the ghost of an ambition forming. Predictably, my hard-shell relatives claimed I was ruining my mind by "thinkin'" too much. Doggedly, I read on. Working a night job, I sometimes skipped school to read because reading was as essential as breathing to me.

On my walk through the streets, I'd passed no one and there was little traffic moving on the boulevard at nine A.M. Squirrels danced on the power lines. Up the block, a sign over a car lot read: *Kars Fur "U"—MUCHACHO MOTORS.* With a sense of sorrow and anger that made my heart race, I realized I still missed the clanking, spectral streetcars that had stopped running along Jefferson for good back in 1956.

I trudged through leaves to the drinking fountain on the corner. You could see the scars in the granite where the old "White" and "Colored" markers had hung. Now, the signs were gone, and there was no water at all. An awful, obvious metaphor . . .

I started back toward the car. I was in Texas for a week's time—to take a look around my old Oak Cliff and feel for its pulse, if there was one left. I also wanted to pay my respects to some unquiet Oak Cliff souls, people I'd measured myself against on one level or another in deep dreams, in freer climes.

II.

The shape of things in Oak Cliff was essentially the same, but the lines had run eerily. Nothing—and everything—had changed. The ethnic configuration now stood at 40 percent white, 40 percent black, and 20 percent Hispanic in a district comprising roughly a third of Dallas's area and population. I drove all over the downfallen suburb, numbed by the decay and patchwork balkanization. Most of the neighborhoods I'd known were streaked with phantasmagoric blight and filled with desperately poor and sometimes dangerous people—the latest incursion of have-nots from *jacales* and East Texas slums. In my notes, I groped for terms to encompass the scope of the disaster: *systemic collapse, municipal cancer, de facto apartheid, social time bomb, a thousand points of dark* . . . Billy Lee Brammer's old boyhood home looked intact in a modest cul-de-sac behind Greiner Junior High, but the block bristled with *For Sale* signs—not a good sign. My daily forays were depressing, educational, and at times very touching. I found no road back to the cracker Eden of the 1950s, but at every turn I encountered Oak Cliff's famous hospitality—and the smell of cooking red beans. Those things hadn't changed. My new conspiracy theory was that after JFK's murder, Official Dallas had snuffed its gulag across the river in cold blood, and the cover-up had lasted until Oak Cliff's outraged secessionist movement of 1990 . . .

The Jefferson business community was part of the overall mess. Its decline marked the transition from backwater to stagnant pool. Dallas's virtual cessation of city services to the area, spanning roughly thirty years, had all but assured the evolution of two almost perfectly segregated worlds—the white-power domain of the new downtown towers and the rainbow-hued world of the faded boulevard. Fair or foul, boom or bust, the shyster pols and "bidness" savants favoring North Dallas interests kept Oak Cliff on a short ration.

I made two sweeps of the business zone, one with Laura Mulry, the executive director of the Jefferson Area Association (JAA). The nonprofit group, jointly funded by the Texas Urban Main Street program and the City of Dallas, was the sole semiofficial agency promoting local restoration and revitalization, its major aims being capital reinvestment and cultivation of an old-town flavor. In daily practice, the JAA functions as a watchdog and fixer-upper organization coaxing local merchants toward improvement.

A savvy, articulate guide, Mulry pointed out some of the small victories the JAA had wrung from Dallas's bureaucracy: a walking-beat police substation, repair of the plaza across from the Texas Theater, rebricked crosswalks, streetlights along Jefferson that worked again. We also toured her "success stories in rehabbing"—Eugene's Guitars, the Charco Broiler, Ojeda's Cafe, the Bishop Arts District, Jim's Bike Shop, and the Boulevard Emporium.

The prize of the lot was probably Oak Cliff's nicest-looking building— Winnetka Place—a classy office galleria fashioned from a 1920s warehouse. As we strolled along the block outside, Mulry hailed David Hudgins, a fifty-ish JAA volunteer she introduced fondly as her "original streetlight watchdog."

"That's right," Hudgins said. "In '89, there were sixty-five streetlights out on Jefferson in just the mile between Marsalis and Polk. I called downtown to complain and they said, 'How do you know the lights are out?' I said because my wife and I drove up and down and counted."

"And they wondered why we had a crime problem out here," Mulry put in. "It took us six months and our councilperson—Dr. Charles Tandy—but they finally got it lit."

In Mulry's Honda, we cruised around the mostly Hispanic neighborhoods abutting the business zone. To my amazement, she said the JAA already had goaded Dallas into razing the worst of the derelict houses clustered at Tenth and Patton. Further on, she pointed out a raggedy black man crossing against a stoplight. "Mr. Trash Man," she explained. "He's homeless, yes, and mentally deranged. Twenty percent of Dallas's services for the homeless and mentally handicapped are located within half a mile of Jefferson—facilities for the whole city. So we're a magnet for the homeless. It's a serious problem."

Later, I made a second swing through Oak Cliff's downtown, thinking about Laura Mulry and her clients. After two years in charge of the JAA operation, she conceded her job was discouraging. Many of the Latino retailers didn't want to deal with a *gringa*. Blacks often said: "What does this little white chick know?" Mulry was a pleasant young professional woman—bright, dedicated—but there was a sadness coming over her face that matched the dreary street she was trying to regenerate.

Jefferson's shopping district had been second only to downtown Dallas in the early '50s. Now, it was a nut without a kernel. I hiked a mile from Willomet to Beckley and back on both sides of the boulevard. A seedy Western Union office and a MacDonald's were the only national franchises I passed. Skillern's, Sears, J. C. Penney, and all the other blue-chip concerns had decamped by the mid-'70s—leaving in their place, all too often, marginal businesses operated by immigrants selling cheap goods produced by cheap labor in places like Hong Kong and Korea. There was no shortage of ninety-nine-cent stores, *herberías*, pawnshops, TV rental outfits, and bridal-gown salons. The two commonest signs were *Se Habla Español* and *Se Accepta Estampillas*. The JAA's organized face-lifting seemed a brave first step, but I couldn't escape the feeling that Jefferson had more of a history than a future.

I stopped by Ramon's near Madison for a haircut and maybe a breath of comfort. "What happened to your street?" I asked the barber, a sandy-haired man named Bob.

"Aw, just wore out, I guess," he said. "This damn recession didn't help much." Bob pointed east with his scissors. "Guy got killed up here at Zangs the other night for a piece of jewelry. Gang deal, yeah . . . I tell you one thing—we need a change all the way along the line or there'll be some real trouble."

Robert McElearney, the principal architect of Oak Cliff's much-buzzed-about secession movement, had told his tale before—even on the *Today Show*—and it came out smooth as a computer feed. Sarah Haskins, his elderly volunteer assistant, a former Dallas school board member, sat beside him, her jaw clenched in what seemed to be permanent anger. The three of us met in the cathedral-domed main hall of the Oak Cliff Chamber of Commerce, which is probably the suburb's second-nicest-looking building.

"At Councilman Tandy's request," McElearney, the Chamber's president, recounted, "I began to look into how we could get more equitable representation, and out of that eventually evolved our Strategic Agenda—seventy or eighty items that Dallas had been shorting us on. We used their own records for documentation—looked at every penny spent in 1989 and '90—and we found that less than 1 percent was spent here south of the Trinity—"

"That's basic services for 370,000 people," Haskins emphasized with a weary roll of her eyes.

"It was a conscious pattern of neglect," McElearney went on, "so we told Dallas if you don't comply, we're leaving and we've got the votes to do it. We formed the Greater Oak Cliff Citizens Council (GOCCC) with community members to closely monitor the city's compliance. They've just committed $20 million for code enforcement on demolition, so for the moment, secession is more a legal threat than a political movement. But we forced them to acknowledge the inequities, and I think that's what most folks wanted. And maybe it's proved to Dallas that Oak Cliff is a valuable asset. Why else would they fight hard to keep us?"

"One reason is there's absolutely no developable land left to the north," Haskins remarked dryly.

Greater Oak Cliff . . . The GOCCC's master stroke had come in redefining Oak Cliff's legal boundaries. In the proposed new city, the northern boundary would extend across the current Trinity River channel to its old bed — encompassing rich tax-base acreage parallel to the Stemmons Freeway, including the shiny new hotel where I was staying.

"Was there a certain element of payback for Dallas's neglect in setting that boundary?" I asked.

"Yeah," McElearney agreed with a smile. "Two, maybe. One, we wanted to tweak 'em — no doubt about that — and we also felt it was legitimate. Leon Jaworski, who was hired as Dallas's attorney, thought so, too. 'You guys could beat us in court,' he said."

McElearney and Haskins made an interesting contrast. He was erudite, urbane, a polished master of the hincty white executive style. She represented prepluralist Oak Cliff, the way it used to be when its housing, roads, and education ranked with Texas's best — a bygone age of discipline and traditional values.

"What exactly happened to the community to cause the disaster at Tenth and Patton?" I asked.

"It was a decision made at City Hall," Haskins said in a bitterly aggrieved tone. "We had so-called 'leaders' who decided that every big city needed a ghetto and the natural barrier for Dallas's was the river.

"Then we also had block-busting by realtors, white flight, red-lining by the banks . . . Yes, the dry election in 1956 played a part in it. I've watched the deterioration, and it's terrible to say, but I'm tired of it — tired of fighting. I feel very betrayed. If Dallas lives up to its commitments, we'll be on the road. But there's also got to be a change in people. We don't like each other anymore. Everything that's brought up, somebody says, 'That's racist.' Our churches — my own, Cliff Temple Baptist — have got to say, 'Our doors are open to all people.' The black churches have got to do that, too, and they don't. I don't want us to be just another big city. I want us to be an ideal city that we can all look to with pride."

A couple of days later, I read another of Sarah Haskins's statements to John Wiley Price. "We need to reach a point where I can put my hand out to my black brethren and they don't accuse me of being a racist." The Dallas County commissioner — very African, very American — listened noncommittally, but his large, fine hands gestured in dismissal.

"It's not enough just to stretch out a hand," Price said in his office at the Old School Book Depository. "You've got to follow through with action — show that you're doing something to help that area. So I invite not only Miss Haskins, but Mr. McElearney and others like that, to do more. You know — 'Hey, the C of C's going to take on a house in Oak Cliff, make it a model home, push the city on code enforcement, then adopt another' — and so forth. If they want to do that, they can. McElearney used to be with the city — in code enforcement, as I recall. But there's no real interest. Those people don't live in the area."

In shirtsleeves and maroon suspenders, Price maintained a riveting eye contact across his knickknack-covered desk. "See," he said, leaning forward, "I live in Oak Cliff — on East Fifth Street, right across from the park. I've been there now going on twelve, thirteen years. My house has been broken into twice. It's basically the guy next door, you know? I caught him once, couldn't prove it. In my area, we've got a group called the Lake Cliff Neighborhood Association, and we have our anti-thug-and-drug patrol every week. Dope dealers come in and physically remove old ladies, so I've got to help them get their houses back or somebody'll try to take mine tomorrow."

Price's critique of Official Dallas was that "racism is institutionalized." "And institutions perpetuate themselves. My contention has always been, once you raise the bottom, the top automatically moves. When you help people at the lowest strata, the whole human family moves . . . Oak Cliff has a lot to offer. In the next few years, it's going to be tough because of the economy, but more people have to make that commitment to take back their neighborhoods."

I was curious about Price's sense of himself. With his high visibility as an activist—he'd been picketing the *Dallas Morning News* for sixty-six weeks over its hiring policies—did he ever worry about his personal safety? "Nah . . . my spirit's strong. I'm not a hostage. You've got to be very clear about who you are. African Americans have been locked out of the system for too long. Racism is real—we didn't fabricate it. We've only been able to vote in this country for twenty-six years."

Focused, intense, a master of the hincty black executive style, Price seemed incendiary to me only in his intelligence. In other urban settings—in freer climes—a man of his qualities might thrive. But as I left his office and walked out into Dealey Plaza, the melancholy thought occurred to me that Dallas's first elected minority commissioner might do well just to survive.

III.

Corrupt politics debases the plain truth, and debased language in turn empowers corrupt politics. . . . As I parked on Jefferson and walked the two blocks north to Adamson High School, I was thinking about my grammar teachers there in the 1950s. Stiff old biddies, they showed you the muscle-and-blood of language—Latin, even—through strict and frequent class drills, backed up by unceasing homework. What I hadn't understood at the time was that it's rare for the establishment to grant its outcasts access to such useful and subversive knowledge. In the decades since, "dumbing down" along with the rest of America, Official Dallas had moved to plug the leak.

Time and attrition had picked my old alma mater to the bone. In my time, Adamson had dwarfed the neighborhood. Now it was the other way around. The school stood like a becalmed ship in a sea of rotting tenements, two blocks from Tenth and Patton and about the same distance from the scabrous slums along West Davis—"hooks and crooks" territory.

The place struck me as emblematic of the reaming we've all taken after years of moral and economic freebooting.

I talked with Martin Riojas in his office across from the padlocked auditorium. In his late thirties, a sixteen-year veteran of the Dallas school system, he'd served as Adamson's principal for only two months—but long enough to sort out the school's stark problems. A genial man with a worried air, he said that almost half the student body—over 500 out of 1,300—qualified for the poverty-level free lunch program. "We're about 83 percent Hispanic," he said, "and we have a tremendously high dropout rate. Two-thirds that start in the ninth grade don't finish. One of my goals is to at least reduce that. But we lost ten teachers in the September cutbacks—fifty classes a day."

"Are the gangs much of a problem?"

"Yes, they are. But not as much as in the past. We get painted with graffiti occasionally by, oh, the Outlaws or the Royal Knights or whatever. I don't know who the Outlaws are—not our gang. The Royal Knights were in the past, but they're not so evident now. I don't consider the gang situation a high-ranking problem at the moment."

The campus surroundings had reminded me of a daylong pep rally held before an Adamson-Sunset football game in the 1950s. Was that tradition of intense rivalry still cultivated?

"No," Riojas said sadly, "we don't do that anymore. I think it's nice to feel that kind of spirit, but I'm afraid right now we're at the other extreme. The spirit's just not there. Our team is not doing well, no sir."

I kept encountering the strange dwelling within the familiar. . . . What was once grand about Adamson had dimmed to utilitarian drab. I made my way upstairs alone and found my old locker, then leaned for a minute in a window well, lost to memory if not exactly nostalgia. . . .

You were forever defined as being far down the food chain if you hailed from Oak Cliff, so it somehow followed that Adamson in the '50s was relentlessly class-conscious. Mirroring a strict, authoritarian regime, "sosh" cliques and star jocks ruled over the lumpen as if by divine right. The football fraternity tended to be arrogant, bullying swine. I knew about that firsthand because the most vicious of them dealt me endless misery in my job on Jefferson. Tall, gawky, "four-eyed," I shuffled along Adamson's halls well nigh invisibly, developing a gut resistance to being treated like dirt by scum. All the while, the educational process "took" on me and other nobodies in the Class of '53. . . .

The third-floor corridor was empty, silent. I peered into an unused classroom, recalling one of the stiff old biddies who'd taught me how to diagram sentences. I'd worked and reworked an English theme for her about my chance discovery of Clyde Barrow's grave and what it meant to me. Mistaking her shock for enthusiasm, I'd blurted out my hopes of becoming a novelist or maybe some kind of roving correspondent. A kindly woman in most things, she'd tapped me on the shoulder with a blunt finger: "You'd best think about something you can actually accomplish." She'd marked my paper A for composition, D minus for content. . . .

In those years, I still fell off into the blues sometimes about Opal and Big Grover, but mostly I pined for . . . well, romance. Sex was almost always on my adolescent mind, and every day I didn't get laid seemed a dark failure. But beyond sex, I longed for someone to hold precious—a sweetheart as pretty as the bell of a honeysuckle, a golden-hearted girl who'd be my partner in everything. By the time I started working nights at fourteen, considerably reducing my chances, I hadn't found her, but I tried my best to stay hopeful as I looked. . . .

The North Oak Cliff Branch Library at Tenth and Madison, which had replaced the old Carnegie facility in 1987, looked somewhat incongruous in a neighborhood given over to services for the homeless and mentally handicapped. Built in a trendy modular design, the new building called to mind an upscale shopping mall—all glass and reinforced concrete. Oak Cliff, I'd found, was rife with such surreal juxtapositions, a fever dream of rust and spanking new billboard fantasies.

Annette Curtis, the branch librarian, offered me coffee and a thoughtful assessment of a local culture that had turned into its opposite in a generation's tick. She said it saddened her most to see the level of education creeping down. She rated the work required of students at Adamson and Sunset as "shallow"—lacking in "intellectual substance"—compared to the more demanding work assigned to college-bound North Dallas students.

"Can I add a personal note?" Mrs. Curtis asked, her cheeks reddening. "I live here in Oak Cliff, and it just burns me up when people dismiss it without knowing a thing about it. A lot of them react negatively to the name, you know, without ever bothering to cross the river. People in Dallas need to change the way they relate to each other."

In the main reading room, I sat down at one of the computer terminals and nervously tapped in the names of a couple of Oak Cliff writers who were important to me—talismans of a sort. There were three books listed by Horace McCoy, but not his hard-to-find autobiographical novel about Oak Cliff in the 1920s, *No Pockets in a Shroud*.

I typed in my friend Billy Lee's name, and the title flashed up: *The Gay Place* by William Brammer. The book had won the coveted $10,000

Houghton Mifflin Literary Fellowship Award in 1961—extraordinary recognition for a native of Oak Cliff's provincial void. In his palmy days of literary celebrity, Billy Lee had been five years older than me, already launched on a national career, but I'd recognized him at once as another solitary schoolboy who'd stayed home to read, forging out of the common language a voice purely his own. . . . Charming, reckless, crazy Billy, pressing the bohemian flesh at Scholz's beer garden all those storms ago . . . I was still fond of him, still mad at him. . . .

On a private errand, I drove back to my old neighborhood and cruised along Denver again to double-check on Tess's place, inching along to be sure. A fool's errand . . . Her little blue-roofed garage apartment was gone, and so was her mother's place across the street. Vacant lots there now, mounds of trash, grotty weeds . . .

All those years ago, I'd been looking for a girl and found a woman. . . .

IV.

God don't like ugly, baby.
—BO DIDDLEY

I was interested in more than just change, more than just how surface appearances alter over time. Oak Cliff remembered and Oak Cliff disintegrating sprang at me, had me by the throat halfway through the week. By then, I'd visited four cemeteries, with a fifth to come if I could make myself stop avoiding it. The dead included my kin and familiars—Oak Cliff's wild cards, spectral heroes and villains, phantoms I'd loved, deplored, never stopped wondering about. I was standing over Matthew Bailey's marker in the Sunset Gardens section of Restland, near Richardson, within an hour of touching down at the D/FW airport.

It was eerie to think of that man of wild commotion enshrouded in such stillness. I'd attended his funeral in 1960, too old to cry by then and not about to break down in front of the pecksniff Baileys. Matthew was in Hell now, I presumed. Wherever. Thinking about him made me realize how little our explanations explain. In the years since, I'd worn his shade like an inner skin—like memories of the ghosty streetcars on Jefferson or Oak Cliff's furnace-red sunsets—and scarcely a month went by when I didn't recall his smell of cheap pipe tobacco and whiskey. During our last conversation — he'd taken on a load of hundred proof to deaden his pain — he'd blurted out his rancor at the world, or perhaps it was his vision of eternity: "The women won't screw you, sonny boy, but the men will. Ha! Watch out for the sons-of-bitches!" . . .

Bonnie Parker's grave in the Crown Hill Memorial Cemetery, facing a rundown pod mall in Dallas's Walnut Hill area, was decorated with a little dime-store American flag on a wooden staff. She and Clyde had died in a mythic squall of bullets the spring before I was born, but they were still a presence in my mother's house when I was a child. Opal responded viscerally to their narrow, doomed lives, not so much with reason as with heart. I remembered tears coming to her eyes when Bonnie's name would come up, and once, years later in a strange Yankee city, I'd dreamed of the two of them together, smoking cigarettes without inhaling and making up poems. . . .

The Barrow family plot, including the graves of Clyde and his luckless dumbbell brother Buck, lay in the Old West Dallas Cemetery overlooking a gruesomely sleazy stretch of Fort Worth Avenue on Oak Cliff's northern verge. When I'd first discovered the place around 1950, it was overgrown with brush and tangles of knee-high grass — a quiet, murmurous glen sunk in birdsong and neglect. Finding Clyde's marker there had rocked me with a primal force, offering a direct link to my own folks. Afterwards, I'd returned to the cemetery time and again, making it a private sanctuary where I could mull over my feelings about Opal and Big Grover, mourn them, make peace with them a little. . . . Now, the old grounds were fenced and fresh-mown, courtesy of a local church, but the smell of fast food, oil, and metal hung over the tombstones, and dead-eyed pimps watched me come and go from off-plumb doorways. . . .

At the other end of Fort Worth Avenue — the Fort Worth end — Lee Harvey Oswald was buried somewhere in the eighty-seven-acre Rose Hill Cemetery, the exact location kept secret to discourage kooks. I searched fitfully for his plot, then gave it up and spent an hour or so just wandering the rows of stone, letting my thoughts wander, too, hearing what sounded like explosive bursts in the distance . . . Oswald's "crime of the century" lay twenty-eight years in the enigmatic past, and Lee himself had since disappeared into a blur of disputed roles, his true connective threads obscured by decades of cloud cover — myth bleeding into legend turning into smoke. According to the Warren Report, he'd been a misfit driven to kill by resentment, envy, and madness. Perhaps — not wholly inconceivable. But I'd known a dozen Lee Oswalds when I was growing up — quintessential Oak Cliff losers mired in a hopeless system that denied lateral entry. The bottom line was always drawn just above their names. . . . I sat for a while in a patch of shade, smelling gunpowder. Whether Oswald was guilty or not, I just wanted to bow my head an instant for the poor bastard. The *crump-crump-crump* in the distance, a passing caretaker told me, was the sound of gunfire from a police training academy across the road. It went on every day. Even unto the grave, Oswald was destined for steerage—the ultimate patsy. . . . *Family*, I wrote in the mortuary registry.

After the rich achievement of *The Gay Place*—Gore Vidal had called it "the best novel about American politics in our time"—Billy Lee Brammer's future seemed golden. But when I first met him in the early '60s, he was already using speed, talking his second book away in bursts of inspired gabble. *Fustian Days*, as he called it, simply evaporated over time, and Billy Lee fell increasingly under the spell of what Baudelaire calls "the pharmaceuticals of heaven"—specifically, pure crystal meth. I'd last seen Brammer in 1972, looking flayed to the core. Six years later, he'd fatally overdosed at the age of forty-eight.

He was buried next to his working-class parents in the Meditation Park at Laurel Land in far South Oak Cliff. It was early in the day, hushed and cool with a sheen of dew still glistening on the lawns. There was no one around so I just started talking to him.

"Can I come in for a second," I asked, "share a few bad tidings? There's trouble in River City, Billy Lee. Everything has gone to shit and flinders. It's the rankest times I can remember—lean and mean and scary everywhere.

"Remember that old white-trash word 'jicky'? Well, it's a Jicky age. The fat cats and rulingcrats and gravy-sucking pigs robbed the country blind in the '80s—promised us everything, gave us half, and charged us double. Now, there's a global recession and a hole in the ozone. . . .

"Postbust Dallas looks about half torn down and half rebuilt, although it's still the same white man's city with the Trinity as a sort of moat. Oak Cliff is gone or sinking fast. I guess you know I didn't come back to rank the place, but, Jesus . . . it's miserable. Nobody speaks the same language—nobody's in charge, really—and there's no common identity so it's not about anything. Hell, they even lost Stevie Ray Vaughan. I've felt half-sorry for almost everybody I've met.

"People don't talk much about race anymore, but it's still the great divide, and nobody—white, brown, or black—will let go of it. The message I get is that everybody had better lighten up and throw in together against the gangs, say, or maybe just to pick up some of the goddamn trash. If they can't find a common ground as generic humans, they might as well pack it in and head for the graveyard."

I started away, then turned back. "Speaking of which," I said, "you sure messed up, boy."

V.

Memories are old identities.
—WILLIAM BUTLER YEATS

At the age of seventeen in 1926, Clyde Barrow worked briefly as an usher at Dallas's Palace Theater, but soon quit over the paltry $12-a-week salary. Twenty-five years later, I started work as an usher at the Texas Theater for $19 a week—still a pittance, but enough to see me through high school. The experience jerked some complex knots in and out of my young life, and I finished growing up very quickly.

In the early '50s, the Texas was the principal seat of allowable public pleasure in Oak Cliff—a spit-and-polish place where Daddy took Mama to the show on Sundays. Already twenty years old by then, it was well kept up, not even close to being rundown. But as Jefferson withered, the once venerable movie house started falling to pieces, too. In 1989, to avert demolition, the nonprofit, citizen-based Texas Theater Historical Society (TTHS), with aid from the Oak Cliff Chamber of Commerce, bought the old landmark, pledging restoration and development as a cultural arts center. To meet a $3,000 monthly mortgage, TTHS volunteers—many of them teenagers from the area—reopened the theater as a $2 rerun venue.

(In February, the TTHS board filed for Chapter 11 bankruptcy protection, with the Chamber's take-charge Robert McElearney maneuvering for control, and the society's founder terming his efforts a "hostile takeover.")

On a late weekday afternoon before the evening show, Maxine Burroughs, the matronly manager, showed me around. She was a veteran Texas employee, along with her husband, the doorman who'd been on duty when Oswald was apprehended. "Butch and I got involved," she explained, "because there's no place left in Oak Cliff for families and kids to go."

The lobby looked frayed, sad, smaller than I remembered. We mounted the foyer stairs, passing a mawkish amateur mural of JFK, and climbed to the balcony. "Were you here," she asked, pointing at the muddy-colored ceiling, "when the stars still worked? I've only seen pictures of it—little planets and clouds outlined in electric lights. The architects said everything's still up there, just stuccoed over."

I wandered along the center aisle, glancing by reflex toward the last rows in front of the projection booth where the raff of Oak Cliff's hillbilly gene pool had traditionally gathered—the dread "balcony rats." In the watery light, I found my old spot by the A stairwell. While I was still a green hand, but a tall one, I'd been stationed there to keep a lid on the general anarchy. After a couple of grueling break-in shifts, less terrified of the badasses than worried about failing, I'd bought an oversized flashlight that suggested a club. The bluff worked pretty well for a year . . . until a beered-up lummox from West Dallas flung himself at me over four rows of seats, and I did the first thing that Matthew or Spook would've done—bopped him on the ear. The injured party ran bellering to the lobby, alerting the manager, who had him hauled off for drunk. As a sort of reward for "cutting it," I was transferred downstairs to the candy case, a choice job compared to standing aisle. . . .

It troubled me that I couldn't remember the old manager's name. I'd been trying to think of it for a couple of months, and it still eluded me as I followed Mrs. Burroughs back to the main floor.

On a fall night in 1952 as I was closing up the stand, Tess Tyler came out of the auditorium and stopped to shoot the breeze. I called her that because her own name was so student-nurse-y and she had the brisk stride and ginger bangs to go with it. She was a neighbor, in her mid-twenties, divorced, familiar enough at my boarding house to sit down at meals. We had a casual, jokey acquaintance, and we decided to walk home together.

On the way, having our first private conversation, I saw her clear as a person instead of a remote adult. She'd married a well-off Oak Lawn jerk who'd bruised her around and then thrown her away. Under the blowy elms on East Ninth, slowing down to light one of the Tareytons she chain-smoked when her relatives weren't around, we bumped into each other accidentally and then embraced impulsively. We stood holding each other, kissing, both of us shaken. I was speechless. In the shadows, her face was pale and a little too lean—pure-dee Oak Cliff. "You wouldn't tell anybody, would you?" she asked in a faint voice. "No, I swear." "Wait for fifteen minutes. When you come up, be sure Mama's lights are out." . . .

We met that way for five or six months, fugitives in the dark, risking everything not so much for sex as deliverance from love-starved isolation—some shared connection to stave off loneliness. Our times together were tender, painful, glorious, wretched, wise, and foolish—but redeemed, I thought, by the solace and comfort we gave each other. . . . Tess taught me to tie a Windsor knot, comb my hair without a part . . . Sometimes I went to her place just to write while she slept with the radio low. . . .

But we were tap-dancing on the edge of disaster, and the dread of exposure bore in on us. We both knew that her holy-roller mother would shoot us in the name of God if she ever figured things out. After a couple of close calls, we backed off, saw each other less, then not at all. . . . For a while, we took pains to avoid meeting. Then we began exchanging guarded greetings in passing. In the end, we went back full circle to being casual strangers across the boarding-house table. . . .

Mrs. Burroughs beckoned me into the main auditorium downstairs with an expression between a frown and a smile. We stood regarding the infamous spot where Oswald was captured. "It's the fifth seat in the third row," she said. "People come from all over to see it, you know—police officers, school groups . . ."

I walked ahead down the main aisle, resisting a sudden urge to tell her I'd seen enough and had to leave. I moved a few steps further and the name of the old manager came back to me—*Jimmie Rawlins*. As I descended deeper into the dingy gloom of the theater, another pocket of memory opened up, and I crossed to the side aisle and hurried to the fire exit. I parted the mangy curtains and peered inside at a chest-high door set low in a peeling wall.

"What in the world was this place used for?" Mrs. Burroughs asked. "Do you remember?"

"The ushers' dressing room," I said. "It's where we stowed our coats and ties, personal things . . ." The tiny wooden door, unopened for decades, was locked tight as a tomb. Turning away, I let the curtain drop. I realized I was shaking a little. . . .

In my final semester at Adamson, a cheap zipper notebook crammed with my writings disappeared from the cramped little cubbyhole. Jimmie Rawlins, thinking it was schoolwork, helped me search high and low, but it was gone without a trace. The contents included photos of Opal and Big Grover, stories, poems, and part of a novel I'd started at Tess's apartment. Sixty-odd pages long, called *Midnight Show*, it was set in the upper balcony at the Texas on a violence-wracked Saturday night. Writing it, I'd felt fully in possession of myself for the first time — exalted by the idea of work that was a calling.

The loss of the manuscript seared my soul. In dry despair, I didn't have the heart or the know-how to start it over. In dreams, I kept finding the pages and losing them again. I got drunk and bawled at the West Dallas Cemetery. I tried concentrating on Hemingway's concept of grace under pressure, but that didn't help, either. For a long time, I felt unable to assign any meaning to words. . . .

As graduation neared, Spook bought me a "dress-up" suit at the Penney's on Jefferson. When I tried it on for him, we were already set on separate paths. He was about to retire, and he'd recently joined the church of his sisters' dreams. I hid my true feelings about it, but a gulf opened between us that would widen over the years. At my June commencement, we shook hands and patted each other's shoulders, and he said he'd pray for me. . . .

By then, I'd left the Texas and found a slightly better-paying job at the Pig Stand drive-in on Colorado and Zangs, where one of my uncles was the boss. I was going fairly seriously with an Adamson belle whose guiding lights were sanctimony and matrimony. . . . I longed to get away — make tracks for freer climes — but how? Oak Cliff closed around me like a fog off the Trinity. Counting false starts and dead ends, it would be ten years before I lit out for the real territory of my life. . . .

Back in the lobby, a crew of young volunteers was busily preparing to open the concession stand for the night's show. Mrs. Burroughs walked me to the main door.

"It's sorta hard to put into words," she said, "but the Texas is still really a special place. To me, it represents entertainment, people having fun — not just Oswald and all that stuff. . . . I hope you enjoyed the visit, hope it brought back pleasant memories for you."

"Yes," I said, "thank you very much."

Outside, the darkness was lowering on Jefferson, and except for the theater sign and the marquee advertising *Naked Gun* 2½, the neighborhood looked abandoned. A city bus rattled by with no one aboard but the driver. Halfway to my car, I felt a sudden stab of alarm, a prickle at the back of my neck . . . Whirled around. Nobody there.

Grover Lewis relaxes at an outdoor café in Houston. Lewis, who fancied cowboy boots for footwear, is captured in a rare moment when he is wearing street shoes.

Hillbilly Song

From *I'll Be There in the Morning, If I Live*, 1973

> (And now! What
> did we wish to
> say, that we
> were not able
> to say?)
> —ST. JOHN PERSE

You asked me once, Ann,
Over coffee gone cold with talk
In your mother's rain-drowsy
House, who they were, how it
Was with them in their breathless
Time in the wilds of years . . .
Think of old pictures long put
Away; cracked grey snapshots and
Newsreels of the monolithic stillness
Of extinct hearts, vanished light —:
Think of sere skeletons of flowers
Pressed mad with ruin and years
Forgotten in the unspanned leaves of
Spine-broken books, limp eerie albums
Of all our lost tribes in swimming time.
Think of Summer 1934; see the
Square autos in evening creeping
Past stubbled, yellowed yards;
Supper smell, the rich iron smells of
Hunger, American men and their

Women resting after work on
The dusty porches of rent-houses.

— Ours had a groaning canvas glider
Under a flap of trellis,
A pair of scarred kitchen chairs
Inside a hum of insects:

My father drives a brewer's truck,
A good Depression job he has;
His khaki clothes are sweet and
Stiff with salt and the raw drench
Of yeasty workmen's taverns as
He sits talking and laughing,
Tilted back lazily against
The slatted, dust-engrained wall.
My mother, swinging, laughs with him
When he reaches across to embrace
An impulsive arm around her middle,
And still laughing, cradle his hand
A moment easily at the base
of her young, swollen breast.

It is a quiet moment; it is
A trembling moment of stillness
And hush, almost like the sadsong
Fastness of long, icy sleep
. . . Before he feels the first
Shudder of fevery awakening
Blow across her flesh like
The scudding breath from some small
Animal's crazed winter mouth.

For an instant, locked in the
Cloudy glass of his own skin, he
Doesn't move — rests frozen and
Blank to capture a sudden teasing

Image that sunfishes against
The inner lids of his eyes, turned
Opaque now, and somber. A woman he
Knows, a waitress. A beer waitress at Texas
Ted's Cafe; her name is Edna and her
Hair is red, and she'll do that thing, by
God, he knows in his heart she will—
Hasn't she practically said it,
The way she talks? The ways she
Cuts up and prances and puts on
The dog, and godamighty damn, almost
Rubs it in a man's face? Yes, Edna—
Yes, yes—And hungrily, his gaunt,
Austere, damned Southern face still
Fixed in the mask of gone laughter,
His hand, cupping Opal's harvest-near
Breast, fumbles a caressing circle,
Wider and wider sweeping her taut,
Damp flesh till at last he finds
Her roused and quaking sex.
"The baby, Grover—" she murmurs glassily,
Whimpering her fullness of stomach,
But now he lifts her to passive,
Unseeing feet, guides her urgently
Through the rasp of screendoor and
Hollow, dusky resonance of ironing-smell
House to the seed-heavy apocalypse
Of the bed. Edna! Edna! he cries
In the mute, airless tomb of his heart,
Stroking Opal's loins.

Beyond the paper-shaded window,
The first fireflies burn their
Brief, stricken lights. Undressing
Hastily, pale fingers agrope, my
Father hypnotically conjures the
Strange woman's sensuous, wanton

Face, clings to it in his mind's eye,
Frantic that he'll forget it before
He can fit it to Opal's heavy, moist
Breathing, lock it to the labored
Sounds of her solitary undressing
Across the spectral stealth of the room . . .

At last, breathless and dry-mouthed
With private desire in the blue,
Swollen dark, we all lie down together—
My mother, my father, their perishing
Dreams, and I, this unborn prisoner son,
Yet still a sealed autumn's eternity
Locked away in the globey mound
Somewhere between their
Heaving, coupled, lonely skins.

A Cracker's Farewell

A REMEMBRANCE

Robert Draper

Texas Monthly, 1995

t would be nice if we didn't have to wait until a person's death before the logic of his life was made plain — though better late than never, I suppose. The screwball reasoning behind the uneven life of Grover Lewis didn't hit me all at once on April 22, the day I attended his funeral in Kanarraville, Utah. After all, he was buried among his sheepherding in-laws rather than beside his parents in San Antonio. None of his famous literary friends, who included Larry McMurtry and Hunter S. Thompson, had come to see him off. Instead, it was a curious mix of Mormons, Marxists, and artsy outlaws who laid the great Texas writer to rest, serenaded by a trio of fiddlers under a flurry of sleet.

I guess I must have been halfway back to Las Vegas that evening before I grasped the significance of Grover's companions that day, both above and below the soil. From the cradle and now to the grave, he was destined, in spite of his astonishing talents, to reside with the uncelebrated. His was an unwashed greatness, the best imaginable product of a butt-ugly life, and under such circumstances the most you could hope for was a bittersweet finish. If he couldn't lie down with Texans, he would lie down with Utah sheepherders. If he couldn't find a place among the literary celebrities, he'd take the loyal oddballs any day, up to and including the day of his funeral. And perhaps it all looked rather tragic, him being such a good writer and dying with so little fanfare and all that. But I suspect that even Grover, who romanced tragedy rather recklessly, would be compelled to acknowledge that, well, maybe things were kind of sweet there near the end.

How good a writer was Grover Lewis? In the Fifties his closest companion at North Texas State College was Larry McMurtry, and the writing professor who taught them was said to have observed, "Larry's good, but his friend is better." His literary cohorts in the Sixties included McMurtry, Billy Lee Brammer, Bud Shrake, Dan Jenkins, and novelist Sherry Kafka, the latter of whom now says, "Grover was the most talented of all of us — mainly because he was as talented a thinker as he was a writer." Not long after moving away from

Texas for good in 1969, he worked at *Rolling Stone* alongside Hunter S. Thompson, Joe Eszterhas, David Felton, Tim Cahill, Timothy Ferris, and Howard Kohn—arguably the most able group of writers assembled under one roof in the past quarter century. Assessing Grover's status at the magazine, Cahill says simply, "He was the best of us."

For some it might be tempting to make the case that Grover wrote well because he lived poorly. You could say he had a keen ear for dialogue because he had to compensate for congenital near-blindness; you could say he portrayed white trash so exquisitely because that was the house he once called home. And there is no question that the righteous bile roiling in Grover's prose was summoned from his personal storehouse. (Former *Texas Monthly* editor William Broyles Jr., who counts Brammer and Grover as two of his biggest literary inspirations, compares them thusly: "There was a sweetness to Billy Lee, and a high acid content in Grover. But Grover would be the first to point out that he had managed a peculiarly graceful life—abetted by his ironic sense of humor and by his wife, Rae, who, it's generally believed, kept him alive over the past twenty-two years.")

Furthermore, no upbringing, however steeped in agony or privilege, can guarantee a talent such as his. Grover could make a routine hotel coke-snorting scene with the Allman Brothers read like an ode to a Southern cracker's lost innocence. He could render a Sam Peckinpah set as a wasteland of Hieronymus Bosch–like anarchy. By digging deep, he elevated everything he committed to paper. From the sonic rage of his 1963 Beat-era poem "The Wreckage Children" ("What an indictment a man's face can come to be—A ruined contour map of remorse, a white blur of fatality. /Reiser says I look like an American, but I've wept/Seeing myself suddenly in mirrors") to the understated drama of his autobiographical *Texas Monthly* story "Farewell to Cracker Eden" some thirty years later ("Growing up in Dallas' working-class suburb of Oak Cliff in the Forties and Fifties was the second experience in my life that I never got over"), Grover Lewis was a natural who never betrayed his gift.

The ornate fragments of Grover's considerable body of work are scattered all over the literary landscape, though never where you would think to look. *Esquire,* for example, named him one of America's Heavy 100 in 1973, saying he "helped make *Rolling Stone* a citadel of respectable journalism," but *Esquire* never published any of his writing. For that matter, the native Texan's byline did not appear in *Texas Monthly* until 1992. His poetry found a home at *The Nation* in the late Fifties, as did his short stories at *The Carolina Quar-*

terly. At the *Fort Worth Star-Telegram* in the mid-Sixties, he became the first pop music columnist at a Texas newspaper, and in 1968 he penned a brilliant five-part series on bluesman Lightnin' Hopkins for the *Village Voice*. He did little music reporting at *Rolling Stone*, however, concentrating instead on film. When Grover landed a small role in the film adaptation of McMurtry's *The Last Picture Show*, he took his tape recorder with him and eavesdropped on the dreamy-eyed novice thespians on the set, among them Cybill Shepherd, Randy Quaid, Jeff Bridges, and Timothy Bottoms. The resulting opus, "Splendor in the Short Grass," was a towering achievement—Grover's most celebrated work, one of *Rolling Stone's* most momentous pieces, and one of the finest articles ever published in any magazine. In that and subsequent movie stories, Grover pioneered on-location film journalism, a subgenre that has been much abused since its master immaculately conceived it.

But for my money, Grover saved his best work for last. From 1990 until his death, he focused his attention on minor heroes—actor Aldo Ray, screenwriter Gus Hasford, novelist Edward Anderson—who were caught for the briefest time in the limelight before dwindling into anonymity. For those of us who knew Grover, the connection between these works and the personal horrors he described in "Farewell to Cracker Eden" is plain. His heart lay with the down-and-outers, a breed he had known since he became one himself at age eight, when his parents shot each other to death and he was sent off to Fort Worth to live with a wildly abusive uncle. Those years permanently crippled him, and only late in the game did he use his affinity for misfits to his advantage. By then, he had wrecked his body with alcohol and cigarettes and done a similar number on his career. What his kinfolk had started, Grover and his lifetime of grudges had practically finished off—though sweet redemption was to come near the very end.

As dumb luck would have it, that's where I stumbled in. Our paths first crossed in December 1988, by which time, it's fair to say, Grover Lewis had fallen off the literary map. I was writing a history of *Rolling Stone* and making contact with that publication's many luminaries, from Hunter Thompson to Joe Eszterhas. But I couldn't find a trail that led to Grover's doorstep, the reason being that he hadn't left one. Why he had all but stopped publishing articles was a matter of some speculation among fellow writers. Many said it was the booze; others suggested he had become permanently unnerved by the experience of being a few steps from *Hustler* publisher Larry Flynt when Flynt was shot; still others heard that Grover had fallen into the Hollywood screen-writing swamp.

None of these turned out to be true. The Grover Lewis I tracked down in Santa Monica, California, was dried out and as searingly articulate as ever. Though his teeth were bad and his eyesight worse, Grover still had the Moses-like voice everyone had told me about, an imposing instrument slightly offset by the courtly demeanor he had retained from his Texas days. Typical of his fastidious manner as a journalist, he had prepared for our talk by combing his files and making photocopies of pertinent memos. The war stories he told about Thompson, Eszterhas, Annie Leibovitz, and his other peers were insightful, often hilarious, and usually backed up with documents he had saved. He spoke of *Rolling Stone* editor-publisher Jann Wenner with florid contempt—"It would be nice to think that he would die in the gutter," he allowed—and of his own accomplishments with characteristic swagger. For the purposes of my book, I couldn't have asked for more.

Still, the writer in Grover was practically defeated. In addition to the scars he bore from childhood, he now had a full ensemble of professional wounds: straitjacketed by his conservative editors at the *Houston Chronicle* in the late Sixties, estranged from his old friend McMurtry, stung by a book contract with *Rolling Stone* reneged on by Wenner in 1973, and essentially dismissed as a drunk by author Robert Sam Anson. Too proud to accept a lucrative offer by Helen Gurley Brown to write for *Cosmopolitan* and otherwise effectively blacklisted as a boozer throughout the gossipy publishing industry, he wallowed bitterly through the Eighties. For the first time ever, Grover Lewis had lost confidence in himself. It was a disquieting experience for me as a young writer to see a legend embalmed in rancor and self-doubt. As I left his house that afternoon, I suspected I wouldn't be laying eyes on Grover again.

Two years later, while reading from my just-published *Rolling Stone* history at a publicity function in Berkeley, California, I looked out into the audience and saw Grover and Rae Lewis. He was grinning, almost radiant with joy. My book, he proclaimed after the reading, had restored his literary reputation; the wrongs by Wenner, Anson, and the rest had been made right. A few weeks later, Rae wrote to thank me herself and to tell me that Grover was writing feature stories again.

Shortly after *Texas Monthly* hired me in 1991, I made it a point to solicit work from him. Those of us who had a hand in "Farewell to Cracker Eden" are still limping a little from the experience. The manuscript came in at three times the prescribed length, and Grover fought to the death over every change. Still, the story's evocation of Oak Cliff and its orphan scribe was hypnotic, and it delighted but came as no surprise to us when the piece eventually caught the attention of heavyweight New York editor Judith Regan, who had made her name publishing Rush Limbaugh and Howard Stern and who had never before heard of Grover. "My philosophy is that whatever connects us to the human spirit is ultimately commercial," she would later tell me. "And the pain that Grover suffered as a kid and told so dramatically in that article convinced me that his story had commercial potential as a book."

Grover phoned us last fall to say that he had signed a contract with Regan to write his memoirs. When we didn't hear from Grover for the next six months, we figured that was good news. It seemed that Grover was back in the saddle—sitting, in fact, taller than ever. We didn't know about the back injury he had suffered in November or about the diagnosis in February that the injury was a metastasized sign of lung cancer. We didn't know Grover was suffering the indignities of a painful death until Rae phoned our office on April 10, sobbing as she informed us, "I don't think he'll make it through the weekend."

She was right. Grover died on Easter Sunday. He had completed a grand total of eleven pages of his memoirs. That story is lost to us, as is its inimitable teller. I'll mourn the passing of both, but it relieves me to no end to be able to report that Grover Lewis died on the upswing, out from under the publishing world's manhole cover. He went out a writer—unsung, perhaps, but it was in the writing and not in the applause that he found where he belonged.

Thanks for the Use of the Hall

From *I'll Be There in the Morning, If I Live*, 1973

Only a gray shadow
Remains of the tent:
Hard echoes of laughter
Heard through the faded film
    of blue smoke,
A cabal of thin-lipped barkers,
The wretched marks howling
    their terrors
To all who would clap.

It was really a very fine circus.